Motorcycle Maintenance TechBook

by Keith Weighill LCGI

(4071-256-2AH1)

44085

© Keith Weighill 2008
© Haynes Publishing 2008

ABCDE
FGHIJ
KLMNO
P

A book in the **Haynes Service and Repair Manual Series**

ISBN 1 84425 071 7

British Library Cataloguing in Publication Data
A catalogue record for this book is available from the British Library.

Printed by **J H Haynes & Co Ltd**, Sparkford, Yeovil, Somerset BA22 7JJ, England

Haynes Publishing
Sparkford, Yeovil, Somerset BA22 7JJ, England

Haynes North America, Inc
861 Lawrence Drive, Newbury Park, California 91320, USA

Haynes Publishing Nordiska AB
Box 1504, 751 45 UPPSALA, Sweden

Contents

Acknowledgements

This book could not have been produced without the help and encouragement of many people, namely Helen, Tim, Paul, Chas, Rob, Owen and Regine, plus many others who gave assistance – my thanks for your time and the use of your pride and joy.

I would also like to thank Merton College for the use of their facilities and NGK Spark Plugs (UK) Ltd who supplied the colour photos of spark plug conditions.

Finally, yet most importantly, my thanks go to my wife Teresa for proof reading the book and putting up with her husband being locked to a computer for so many hours.

Keith Weighill, Spalding, Lincolnshire. 2004

About the Author

Keith has always said that he is a very lucky man in that he has two great loves in his life. His wife, to whom he has been married for over thirty years and the second, has two wheels and an engine. When he was about six, his parents bought him a Meccano set and this started his love of all things mechanical. He studied City and Guilds motorcycle mechanics at Merton College and passed with distinctions in all three subjects. This led to a job in the motorcycle trade where he worked on the big four Japanese makes of motorcycle with occasional work on American and Italian machines.

He was taken on as a lecturer, at Merton College, where he worked for almost twenty years. During this time, there were great changes in the City and Guilds courses and the introduction of the B/TEC national certificate in motorcycle engineering and NVQs, in all of which he had a part to play. Keith's qualifications include the City and Guilds 389 motorcycle mechanics certificate, B/TEC national certificate in motorcycle engineering, and he holds a licentiateship from the City and Guilds in vehicle and plant.

Liasing with manufacturers and attending their training courses has kept Keith up-to-date with new developments in motorcycle technology. Although he saw the introduction of disc brakes, electronic ignition, single shock rear suspension and fuel injection he believes that motorcycle mechanics is really quite easy, just don't tell everybody! With the correct instruction, anyone can carry out basic motorcycle maintenance and get great satisfaction from doing the job themself. He is still riding today and is looking forward to the Hydrogen powered motorcycle.

Introduction

The aim of this book is to guide you through servicing and minor repair tasks on your motorcycle or scooter, providing useful hints and helpful advice gathered from years of experience. Advice is also given on setting up a toolkit and equiping your home workshop. This book is not intended to take the place of a model-specific workshop manual or the owner's manual, either of which will be necessary as a source of technical data or specific procedures.

The text is illustrated with photographs of everyday machines, chosen because their components are common to most models. In some cases the examples are in poor condition, but do serve to illustrate the typical wear you might expect to find on machines in regular use.

The Chapters are divided into numbered sections, which correspond to a contents list at the beginning of each chapter. References to the left or right side of the motorcycle assume you are sitting on the seat, facing forward.

Whilst every attempt is made to ensure that the information in this book is correct, no liability can be accepted by the author or publishers for loss, damage or injury caused by any errors in, or omissions from, the information given.

Professional mechanics are trained in safe working procedures. However enthusiastic you may be about getting on with the job at hand, take the time to ensure that your safety is not put at risk. A moment's lack of attention can result in an accident, as can failure to observe simple precautions.

There will always be new ways of having accidents, and the following is not a comprehensive list of all dangers; it is intended rather to make you aware of the risks and to encourage a safe approach to all work you carry out on your bike.

Asbestos

● Certain friction, insulating, sealing and other products - such as brake pads, clutch linings, gaskets, etc. - may contain asbestos. Extreme care must be taken to avoid inhalation of dust from such products since it is hazardous to health. If in doubt, assume that they do contain asbestos.

Fire

● Remember at all times that petrol is highly flammable. Never smoke or have any kind of naked flame around, when working on the vehicle. But the risk does not end there - a spark caused by an electrical short-circuit, by two metal surfaces contacting each other, by careless use of tools, or even by static electricity built up in your body under certain conditions, can ignite petrol vapour, which in a confined space is highly explosive. Never use petrol as a cleaning solvent. Use an approved safety solvent.

● Always disconnect the battery earth terminal before working on any part of the fuel or electrical system, and never risk spilling fuel on to a hot engine or exhaust.

● It is recommended that a fire extinguisher of a type suitable for fuel and electrical fires is kept handy in the garage or workplace at all times. Never try to extinguish a fuel or electrical fire with water.

Fumes

● Certain fumes are highly toxic and can quickly cause unconsciousness and even death if inhaled to any extent. Petrol vapour comes into this category, as do the vapours from certain solvents such as trichloro-ethylene. Any draining or pouring of such volatile fluids should be done in a well ventilated area.

● When using cleaning fluids and solvents, read the instructions carefully. Never use materials from unmarked containers - they may give off poisonous vapours.

● Never run the engine of a motor vehicle in an enclosed space such as a garage. Exhaust fumes contain carbon monoxide which is extremely poisonous; if you need to run the engine, always do so in the open air or at least have the rear of the vehicle outside the workplace.

The battery

● Never cause a spark, or allow a naked light near the vehicle's battery. It will normally be giving off a certain amount of hydrogen gas, which is highly explosive.

● Always disconnect the battery ground (earth) terminal before working on the fuel or electrical systems (except where noted).

● If possible, loosen the filler plugs or cover when charging the battery from an external source. Do not charge at an excessive rate or the battery will be severly damaged.

● Take care when topping up, cleaning or carrying the battery. The acid electrolyte, even when diluted, is very corrosive and should not be allowed to contact the eyes or skin. Always wear rubber gloves and goggles or a face shield. If you ever need to prepare electrolyte yourself, always add the acid slowly to the water; never add the water to the acid.

Electricity

● When using an electric power tool, inspection light etc., always ensure that the appliance is correctly connected to its plug and that, where necessary, it is properly grounded (earthed). Do not use such appliances in damp conditions and, again, beware of creating a spark or applying excessive heat in the vicinity of fuel or fuel vapour. Also ensure that the appliances meet national safety standards.

● A severe electric shock can result from touching certain parts of the electrical system, such as the spark plug wires (HT leads), when the engine is running or being cranked, particularly if components are damp or the insulation is defective. Where an electronic ignition system is used, the secondary (HT) voltage is much higher and could prove fatal.

Remember...

✗ **Don't** start the engine without first ascertaining that the transmission is in neutral.

✗ **Don't** suddenly remove the pressure cap from a hot cooling system - cover it with a cloth and release the pressure gradually first, or you may get scalded by escaping coolant.

✗ **Don't** attempt to drain oil until you are sure it has cooled sufficiently to avoid scalding you.

✗ **Don't** grasp any part of the engine or exhaust system without first ascertaining that it is cool enough not to burn you.

✗ **Don't** allow brake fluid or antifreeze to contact the machine's paintwork or plastic components.

✗ **Don't** siphon toxic liquids such as fuel, hydraulic fluid or antifreeze by mouth, or allow them to remain on your skin.

✗ **Don't** inhale dust - it may be injurious to health (see Asbestos heading).

✗ **Don't** allow any spilled oil or grease to remain on the floor - wipe it up right away, before someone slips on it.

✗ **Don't** use ill-fitting spanners or other tools which may slip and cause injury.

✗ **Don't** lift a heavy component which may be beyond your capability - get assistance.

✗ **Don't** rush to finish a job or take unverified short cuts.

✗ **Don't** allow children or animals in or around an unattended vehicle.

✗ **Don't** inflate a tyre above the recommended pressure. Apart from overstressing the carcass, in extreme cases the tyre may blow off forcibly.

✔ **Do** ensure that the machine is supported securely at all times. This is especially important when the machine is blocked up to aid wheel or fork removal.

✔ **Do** take care when attempting to loosen a stubborn nut or bolt. It is generally better to pull on a spanner, rather than push, so that if you slip, you fall away from the machine rather than onto it.

✔ **Do** wear eye protection when using power tools such as drill, sander, bench grinder etc.

✔ **Do** use a barrier cream on your hands prior to undertaking dirty jobs - it will protect your skin from infection as well as making the dirt easier to remove afterwards; but make sure your hands aren't left slippery. Note that long-term contact with used engine oil can be a health hazard.

✔ **Do** keep loose clothing (cuffs, ties etc. and long hair) well out of the way of moving mechanical parts.

✔ **Do** remove rings, wristwatch etc., before working on the vehicle - especially the electrical system.

✔ **Do** keep your work area tidy - it is only too easy to fall over articles left lying around.

✔ **Do** exercise caution when compressing springs for removal or installation. Ensure that the tension is applied and released in a controlled manner, using suitable tools which preclude the possibility of the spring escaping violently.

✔ **Do** ensure that any lifting tackle used has a safe working load rating adequate for the job.

✔ **Do** get someone to check periodically that all is well, when working alone on the vehicle.

✔ **Do** carry out work in a logical sequence and check that everything is correctly assembled and tightened afterwards.

✔ **Do** remember that your vehicle's safety affects that of yourself and others. If in doubt on any point, get professional advice.

● If in spite of following these precautions, you are unfortunate enough to injure yourself, seek medical attention as soon as possible.

Chapter 1
Tools

Contents

1   Building up a toolkit

Good quality tools are as important to a motorcycle rider as a good set of riding clothes and helmet. The best and usually most expensive tools are really the preserve of the person who makes their living servicing and repairing motorcycles. You, however, will be servicing your machine following the manufacturer's recommendations on a time or mileage basis, but this doesn't mean that those old spanners and hammer that were found at the back of the shed will do!

Purchase what you can afford, bearing in mind that your toolkit can be expanded as time goes on. Note that paying a little extra for reasonably good quality tools will pay dividends in knuckles that do not get skinned, bolts, screws and nuts that do not get chewed up and time saved using the correct tool in the correct place.

Where can you purchase tools? There are various places where tools can be purchased, high street automotive stores and hardware stores (ironmongers); in addition to the tools they have in stock there are often others which can be ordered from tool suppliers' catalogues.

Your local motorcycle dealer will stock tools that are specific to the motorcycle and will be able to order manufacturer's service tools, such as a socket for tightening the steering stem lock nut. Mail order firms now stock a large range of tools, and some companies are specifically geared to the needs of the motorcyclist. Another place to browse for tools is the internet.

New machines are supplied with a toolkit which usually comprises a few open-ended spanners, a plug spanner, pliers and screwdriver, all kept in a neat plastic wallet. Although this

When making a purchase always ensure that the tool meets the national safety standards and is of a reputable brand.

is useful as a 'get you home' kit should you have a breakdown, it cannot realistically withstand the use of regular servicing. Keep this on your machine, and if you find the kit missing when buying a second-hand machine, make up a similar kit of useful tools to store on the bike.

The following sections of this chapter by no means describe the 'be all and end all' toolkit, but are a good basis for the majority of service tasks.

2   Spanners, sockets and screwdrivers

Spanners

A set of chrome-vanadium, drop forged spanners is a necessity and will be the starting point for your toolkit. Some spanners in the set will rarely be used but buying them as a set is usually the cheapest option. Spanner sets usually start with an 8 mm and end with a 19 mm, but a 22 mm spanner is a useful addition.

You will notice that there is a doubling of some spanners sizes; the 10 mm, 12 mm and 14 mm are the most often used sizes and it is well worth buying these in separate sizes in addition to the set.

Combination spanners are shown which have one open end and one ring end. Wherever possible always use the ring end as this is safer and gives a more secure fit on the nut/bolt head. As this is not always possible, this type of spanner offers the best of both worlds. An adjustable wrench is also shown in the photo; don't turn your nose up at this spanner as it can be a very useful addition to the toolkit.

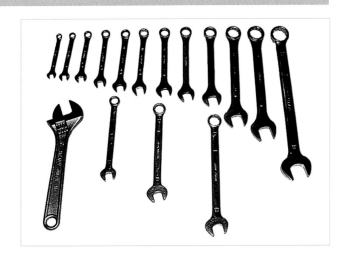

Sockets and Socket sets

The difficult decision is whether to buy sockets as single items, to start with a small set and build it up, or to purchase a large set like that shown.

Single sockets tend to be more expensive than a set, but you can spread the cost over time and you will only purchase the sockets you need for your machine. A small set gives you a reasonable amount of sockets to start, with the advantage of adding to or replacing as funds allow.

Whichever route you chose, purchase the best quality that you can afford. These tools are likely to last a lifetime and money spent on quality rather than quantity will pay dividends in tools that are not broken, nuts/bolts that are not damaged and a lack of injury to yourself.

Many socket sets are intended for car use. Because a motorcycle has a great deal of engineering in a very small space 1/4 in. or 3/8 in. drive sockets are preferable to 1/2 in. drive sockets which tend to be a little bit too big and cumbersome.

Most sockets are of 12-point construction (B), which means that the socket grips on the corners of the nut/bolt head, and not on the flat sides. In most situations this is perfectly all right, however there are times when the nut/bolt is so tight that you start to round off the head. If you continue all that happens is that the head is ruined and you now have a real problem. The socket (A) is of 6-point construction and grips the nut/bolt head on the sides. This type of construction is virtually universal on the larger sockets.

The socket (D) has a 3/8 in. drive end whereas the socket (C) has a 1/2 in. drive. The largest 3/8 in. drive socket that should be used is 22 mm, larger sizes should have a 1/2 in. drive.

| A | B | C | D |

To complete your collection various 1/2 in. drive sockets can be purchased as required, together with a 1/2 in. drive handle or ratchet. Do NOT be tempted to use a 3/8 in. drive ratchet and adapter – it will not be able to withstand the strain.

To prevent single sockets from rattling around in the bottom of your toolbox use a bar with spring clips to hold them captive. The centre (black) set is of 6-sided construction with a 3/8 in. drive. Their black colour denotes that they can be used on a compressed air ratchet. The bottom set is a 1/4 in. drive; the flexible driver is not strictly necessary, but a useful addition.

'T' Bar Sockets

These tools virtually describe themselves; the socket is a 6-point type that is built into the end of the shaft. The handle is welded to the shaft and the tool is almost indestructible. It can be used instead of a long extension bar and socket, without the risk of the socket falling off the bar.

The one great advantage of the 'T' Bar is the speed with which it can be used. Pretty much in the realm of the professional mechanic, but once used you will always want to use them whenever possible. Sizes range from 8 mm to 19 mm.

Valve adjusting spanner

A small flat spanner made from thin section steel, about 5 inches long with a square section cut out of the head.

For use on four-stroke engines with screw and locknut valve adjustment (see Chapter 3, Section 2) where the adjuster screw has a 4 mm square head. This tool is an exact fit and much better than trying to use long-nose pliers.

The open jaw crows foot wrench

There are instances where it is IMPERATIVE that nuts are tightened to a specific torque setting, yet there is insufficient room to fit a socket and torque wrench.

Some may chose to tighten the nuts by hand using a spanner, and trusting to luck that they are all tightened by a reasonable and equal amount. However, this rarely works as we tend to over-tighten nuts/bolts and it is virtually impossible to get any consistency when tightening by hand.

The open jaw crows foot wrench overcomes this problem. It is an open-ended spanner with a 3/8 in. drive square section in the body. They can be purchased from your local tool supplier or hardware store and are available in various sizes. Ring end types are also available. The two most commonly used types are shown in the photo (14 mm on the left and 12 mm on the right).

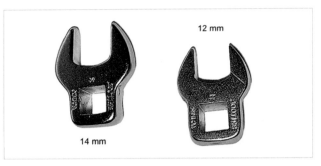

Set the torque wrench to the required setting and fit it to the tool so that its body is in line with the tool jaws.

There are some situations where even this tool cannot be used with the torque wrench directly connected, and a long extension bar from your socket set must be used.

> **HINT**
>
> Manufacturer's often express a torque setting in terms of a range e.g. 20 to 25 Nm, instead of a single figure. In this case, set the torque wrench to the lower value and tighten all the nuts/bolts in sequence, then set the torque wrench to the higher setting and repeat tightening the nuts/bolts. This will ensure that all nuts/bolts are fully and evenly, tightened down.

Screwdrivers

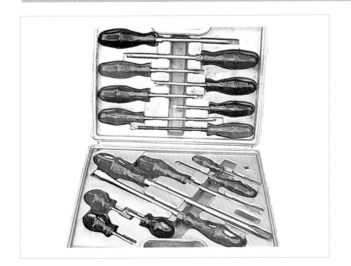

Screwdrivers can be purchased singly or as a set, either as flat-bladed or crosshead design. The advantage of a set is that you tend to get everything you need in one go, and often a nice case or box to keep them in. If you keep them in their box you will always find the screwdriver that you want without hunting through various tool boxes or drawers.

The larger screwdrivers often have a six-sided spanner adapter built into their shaft. This can be a real boon when undoing stubborn screws because is allows hand pressure to be applied to the end of the screwdriver, whilst twisting the shaft using a spanner.

When trying to undo a stubborn screw, select the correct size screwdriver, ensure it is square onto the screw and use a ring-ended spanner on the shaft to help unscrew it. If this doesn't work you will have to use an impact driver (see Section 3).

One of the biggest causes of damaged screw heads, and a major cause of increased time, cost and frustration, is the use of a crosshead type screwdriver that is TOO SMALL for the screw head. It is very easy to select a screwdriver that is too small as the eye tells the brain that a larger one cannot surely fit properly. Ignore what your eyes are telling you and select a driver that is a tight fit in the head. If the driver selected can be 'wiggled' in the slot without turning the screw, select the next size up.

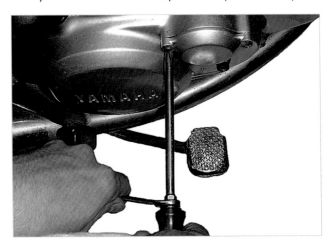

3 Drifts, chisels and hammers

Bars or drifts (A to C) are used to drive components from position, whereas the cold chisel (D) is used to cut metal cables and to separate very close components (see **Cold Chisel** overleaf).

Drifts

One use of a drift is when removing a wheel spindle which has become stuck or corroded in position.

Don't hit the threaded end of the spindle with a heavy object; all you will do is damage the thread. You may eventually succeed in removing the spindle but it will be ruined, as it will be impossible to fit the nut onto its damaged threads.

First check that you haven't overlooked a lock nut or bolt that is holding the spindle in place. Replace the nut and thread it on the spindle until it is flush with the end of the spindle. Now you can hit the nut without damage to the thread.

When the nut is tight against the swinging arm or front fork, loosen the nut by half a turn and carry on. Do not hit the nut after you have turned it halfway off the spindle.

With the spindle close to the swinging arm or front fork, remove the nut and use small diameter steel or aluminium bars (drifts) to continue the process.

Once the spindle is out have a look to see why it fought so hard to stay where it was. You will probably find that it is heavily corroded, and lacking any grease. Before you refit the spindle, make certain that it is clean and use a general purpose or molybdenum disulphide based grease to lubricate it. Doing this will ensure that removal is easier in the future.

Cold chisel

A cold chisel is shown being used to flatten the tabs of a lock washer so that the nut can be removed. Do NOT use a flat-bladed screwdriver for this job.

Insert the cold chisel between the nut and the washer tab so that the tab is prised away from the nut. This will not always completely flatten the tab, but further application using a small diameter steel bar will complete the task.

Note that the type of lock washer shown is a 'use once only' device and must be replaced with a new one if it is disturbed.

Impact driver

Used correctly this tool can be a real 'life saver' when you are faced with a nut or screw that will not come loose. There are a variety of screwdriver bits and the tool can be adjusted for use on left and right-handed screws.

If after one sharp tap with a hammer the screw does not come undone check that you haven't REVERSED the tool and are instead TIGHTENING the screw even further.

This tool will also undo nuts. Removal of the head of the tool (just prise it off) will reveal a 1/2 in. socket drive, fit a socket to it and it will then undo stubborn nuts or bolts.

To use, first select an appropriate screwdriver bit, fit it into the tool and apply the tool to the screw ensuring that it is held square onto the screw. Apply a twisting motion to the handle in the direction that will undo the screw. This will pre-tension the tool. Look at the screw and not the back of the tool and give the tool a sharp tap with the hammer. Don't 'tickle' it or attempt to drive the tool through the case, a sharp, firm tap is all that is required!

Hammers

The rubber mallet (A) – Used where it is necessary to break a seal, such as that between the cylinder head and the barrel when dismantling a two-stroke engine. The use of a metal hammer will only damage the castings even if the seal does break.

Small hammer (B) – A lightweight general-purpose hammer that has uses in the home as well as on the motorcycle.

Copper/Rawhide mallet (C) – A combination head with one relatively hard face and a soft face.

Large hammer (D) – A heavyweight hammer used with drifts, chisels and impact drivers.

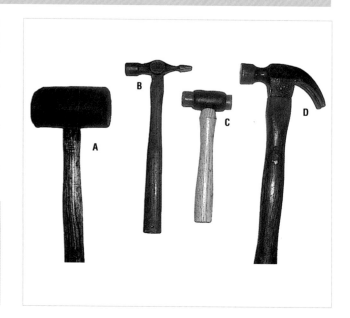

HINT

RESIST the temptation to hit stubborn components with a hammer, even if at first sight they appear to be stuck or corroded in place. It may be that you have forgotten to remove or slacken some part and you may do damage to the machine or even hurt yourself. Decide which hammer is appropriate for the job before you start.

4   Pliers and other gripping devices

Pliers and cutters

Depending on their head design, pliers do the job of holding, clamping or cutting. The accompanying photo shows a selection of the common types.

Hose clamp (A) – used to clamp rubber brake hoses when they are to be replaced.

Side cutters (B and C) – used to cut electrical wiring, or metal cables in the case of the larger set.

Long nose pliers (D) – for those awkward to get to places.

Combination pliers with insulated handles (E) – its uses are many and varied.

Adjustable pipe wrench (F) – used to fit 'E' clips and to fold over locking washers such as those used to secure sprocket nuts.

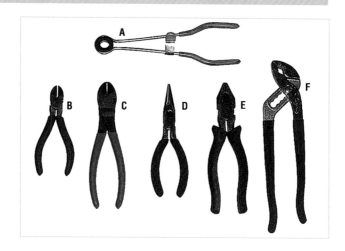

Self-locking 'Mole' grips

A pair of self-locking grips, or as they are known by their popular trade name 'Mole grips', will be found in virtually every professional mechanic's toolkit. It is probably one of the first tools they purchased. Like the adjustable spanner, it is a very versatile holding tool, with the ability to act as a portable vice.

Circlip pliers

Circlip pliers are essential to remove and install circlips without damaging them and without risk of them pinging free. Do NOT try to use screwdrivers to remove circlips.

There are circlip pliers for internal and external circlips as well as different sizes. The combination set shown has interchangeable heads so that they can be used for internal and external circlips, plus two sizes of straight and angled 'fingers' for different sized circlips.

HINT

Circlips are pressed from metal sheet and this action produces a round and a square edge. When fitting, inspect the clip to determine which side has the square edge. Fit the circlip with this edge in the direction of thrust.

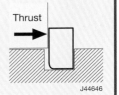

Thrust

J44646

Bench vice

Certain bench tasks, such as replacing fork oil seals, require components to be held firmly whilst work is carried out. This is where the bench vice comes into its own as it acts as another pair of hands.

A bench vice with 4 in. jaws will be adequate for most applications. Note the use of a pair of aluminium 'soft jaws' covers to prevent the serrated jaws doing damage to the components. Manufactured soft jaws can be purchased instead of making your own.

5 | Measuring tools

Metric micrometer

A micrometer is a precision measuring tool, capable of measuring to 0.01 of a millimeter. It is used to accurately measure the thickness of a component to determine if it has worn beyond the service limit. Typical examples would be brake disc thickness or piston diameter.

Micrometers are available in different size ranges, 0-25 mm, 25-50 mm and upwards in 25 mm steps; some large micrometers have interchangeable anvils to allow a range of measurements to be taken. A 0-25 mm micrometer will be sufficient for most jobs on a motorcycle, with the exception of measuring piston diameter.

A Frame
B Anvil
C Spindle
D Spindle lock
E Sleeve fixed to frame (main scale)
F Thimble
G Ratchet

When closed (anvil and spindle head lightly touching), the index line on the sleeve and the 0 on the thimble must align exactly or the micrometer will be out of adjustment.

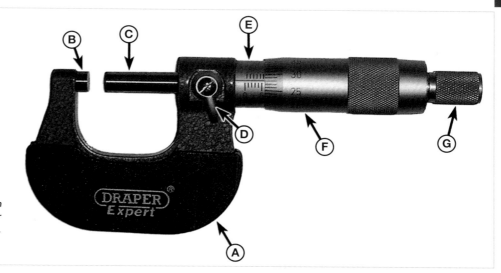

The most common type is the analogue micrometer which is described below, although digital types are now available. The component parts of the analogue micrometer are shown in the accompanying photo.

Reading the micrometer

1 Remove the micrometer from the component being measured. On the main scale, read the lower mark that the thimble scale has completely passed. In the photo below it is 5 mm. Do NOT count the '0' mark.

2 Check if there is an upper mark showing between the thimble scale and the lower (5 mm) mark. If so add 0.5 mm to the first reading. See **Note**.

3 Finally, read the thimble scale. Read the mark on the thimble that is closest to the index line and add this to your other readings. In the example shown this is calculated as:

$$\begin{array}{r} 5.00 \\ 0.50 \\ 0.28 \\ \hline = 5.78 \text{ mm} \end{array}$$

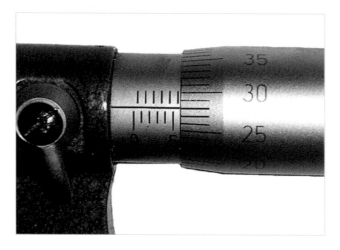

Note

One of the biggest problems encountered when reading a micrometer is whether a 0.5 mm increment has been passed. As the thimble is turned INWARDS, a 0.5 mm mark will start to disappear every time the number 5 on the thimble scale passes the index line.

If the thimble stops BEFORE the 0 on the scale reaches the index line, INCLUDE the 0.5 mm with your measurements. In the photograph below, the micrometer reading is 1.52 mm.

IF the thimble stops with the 0 on or above the index line Do NOT count the 0.5 mm. Read the main and thimble scales ONLY. In the photograph below, the micrometer reading is 1.48 mm.

HINT

Holding the micrometer in this way may look and even feel strange but with practice, it will become second nature. It gives a secure grip to the micrometer and allows your other hand free.

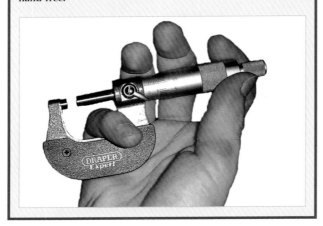

Care of the micrometer

✦ Ensure that the part to be measured and the faces of the anvil and spindle are clean and dry.
✦ Never measure any part that is hot or cold; the reading should be taken with the part at room temperature.
✦ Ensure that the anvil and spindle are in full contact with the part to be measured. Hold the micrometer at 90° to flat surfaces and centred on the diameter of circular surfaces.
✦ Never store the micrometer with the spindle tight against the anvil, always leave a gap. Normal temperature changes could cause damage to the faces, distort the thimble threads or frame with a consequent loss of accuracy.
✦ Use light pressure only. Until you get the 'feel' of the micrometer, do not be afraid to use the ratchet mechanism.
✦ Don't clean any precision tool with compressed air, as dirt and grime will be forced into the tool causing all sorts of unpleasant conditions.
✦ Your micrometer has cost you a lot of money; keep it in its protective case and away from other tools to prevent damage.

Gauges

Feeler gauges

Feeler gauges can be purchased as a metric set (mm) or as an imperial set (1/1000's of an inch). Whichever you purchase is a matter of personal preference, although most manufacturers express clearances in metric.

A multiple set, like that shown, will have gauges ranging from 0.02 mm to 1.00 mm ascending by approximately 0.02 mm per gauge. Cheaper sets do not have such a large range therefore complete accuracy, when carrying out valve clearances, cannot normally be achieved. On the set shown, having extended the required gauge, the black screw can be tightened to lock the gauge for easy use.

Keep the gauges oiled and closed when in your toolbox, preferably in a plastic box with other small tools.

Tyre tread depth and pressure gauges

The tyre pressure gauge (upper) and tread depth gauge (lower) are relatively inexpensive but can be somewhat delicate. Keep them away from your usual tools in a separate box to prevent damage to them.

Refer to Chapter 4 for information of how to read these gauges. Note that the extended centre of the depth gauge is not a screwdriver, lever or probe. RESIST the temptation to use it for anything other than checking depths.

Engine compression tester

When faultfinding problems such as poor starting or lack of power, a mechanic will often conduct a compression test of each cylinder. Sometimes the results will pinpoint the cause of the problem, but more importantly it may indicate that there is nothing wrong with the mechanics of the engine and that the fault lies elsewhere. This can save a lot of time and expense needlessly stripping the engine when the problem may have been in the fuel system or electrics.

Regular checks at the service intervals and recording of the results will give an indication of the state of health of your engine's internals. The tool shown uses a 14 mm fitting and for many multi-cylinder engines, a suitable spark plug adapter will be required.

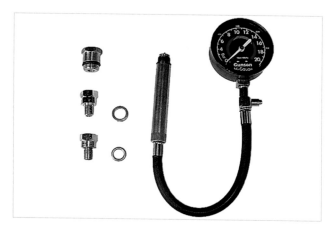

Carburettor balancer

On four-stroke engined machines with two or more cylinders fed via individual carburettors, the carburettor butterfly valves must be balanced (or synchronised) so that the air flow through each inlet manifold is the same. This will ensure optimum power, throttle response, fuel economy and reduced exhaust emissions. Balancer gauges measure the vacuum present in each cylinder's inlet manifold via hoses which connect to take-off points.

The manometer carburettor balancer (see top right photo) uses four, accurately machined steel rods running in clear tubes. Note the different size take-off point adaptors supplied with the balancer; select the adaptor which fits the thread size in the inlet manifold. Some machines are fitted with brass take-off stubs sealed by rubber caps; in this case all that is necessary is to pull off the caps and fit the balancer hoses directly to the take-off stubs.

Vacuum gauge sets (see below) do the same job as the manometer, but display the gauge reading on clock-type gauges. Most sets come as standard with four gauges mounted on a bracket, this being suitable for two, three or four cylinder engines.

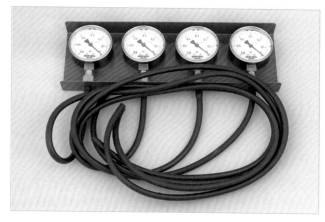

Note that whichever type of gauge is used to balance the carburettors, the object is to adjust the carburettors so that the readings are the same for each cylinder. The actual reading on the gauge scale is less important.

6   Torque wrenches

Torque wrenches are not cheap items, but they are necessary to ensure that critical fasteners are tightened to the setting specified by the manufacturer.

Risks of OVER-TIGHTENING
✦ The threads being over stressed resulting in their damage.
✦ The bolt becoming overstretched, causing it to form a 'waist' in its length which will ultimately break.
✦ Snapping the bolt completely. If the rest of the bolt is inside the component this is going to be expensive to get out.
✦ Distortion of gasket faces.

Risks of UNDER-TIGHTENING
✦ Nuts and bolts that are NOT tightened sufficiently run the risk of coming undone and even falling off. Inside an engine, this can have serious and expensive consequences.
✦ If it is a chassis nut/bolt that is too loose, it may cause you to have an accident.

The two torque wrenches shown overleaf will cover the range of torque settings found on a motorcycle. These types have a positive click system of indicating when the required setting has been achieved. Once you have reached the correct tightness, the tool will 'click' once. This is it, do NOT tighten the bolt/nut any further, operating the torque wrench so that 2 or 3 clicks are heard is not necessary and will over tighten the bolt.

The smaller wrench has a 3/8 inch drive whereas the larger one has a 1/2 inch drive and a 1/2 inch to 3/8 inch adaptor will be needed. When deciding which size torque wrench to use, choose a wrench that does NOT have the required setting at either the beginning or the end of its range. It is preferable to use a large setting on a small wrench rather than a small setting on a large wrench.

> **HINT**
>
> Torque wrench settings are expressed in Nm (Newton metres), kg-m (kilograms force metre), lb-ft (pounds force feet) or lb-in (pounds force inch). If the torque setting specified by the manufacturer differs from the scale on your torque wrench it will be necessary to convert the torque figure into the same units as on the torque wrench. See the page of Conversion factors at the end of the manual.

Bolt or Screw?

The threaded portion is the deciding factor as to whether it is a bolt or screw, not the shape of the head.

On the far left (A) is a hexagon headed screw; note that the threaded portion is the complete length of the screw. Next to it (B) is the same thread size but this is a bolt because the thread does not go from top to bottom. Note also that this is a rolled, not cut thread (stronger construction) and has a fitted spring type lock washer. The one on the far right (D) is a pan head (cross head) bolt whereas the item C is a pan head screw.

This may appear to be superfluous information but it really is important that the correct bolt/screw is used in the correct application. Failure to use a bolt/screw of the correct length and tensile strength may cause serious damage if it cannot withstand the torque applied to it (breaks off in the hole) or the component is loose and comes off.

Measuring fastener sizes

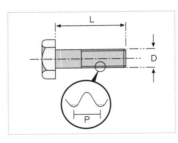

Never refer to the head size or spanner size used on the bolt. Always refer to the thread diameter (D) on bolts or hole size for nuts. The length (L) of bolts/screws or Allen screws excludes the head, the only exception being countersunk heads where the overall length includes the head. Pitch (P) is the distance between the peaks of the thread.

Thread size (dia.)	Typical head size	Typical thread pitch
M5	8 mm	0.8 mm
M6	8 mm or 10 mm	1.0 mm
M8	12 mm or 13 mm	1.25 mm
M10	17 mm	1.25 mm fine/1.5 mm std.
M12	19 mm	1.75 mm

Selecting the correct torque setting

Many of the nuts, bolts and screws on a motorcycle have a specific torque setting and this value will be given in your owners manual or workshop manual. These settings should be strictly adhered to for safety reasons. There are, however, other nuts/bolts on the machine that the manufacturer will not give a specific torque setting for, as these tend to be such items as mudguard-mounting bolts etc. that are conventional engineering quality bolts.

Manufacturers often suggest torque settings for standard sizes, but it is essential that when selecting the correct setting the THREAD size is chosen and NOT the head size. See 'Measuring fastener sizes' for a list of common thread size, head size and pitch combinations.

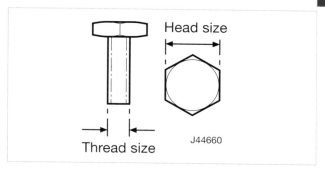

For example, a 6 mm (thread size), grade 7 bolt will have a 10 mm head size – the torque setting for a 6 mm bolt is only 0.8 to 1.2 kg-m. If the head size is inadvertently selected, a torque setting of 4.0 to 6.0 kg-m will be applied and it is guaranteed that you will snap the bolt off in the component. The following is a list of the torque values for nuts/bolts where the manufacturer DOES NOT specify a setting.

Bolt Diameter (mm)	Conventional or '4' marked bolt			High quality or '7' marked bolt		
	Nm	kg-m	lb-ft	Nm	kg-m	lb-ft
4	1 – 2	0.1 – 0.2	0.7 – 1.5	1.5 – 3	0.15 – 0.3	1.0 – 2.0
5	2 – 4	0.2 – 0.4	1.5 – 3.0	3 – 6	0.3 – 0.6	2.0 – 4.5
6	4 – 7	0.4 – 0.7	3.0 – 5.0	8 – 12	0.8 – 1.2	6.0 – 8.5
8	10 – 16	1.0 – 1.6	7.0 – 11.5	18 – 28	1.8 – 2.8	13.0 – 20.0
10	22 – 35	2.2 – 3.5	16.0 – 25.5	40 – 60	4.0 – 6.0	29.0 – 43.5
12	35 – 55	3.5 – 5.5	25.5 – 40.0	70 – 100	7.0 – 10.0	50.5 – 72.5
14	50 – 80	5.0 – 8.0	36.5 – 58.0	110 – 160	11.0 – 16.0	79.5 – 115.5
16	80 – 130	8.0 – 13.0	58.0 – 94.0	170 – 250	17.0 – 25.0	123.0 – 181.0
18	130 – 190	13.0 – 19.0	94.0 – 137.5	200 – 280	20.0 – 28.0	144.5 – 202.5

Castellated nuts with split pins or 'R' clips

Where a castellated nut is used, such as on a wheel spindle, a split pin or 'R' clip is fitted to lock the nut in place and prevent it loosening. When tightening the nut to the specified torque setting the following procedure is suggested to ensure that the nut slots align with the hole in the spindle.

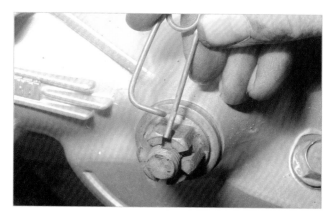

The manufacturer will usually give TWO torque settings for the tightness of this type of spindle nut. An example would be 36 to 52 Nm.

Set the torque wrench to the LOWER setting (36 Nm) and tighten the nut. If the hole and nut castellations line up proceed to fit the split pin or clip. If not, set the torque wrench to the HIGHER setting (52 Nm) and continue to tighten the nut. Tighten it by only a small amount at a time – remove the socket and check if the holes line

up. Continue to do this, a little at a time until the holes do line up. If the upper torque setting has NOT been reached, the nut will be tightened to BETWEEN the manufacturer's torque setting. All that is now needed is to fit the split pin or 'R' clip.

HINT

One problem when tightening the rear wheel spindle to its torque setting, is that the wheels can be pulled out of alignment. If the torque wrench is vertical when operated there is a tendency for it to be pulled backwards which pulls on the wheel spindle changing the wheel alignment.
To prevent this, never let the torque wrench handle pass the horizontal position when tightening the spindle nut. Pushing downwards will not change the spindle position. Use this technique to tighten the spindle nut with a spanner or socket and bar prior to using the torque wrench.

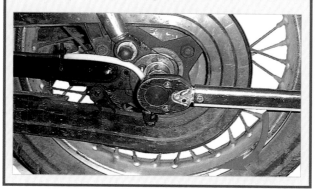

7 | Electrical testers and equipment

Soldering iron

A 25 Watt or 40 Watt iron will be necessary for any soldering tasks on a motorcycle.

The solder bit on the tool shown is 1/8 inch wide and is small enough to repair the internals of handlebar switch units. A 1/4 inch wide bit would be more useable for cable soldering, but would then be too large for the small solder connections within the switchgear.

You will also need an amount of multi-core solder and a soldering iron stand. The stand may not appear necessary, but it will protect the work surface and your hands from accidental contact with the hot soldering iron.

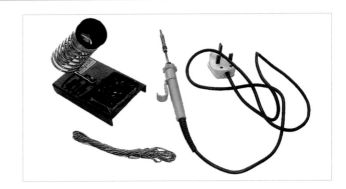

Battery hydrometer

The hydrometer is used only on conventional batteries which have removable filler caps (not on maintenance-free batteries). It measures the specific gravity of the electrolyte and will give a good guide to the state of charge of the battery

The hydrometer will need to be small as the amount of liquid that a motorcycle battery contains is much smaller than that of a car battery, also the filler cap size is smaller than that of a car battery.

This hydrometer has a calibrated float that gives the information required; other types use a number of balls that float depending upon the density of the liquid.

Multi-meter

Analogue and digital multi-meters are available. The analogue type uses an arm or pointer which moves across a scale and some skill is needed to read the meter accurately. The digital multi-meter shows the measurement as a series of numbers and is much easier to read than its analogue counterpart. Both types are delicate and should be treated with great care as they are very easily broken. Keep the multi-meter in its case for protection and store it away from other tools.

The following measuring functions and ranges are necessary for motorcycle use. Most meters will be able to measure Volts and Ohms, but for serious motorcycle use, the fourth specification is a necessity.
+ Ohms, reading in units, tens and thousands
+ DC Volts, 0 to 25V range
+ AC Volts, 0 to 250V range
+ DC Amps, 0 to 10 A range

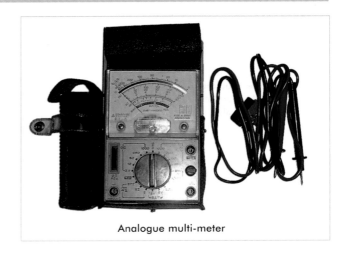

Analogue multi-meter

Digital multi-meter

Analogue meter – preparation for use

There are TWO important things to do BEFORE using the analogue multi-meter.

Line up the needle to the zero position on the scale using the screw (arrowed in the photo below). This sets the datum line from which to read the meter. **Note:** *This meter has been deliberately set with the pointer away from the zero mark to illustrate the characteristic of this type of meter.*

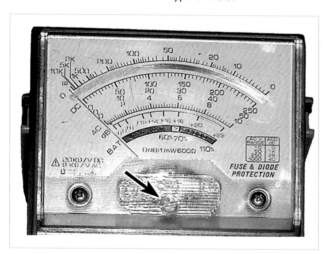

When using Ohms (Ω) function, use the main switch to select the Ohms scale required (x 1, x 10, or x 1000) then place and hold the two probes together. The needle will swing to the right-hand side of the scale and will need to be adjusted via the adjuster wheel if the needle and the zero mark do not line up.

Reading the meter

The multi-meter has far more functions than we are likely to use. The three scales mainly used are:

A Ohms (Ω) – Measures the resistance of a component. Note that the scale reads backwards to the other scales.

B DC volts – Measures direct current voltage, i.e. items powered from the battery circuit. This has three scales 0 to 10, 0 to 50 and 0 to 250 depending on the switch position. When the switch is in the x2.5 position read the 0 to 250 scale as 0 to 2.5. When the switch is in the x1000 position read the 0 to 10 scale multiplying the value by 100.

C AC volts – Measures alternating current voltage, i.e. power output from the machine's charging system. Marked in red on the scale.

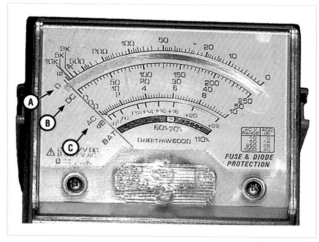

Connecting the probes

Whether the multi-meter is digital or analogue it is imperative that the probes are correctly connected to the meter before use and that the setting is selected BEFORE connecting the leads to the component to be tested.

Referring to the accompanying photos note the probe connection points:

A Black lead to common negative (-) terminal of meter.
B Red (positive) lead to V/Ω/mA terminal of meter.
C Red (positive) lead to 10A DC terminal of meter (for red **10 Amp** scale).

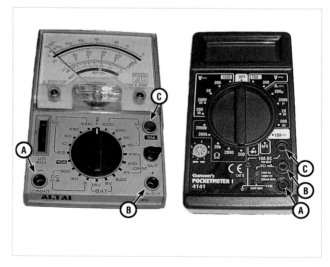

Battery charger

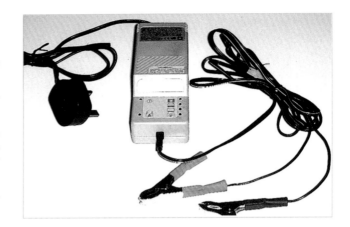

Aim to purchase a good quality battery charger which is suitable for use on motorcycle batteries. Section 5 in Chapter 5 explains the differences between the constant voltage and constant current chargers and their suitability for motorcycle use. The charger shown indicates the battery's state of charge via a series of LEDs and charges at a safe rate for the battery capacity.

If your machine has a 6 Volt battery check that the charger can be switched from 12V to 6V usage.

8   Fabricated (home-made) tools

Fork oil level gauge

It is difficult to measure out the exact quantity of fork oil specified by the manufacturer, and particularly to ensure that it is identical in each fork leg. A typical example would necessitate filling each leg with 210 ± 2.5 ml and then ensuring that the distance from the oil to the top of the fork stanchion measured 144 mm in each leg.

The fork oil change procedure in Chapter 4 illustrates the use of the oil level gauge shown below. The fork oil quantity is exceeded slightly and the gauge used to draw out the excess, thus ensuring that the oil level in each leg is identical and at the exact distance from the top of the stanchion.

To make the fork oil level gauge you will need:
- ✔ A plastic syringe without the needle, 10 – 25 ml capacity is sufficient.
- ✔ A length of clear plastic hose with a bore diameter slightly smaller than the outside diameter of the syringe nozzle. Length must exceed the fork oil level figure specified by the manufacturer.
- ✔ A length of thin but stiff wire (welding rod is ideal).
- ✔ Cable ties.
- ✔ Side cutters, pliers and steel rule.

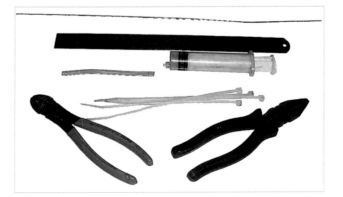

1 Fit the plastic pipe to the end of the syringe. If it is too tight to fit, place one end in very hot water for a few minutes – this will soften the pipe and make fitting easier.

2 Using the steel rule, measure from the base of the syringe and cut the pipe off at the exact fork oil level figure (e.g. 144 mm in our above example).

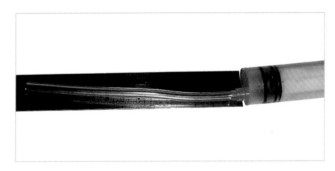

3 Lay the welding rod alongside the syringe/pipe and if necessary put a small bend in it so that it follows the shape of the tool. Secure the wire with two large cable ties around the body of the syringe. Use small ties to secure the wire to the pipe as shown, but don't overtighten them otherwise you may restrict the flow of oil.

Remote fuel tank

It is very difficult to supply fuel to the carburettors when balancing them because it is virtually impossible to position the fuel tank safely, fit the balancer gauge and still access the adjusters. Complete removal of the main fuel tank and fitting a remote fuel tank removes all obstacles and is a lot safer.

To make a remote fuel tank you will need:
✔ An old two-stroke oil tank (purchased from a breakers). Clean its inside thoroughly.
✔ A few lengths of petrol resistant clear plastic hose. 6 mm or 8 mm inside diameter fuel hose should fit most machines.
✔ A simple on – off fuel tap. The type illustrated was purchased from a lawn mower repair shop.
✔ A variety of petrol resistant 'T' and 'Y' pieces for use where two fuel taps are used.

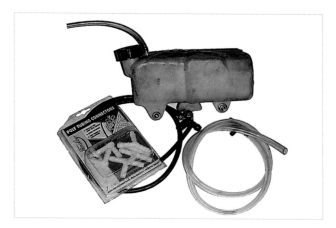

First consider how you are going to mount the remote tank. It must be mounted above the level of the carburettors. In the example shown the two mounting bolts secure the tank to a floor stand. Other options would be to hang the remote tank from the handlebars, or to rest the tank on the seat having first covered the seat with cloth or plastic sheeting. Whatever you do, make sure that the tank is held securely and cannot tip over.

Having removed the main fuel tank from the machine, check that the remote fuel tap is switched OFF, then connect it to the fuel hose from the carburettors and the hose from the remote tank. Fill the remote tank with fuel and check that there are no leaks.

Before you run the engine make certain that the tap is in the ON position or you will run the carburettors dry and probably overheat the engine.

When you have finished using the tank turn the remote fuel tap OFF before you remove the tank. Drain the fuel back into your main tank.

> ⚠ **Petrol (gasoline) is an extremely flammable substance – NO naked flames when you are working with this substance and don't even think of lighting a cigarette until you have finished, you are outside the garage and the fuel is safely stored in the main tank.**

Copper scraper

A steel scraper can easily damage aluminium surfaces unless care is taken. A copper scraper is much softer, will not damage the mating surfaces of aluminium components and can be curved so that it can be used to clean other surfaces, e.g. exhaust ports.

A scraper can be made from a piece of 1/2 inch copper tubing about 8 inches long.

1 Use a hammer to flatten one end of the tube, turn it over and flatten the other side. Use a file to create a 'knife' blade on this end.

2 Repeat this on the other end of the tube.

3 Hold one end of the scraper with a pair of insulated pliers and heat the other end in a gas flame for a minute or two to soften the copper.

4 Place the scraper on a stone floor and place a steel bar over the hot end. Using a pipe wrench, fold the sides of the hot end so that a curve is formed.

5 Dunk the hot end into cold water to anneal it, and you have a very good scraper at virtually no cost.

9 Workshop equipment and miscellaneous tools

This section includes a variety of tools necessary to carry out specific maintenance tasks. Some will be rarely used and should be purchased as required. It is worth considering a joint purchase with other riders for some of the more expensive tools.

Workshop equipment

Organisation

A small parts chest with a variety of plastic trays is ideal for storing small components in an organised manner.

The number of small components you will need or will accumulate when servicing your motorcycle is extensive. These items include a variety of split pins, cable connectors, nuts, bolts and washers, spare fuses and bulbs, to name but a few. Equally, there are a number of delicate or small tools which would be damaged if stored in your toolbox, not to mention difficult to find, and these are best stored separately.

Toolbox

If your spanners came in a tool roll and your sockets and screwdrivers in boxes then you have the beginnings of tool organisation. As your toolkit expands, some means of keeping your tools together will be necessary. If you have a garage you may wish to mount all your tools on boards, screwed to the wall.

A metal toolbox like the type shown is sturdy, relatively cheap and large enough to hold many tools. Smaller tools can be kept in the tray with the larger items kept in the main body of the toolbox. The type and cost of toolboxes differs considerably, ranging from the cheap and simple box to the cabinet and tool station used by many professional mechanics.

Bike stands and supports

A number of machines are not fitted with a centrestand. Many tasks can be safely undertaken with the machine on its sidestand, but there will be occasions when the machine needs to have its wheels elevated. Typical occasions would be when adjusting the steering head bearings or removing a wheel.

Ideally purchase one of the many bike stands (paddock stands). They are specifically designed for this purpose, will support the machine securely upright and the machine can usually be put on the stand by one person. A rear paddock stand is shown below.

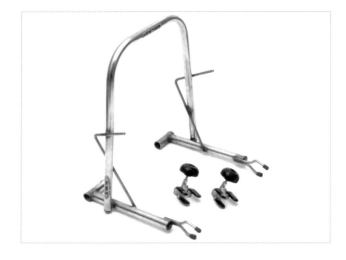

The bike stand shown below locates in the engine mountings or swinging arm bosses.

A trolley jack can be used to raise one or other of the wheels but it should NOT be the only means of supporting the machine. The trolley jack shown below should only be used on a firm flat surface. Its cup should be placed so as not to put strain on any part of the machine; if raising the machine under the engine, a flat piece of wood should be placed between the jack cup and the sump. Have an assistant steady the machine as it is raised, then place axle stands under the footrests or frame tubes as additional support so that the machine is not resting on the trolley jack.

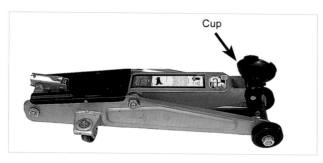

Cup

Axle stands can be used to support each side of the lower frame tubes, under the engine. Their three legged construction gives good stability without taking up a lot of space. The central tube of the stand has a variety of holes allowing up to about six different heights to be used. To prevent possible damage to the frame tubes place a thick piece of rubber (old inner tube) between the stand and frame.

 Warning: Whichever type of stand is used, check that the machine is in no danger of toppling off the stand before you start working on it. Tie-down straps can be used for additional security if the machine is on a raised platform, such as an hydraulic ramp.

Bowls, jugs and funnels

For the purpose of draining the engine oil some form of container will be needed. Dedicated oil drain containers are available, although an old washing up bowl or oven tin is just as good, just make sure that it is large enough to hold the volume of oil you are draining. When you have finished draining the oil, transfer it to a sealed container for disposal at your local re-cycling plant.

A couple of plastic measuring jugs and funnels will be useful for measuring and pouring fluids. Use one jug and funnel for engine oil and a second pair for the cooling system to ensure that oil and coolant do not get mixed.

Brushes

The wire brush shown in the centre of the photograph is an obvious addition to any toolkit, but you may wonder why the paint and toothbrushes.

A small paintbrush is useful for cleaning the area around a spark plug prior to removing it, or anywhere on the machine where it is necessary to remove dust or road dirt from difficult to get at places. A paintbrush is also very useful for working degreaser into very dirty or oily areas of the engine. Equally a small (1/2 inch) brush is useful for applying fresh grease to pivot pins etc. Note that cutting the bristles back will help to stiffen the brush.

Old toothbrushes are perfect for cleaning those difficult to get to places such as around the brake caliper pistons.

Miscellaneous tools

Tyre levers, Scrapers and Steel rule

If you change your own tyres then a pair of tyre levers will be a necessity. Note that many people choose to have tyres fitted by a tyre fitting specialist who will have the skill and equipment to fit tyres safely and without damage to the rim and can also balance the wheel afterwards.

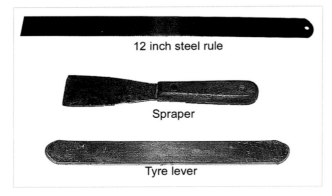

12 inch steel rule

Spraper

Tyre lever

When an engine cover is taken off all old gasket material should be removed before the new gasket is fitted. One problem associated with modern gaskets is that they rarely come away clean, leaving parts of the gasket on the joint surfaces. Careful use of a scraper will remove any old gasket material or jointing compound. Failure to remove these deposits will most likely cause the joint to leak.

The steel rule is used for measuring drive chain tension, lever free play, brake pedal height etc. It can also be used, together with feeler gauges, as a 'straight-edge' for checking for distortion across a gasket face.

Foot-operated air pump

Although you can use the garage forecourt airline for inflating your tyres, there are likely be occasions when having your own pump close to hand will be more convenient as it has many uses around the home.

The pump shown is a high pressure, double barrelled type which is ideal for the higher pressures used on motorcycle and bicycle tyres but costs a bit more than the single barrel type. Don't rely on the pump's gauge, check pressure with your own tyre pressure gauge when you have inflated the tyre.

Hacksaws

The two hacksaws shown can be used to cut bolts down to size and for a myriad of other engineering uses. You may want to keep the smaller one (junior hacksaw) in your toolbox as it is most suitable for motorcycle use.

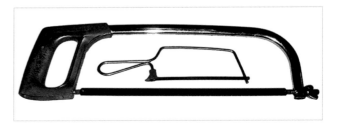

When fitting a new hacksaw blade, the teeth must point forwards as this tool is designed to cut on the forward stroke. Keep the saw square onto the part to be cut but do not exert great pressure as this will only break the blade. Take your time, cutting with a smooth rhythmic action and LET THE TOOL DO THE WORK.

Utility knife

A metal or plastic-bodied utility knife has the facility to store a variety of spare blades inside its handle. It is usually supplied with a safety device to cover the exposed blade when not in use, or has a retractable blade. If your knife doesn't have a blade cover ALWAYS remove and store the blade in the knife body when you finish using it.

Torch (flashlight)

There are many dark recesses on a motorcycle and a torch is often invaluable when servicing such areas of the machine. You needn't spend a fortune on a torch, a cheap plastic one will do just as well. Alternatively, if your workshop has a source of electricity, a mains-operated inspection lamp will be useful, although beware of its cable trailing across the floor.

You may also wish to keep one of the small pen-light torches in the toolkit on the machine, in case of a breakdown at night.

Inspection lamp and extension lead

The inspection lamp is mostly used by car mechanics where the area under the bonnet can be quite dark. It can also be very useful if you service your machine in a garage or shed, as the lighting in these areas is often quite dim. Be careful of the trailing lead though because it is very easy to trip over it!

The inspection lamp is quite delicate and cannot withstand rough handling, especially when it is hot. Heavy-duty bulbs are available but not too easy to track down.

An extension lead is a good investment. On the type shown, which can be wound into the body for easy storage, it is imperative that the lead is fully extended when in use to prevent the cable overheating which could cause an electrical fire.

Drill

Although the electric drill makes light work of many holes that need to be drilled around the home, it can do major damage to a motorcycle in unskilled hands. If you do snap a bolt off in a component such as a fork leg, get it professionally removed and re-threaded. It requires great skill to use electric drills for this purpose and you will probably only make the situation worse.

An electric drill or hand drill is only really necessary for motorcycle use when fitting 'L' plates, a new licence plate or a top box etc.

Oil can

A pump type oil can filled with motor oil is ideal for lubricating the exposed pivot points on a motorcycle. A flexible hose allows the lubricant to be applied to awkward to reach places.

When filling the can, only fill the body to 3/4 of its capacity, as the plunger assembly needs an air space to enter the body.

Grease gun

Where grease nipples are fitted, such as in the rear suspension linkage of a mono-shock system, a grease gun is necessary to apply fresh grease to the bearings.

The type shown is a mini–pistol, pump action type that is ideal for use in small confined areas. Like most grease guns it can have a flexible hose attached for especially awkward to get at locations. Always wipe all dirt off the head of the grease nipple before using the grease gun.

Allen keys

Designed for use with Allen screws which have round heads. The key fits into a 6-sided socket within the head giving a firm grip. They can be obtained in metric or imperial sizes, as keys (see photo) or as sockets (both short and long) for use with a 3/8 or 1/2 inch drive ratchet.

Allen keys can be purchased singly, but a set will provide a wallet or some other means of preventing their being lost in the depths of your toolbox.

HINT

If a screw is so tight that an ordinary Allen key won't unfasten it, try the following methods:
+ The use of an Allen key socket with a ratchet or bar will increase the torque that can be applied to break the seal and unfasten the screw.
+ Use a piece of tubing (as shown) slipped over the Allen key to increase the leverage applied and break the seal.

'C' spanner

The 'C' spanner is used mainly for adjustment of the steering head bearings and rear shock absorber pre-load. They are available in a variety of sizes so purchase one that will fit your machine or purchase a universal tool.

The use of a 'C' spanner makes the job of adjusting the slotted steering head bearing nut much easier and safer than if using alternative methods, such as a hammer and old screwdriver or drift.

Cable oiler

This is one of those tools that once you have used it you will wonder how you ever managed without it. The tool clamps around the disconnected cable as shown in Chapter 4, Section 6, and aerosol cable lubricant is applied via the fluid entry point.

Telescopic magnet

If you have ever dropped a small nut or washer into the top of your engine and had a lot of 'fun' trying to retrieve it from a small dark corner or cylinder fin, you will understand the benefit of the telescopic magnet.

This tool is also very useful when changing valve shims (see Chapter 3 on valve clearances). Note that it won't work on copper or aluminium washers because they are not magnetic.

Coolant hydrometer

The hydrometer is used to determine the density of the anti-freeze solution, which is a guide to the lowest temperature that will protect the cooling system from freezing. Check the density once a year, before the cold season, and change the coolant every two years. Use the tool to check that the new solution will give adequate protection from freezing.

A mix of equal parts anti-freeze and distilled water will protect the cooling system from freezing at temperatures down to -36°C. One part anti-freeze to two parts water will protect to -17°C. If the motorcycle is subjected to temperatures below -36°C the mixing ratio should be increased to 60% anti-freeze, 40% water. Do NOT use a solution stronger than this.

Oil filter wrenches

If your machine has a 'spin-on' type oil filter, you will need a tool for slackening and tightening the filter.

The two tools on the left are proper filter wrenches, available in different sizes to fit the various sizes of filter. They locate over the 'indentations' on the end of the filter, gripping it so that it can be unscrewed with a 1/2 inch socket adaptor. Those shown have been modified by welding 17 mm nuts in place. The reason for this is that some filters are so close to the exhaust system that a socket bar will not fit, although a normal spanner can be used.

The chain wrench, shown on the right in the above photo, can be used to slacken the filter, particularly in cases where there isn't sufficient access for a filter wrench. Note however, that the chain wrench will damage the filter body and must not be used for tightening the new filter. A strap wrench (see below) is a good alternative to the chain wrench.

Holding tools

This strange looking tool is a modified mole wrench. Proprietary versions can be purchased and go under the name of clutch holding tools. Note that even if you never dismantle the clutch, this tool has other uses.

In the 'Chain and sprockets replacement' section of Chapter 4, the tool is shown holding the gearbox sprocket whilst its retaining bolts are slackened and tightened. The two pegs on the reverse side of the tool can be used to hold components to prevent their rotation whilst their retaining nut or bolt is slackened, a typical example being the generator rotor. In the home-made example shown, the two arms of the tool have

been drilled to accept two 8 mm rods brazed to the reverse side of the arms.

Chain separator

A chain separator tool is essential for fitting a new chain to a machine equipped with a riveted link drive chain. There are several types available, some aimed at the DIY market which often come as a kit, and others which are more expensive and suitable for regular use by a professional mechanic.

Most tools are suitable for separating the old chain and riveting the new joining link into place. It is essential that the instructions supplied with the tool are followed correctly and the new joining link is securely riveted in place. See Chapter 4 for details of chain separation and joining using a typical DIY tool.

Fishing scale (spring balance)

Why is a fishing scale (used to weigh fish) included in a book about motorcycle maintenance? Its use on a motorcycle is for checking the tightness of the steering head bearings. It is easy to see if the bearings are too slack, but not so easy to tell if they are too tight. See Chapter 4, Section 3 on steering head bearings for details of how to use the tool.

This tool comes in four different sizes to cover various weights. The smallest is ideal for motorcycle use, as it will weigh from zero to 4 pounds in ounce divisions. Metric version are also available. See your local fishing tackle shop for details.

Brake bleeding kit

Whether bleeding the braking system of air, changing the brake fluid at its two-yearly interval or replacing the hoses at their four-yearly interval, the use of a brake bleeding kit will greatly simplify the operation.

A one-way brake bleeding kit is shown. Because of the one-way ball valve, fluid and air will NOT be drawn back into the system upon release of the brake lever (or pedal if working on the rear brake). This makes single person brake bleeding a very simple task (see Chapter 4, Section 12 for how to use of this tool). The glass jar is to collect the dispelled fluid.

 Warning: Brake fluid drained from the system must never be re-used. ALWAYS pour old fluid into a sealed container and take it to your local re-cycling centre for disposal.

Brake caliper piston retracting tool

When fitting new brake pads or servicing the brake caliper it is difficult to retract the piston(s) into the caliper body so that the new (thicker) pads can be fitted. Using screwdrivers as levers between the pads or pistons CAUSES DAMAGE and should not be attempted.

Releasing the fluid pressure by slackening the bleed screw and using a flat blade type tyre lever is one way, but still a bit

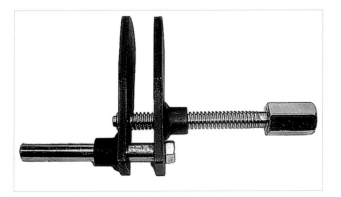

brutal and the brakes will need bleeding afterwards because air will have entered the system via the bleed screw. Using the piston retracting tool shown is a far better method of achieving this. The tool has two blades that fit between the body on one side and the piston(s) on the other, or between the pistons on an opposed caliper design. Rotating the screw opens the two blades and pushes the piston(s) back into the caliper.

Re-threading file

This tool is quite expensive and is usually the preserve of the professional mechanic or motorcycle restorer. It is used where a thread has been bruised (usually by a previous owner with a hammer) and the nut will not screw on or the bolt will not screw into its hole. Bolts can of course easily be replaced, whereas a damaged crankshaft thread is a different matter altogether.

The re-threading file is made from carbon steel and can be purchased in METRIC, UNC or UNF thread forms. The thread pitch sizes of the metric version range from 0.75 to 3.0 mm.

Match the teeth on the thread file with a GOOD section of the thread pitch on the damaged item, try various teeth until one set fits snugly in the bolt thread. The thread pitch on the crankshaft shown is 1.25 mm with the corresponding pitch on the thread file being used. Lay the file against the damaged item and using a stroking motion, work your way around the thread. Depending on the amount of damage (bruising) this will take either a few minutes or a very long time. What is important is that you check the condition of the thread by trying to fit a nut every few minutes. Do not force anything – patience is the key to repairing threads.

10   Heat shrink sleeve

Heat shrink sleeve can be used to cover solder joints, wire connectors and as a repair to control cables that have damaged outer sleeves. It is not the easiest product to track down, but electrical shops and electrical wholesalers will often keep it in stock.

If you are covering a damaged control cable, ensure that you catch it early on before water gets inside and rusts the inner wire. The accompanying photo of a chafed control illustrates the type of damage which can be covered.

If the inner cable has rusted and the inner cable action is stiff, the cable should be replaced – applying a heat shrink sleeve at this stage will not help. See Chapter 4, Section 6 for details.

Items required

✔ A hairdryer – a normal household type, preferably with an air nozzle is ideal. The one used in this instance was a 1200W unit.
✔ Heat shrink approximately 1 1/2 to 2 times the width of the cable to be covered and twice the length of the damage or joint.

Procedure

1 Slide the cut length of heat shrink sleeve over the area to be covered, ensuring that the joint or damaged section is central.

2 Switch the hairdryer on to its high setting and starting at one end, move the dryer up the sleeve keeping its nozzle about 1/2 inch from the sleeve. Move slowly and marvel as the covering shrinks to fit the cable.

3 Once you have reached the top of the sleeve slowly work back to the beginning by which time the sleeve will be a tight fit around the cable/joint.

4 The completed covering – nice and tight on the control cable. Water will be kept out and the sleeve will take on the shape of whatever it is covering.

11   Personal protection and safety

We all think that accidents are things which happen to other people and never to us. Care taken about personal protection can save years of pain and even disfigurement. Take a few minutes to read the Safety first page at the beginning of this manual.

Hand and eye protection

When servicing a motorcycle you will come into contact with many harmful substances, such as the dilute sulphuric acid in the battery, carbon particles in old engine oil, the hydraulic fluid in the braking system to name but a few. It is important to protect your hands from contact with these substances.

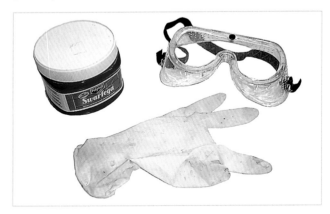

Rubber disposable gloves as used in hospitals, the food industry and many garages will not only keep your hands clean but also protect your skin from contact with oils and greases which can cause skin disorders.

During its life in the engine the oil becomes worn out and picks up many potentially dangerous substances. Carbon particles, from the hotter parts of your engine, together with water vapour and other by-products of combustion combine to contaminate the oil. Always wear rubber gloves when changing the oil to prevent it getting on your hands. This applies equally to handling fresh oil and when applying grease or chain lubricant.

If you discover that you have an adverse reaction to the rubber glove material or just cannot get the hang of working with them, the use of a BARRIER CREAM rubbed onto your hands will act to keep the oil etc. away from your skin. It has an added benefit in that washing your hands with soap and water gets the muck off quite easily.

When you have finished your service unless you have been wearing rubber gloves or barrier cream, your hands will be covered with dirt and grime. This can be quite difficult to remove with just soap and water. Products such as Swarfega seem to melt the grime leaving your hands nice and clean. Although they do a great job of removing the grime, it is much better to not get it on your hands in the first instance.

If there is even the remotest possibility of eye injury when carrying out a particular service operation, a set of safety goggles should be worn.

Clothing

When you work on a motorcycle you are going to get dirty, either from the condition of the machine or by contact with the oils and greases used when servicing. Even the cleanest of machines will have a greasy chain or have road dirt and grime in various places.

Purchasing a set of full overalls will protect your own clothing and exposed parts of your body. They are not expensive, can be easily washed and give a sense of confidence in your own abilities. Steel toe-capped, work boots are not necessary but will protect your feet should you inadvertently drop a heavy object onto them.

12   Oils, greases and fluids

Each oil manufacturer produces an extensive range of lubricants and many have a motorcycle product range. Always aim to purchase motor oils designed for motorcycle use.

Whichever product you use, be guided by the motorcycle manufacturer who works very closely with the lubricant industry to select the best product to keep your machine in tip-top condition. The following is a selection of the many products you will need to service your machine.

Oils and Greases

Fork oil – This comes in various weights (viscosities). Consult your manual for the type for your machine.

Gear oil – Used in shaft drive units. It should also be used in machines with a separate gearbox where specifically stated by the machine manufacturer.

Two-stroke oil – Two-stroke engines use a separate oil supply for the engine and gearbox. The engine oil must be light as it is pumped into the inlet tract (from a separate tank) lubricates the internals and is then burnt in the combustion chamber. Refer to Chapter 3, Section 6 for more details.

Four-stroke engine oil – Most four-stroke engines use the same oil supply for the engine and gearbox. The oil will be of a multi-grade viscosity and either a straight mineral oil, semi-synthetic or fully synthetic type. Refer to Chapter 3, Section 6 for more details.

Greases – Copper grease, molybdenum disulphide grease, multipurpose grease and silicon grease are four commonly used types. All have specific applications, so ensure you use the correct type.

Chain wax or chain grease – Specially formulated for use with motorcycle final drive chains. Usually supplied in aerosol form.

Fluids

Thread locking agent – Used to ensure that nuts, bolts etc. stay tight. Do not over use this product as it fills the thread area and may make future removal extremely difficult.

Chrome cleaner – Used for the cleaning and protection of chrome plated components.

Coolant – Packaged either as ready mixed antifreeze and distilled water OR as straight antifreeze which requires mixing with distilled water in the correct ratio. Refer to Chapter 3, Section 4 for details. Do NOT mix different brands of antifreeze as the characteristics may vary. Read the label to ascertain the protection that the antifreeze will give.

Cooling system sealant – Can be used in an emergency to caulk small leaks from the radiator.

Brake and clutch hydraulic fluid – This must be used with care as most fluids will dissolve paint. Always use the type specified by the manufacturer. Refer to Chapter 4, Section 12 for details.

Brake cleaner – Leaves no residue and is used on disc and drum brakes. Note that brake dust is still dangerous even though asbestos is no longer used.

Light penetrating oil – Aerosol lubricant for a variety of applications.

Gasket sealants – Used as a sealant for rubber cam-cover gaskets and for engine covers where no gasket is used.

Chapter 2

Schedule

Service schedule & records

Contents

1 Service data

Unless you are familiar with finding your way around the workshop manual for your machine, you may prefer to extract the relevant service data and record it on a separate sheet. It can then be kept in your toolbox where it will be readily to hand. Store it in a plastic sleeve to protect it from dirty finger marks.

The following chart lists the basic items you will need to record, although it will need to be modified to suit your specific model. A similar chart can be created to record torque wrench settings for the chassis components (see Section 5).

Bike data

Make/model	
Engine number	
Frame number	
Ignition key number	
Steering lock key	
Minor service mileage interval	
Major service mileage interval	

Chassis specifications

Chain and sprockets	
Chain slack	
Chain size	
Number of links	
Front sprocket – no. of teeth	
Rear sprocket – no. of teeth	
Brakes	
Fluid type	
Friction material minimum thickness	
Pads	
Shoes	
Disc run-out (maximum)	
Disc thickness (minimum)	
Front brake lever freeplay	
Rear brake pedal freeplay	
Rear brake pedal height	
Front forks	
Fork oil type	
Fork oil quantity (per leg)	
Fork oil level	
Fork spring free length	
Clutch lever freeplay	
Tyre sizes	
Front	
Rear	
Tyre pressures (cold)	
Front	
Solo	
With passenger/luggage	
Rear	
Solo	
With passenger/luggage	
Tyre tread depth (minimum)	

Engine specifications

Engine oil	
Type/viscosity	
Quantity at oil change	
Quantity at oil and filter change	
Drain bolt torque wrench setting	
Gearbox oil	
Type	
Quantity at oil change	
Spark plug	
Type	
Gap	
Torque wrench setting	
Valve clearances (cold)	
Inlet	
Exhaust	
Engine cylinder compression	
Minimum (service limit)	
Maximum difference between cylinders (multi-cylinder engine)	
Coolant	
Antifreeze and distilled water ratio	
System capacity	
Engine idle speed	
Throttle freeplay	
Fuel level or float height	

Electrical specifications

Battery	
Capacity	
Charging rate	
Fuses	
Main	
Ignition/starter	
Headlight	
Signal/tail lamp/brake lights/horn	
Cooling fan	
Lights (bulbs)	
Headlamp	
Position lamp (parking)	
Stop/tail lamp	
Turn signal	
Instrument illumination	
Warning lights	

2 Checklist and records

A checklist is useful to ensure that nothing is missed from the service. Using the typical list shown below as a guide, make up a checklist for your machine and use a fresh copy each time to tick off items relevant to the service interval.

Keep your service sheets to remind you of the work that was carried out at the previous service and use it to record any comments or observations. If you like to keep track of how much you are spending on maintaining your machine, you can also attach receipts for any new items purchased.

HINT

Keep records of all service work that you carry out and receipts for new components purchased. Not only will this give a true record of the machine's service life, but it may even stand you in good stead when the time comes to part with the motorcycle.

Type of service:		Mileage:		Date checked:	/ /	
Air filter cleaned/replaced	☐		Engine idle speed correct			☐
Battery terminals greased	☐		Engine oil filter replaced			☐
Brake caliper bolts tight	☐		Engine oil changed			☐
Brake calipers cleaned	☐		Engine oil level correct			☐
Brake fluid level (front) correct	☐		Footrests/gear lever/brake pedal greased			☐
Brake fluid level (rear) correct	☐		Front wheel spindle clamp screws tight			☐
Brake pads (front) checked	☐		Headlamp aim correct			☐
Brake pads (rear) checked	☐		Lights checked			☐
Brake fluid (front) changed	☐		Rear brake light switch adjusted			☐
Brake fluid (rear) changed	☐		Rear wheel spindle nut tight			☐
Carburettors balanced	☐		Rear suspension bolts greased/tightened			☐
Chassis nuts/bolts tight	☐		Spark plugs cleaned/adjusted/replaced			☐
Choke cable adjusted	☐		Steering head bearings checked/adjusted			☐
Clutch cable adjusted	☐		Sump plug tight			☐
Coolant changed	☐		Throttle cable adjusted			☐
Coolant level correct	☐		Tyre pressure (front) checked			☐
Cylinder compression checked (see below)	☐		Tyre pressure (rear) checked			☐
Drive chain guide wear rate checked	☐		Tyre valve caps fitted			☐
Drive chain tension correct	☐		Wheel alignment checked			☐

Cylinder compression pressure

Keep a record of the figures obtained when carrying out a cylinder compression test. Make up a chart similar to that shown below, to suit the number of cylinders. Carry out the test as described in Chapter 3.

	Cylinder 1	Cylinder 2	Cylinder 3	Cylinder 4
Dry reading				
Wet reading				
Maximum difference between cylinders (deduct the lowest reading from the highest reading)				
Date / /		Mileage		

3   Service schedule

Shown on the opposite page is a typical service schedule for a four-stroke, air-cooled engined machine. Each machine will have a different service schedule, so it is essential that you follow the schedule in the owners or workshop manual for your model. The manufacturer will have devised a schedule specific to the mechanical characteristics of the machine, its performance and intended use, thus ensuring that the machine can be kept in tip-top condition.

Service intervals are usually expressed in terms of distance covered (miles or kilometres) and time. Follow the mileage or months (whichever comes first). Note that extending the times/mileages between services will be more costly in the end.

The service intervals for motorcycles tend to be shorter than for cars. This is to some extent because motorcycles rev to approximately twice the engine speed of cars and thus subject the engine to greater stress and wear. Unlike a car engine, the engine and gearbox of most four-stroke motorcycles is lubricated by the same oil. The oil has to withstand the very high temperatures of the engine whilst withstanding the tearing action applied to it as it lubricates the gearbox. Another very obvious reason for the shorter service intervals is that many components on a motorcycle are exposed to the weather elements.

Pre-ride checks

In addition to the items specified in the service schedule, your owners manual will also give a list of pre-ride checks which you should perform every time you ride the machine. Many of these are common sense, but if you get into the habit of checking them regularly you will be able to pick up things before they develop into serious faults.

✔ Check the engine oil level
✔ Check the brake fluid level (hydraulic brakes)
✔ Check the coolant level (liquid-cooled engines)
✔ Check the tyre pressures
✔ Check that the steering and suspension operate correctly
✔ Check the operation of the brakes
✔ Check that the drive chain doesn't look too slack
✔ Check that the throttle grips snaps shut when you release it
✔ Check that all lights work and that the horn works
✔ Check that the stand is held securely up when retracted

HINT

If you have purchased a second-hand machine which doesn't have a service history, it is advisable to carry out a full service then settle into the schedule given in the owner's manual.

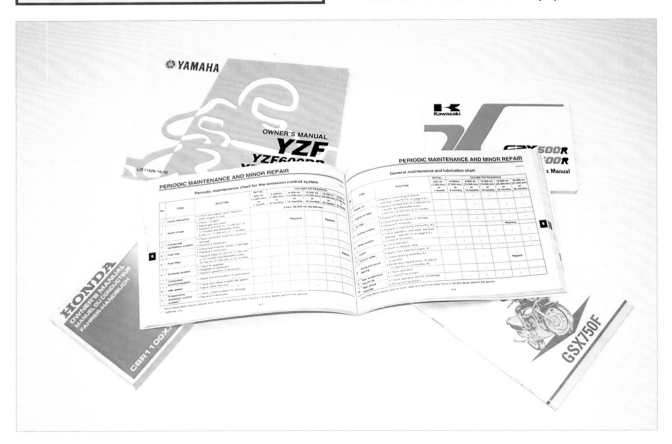

In the following service schedule example the minor service would be every 6000 km (4000 miles) or 12 months, and the major service every 12,000 km (7500 miles) or every two years. Note that the list of items in the 1000 km (600 mile) column relate to the machine's first service from new (initial service) and would usually be carried out by the dealer under the terms of the warranty. This initial service is not repeated, once done maintenance is then carried out at 6000 km/4000mile and 12,000 km/7500 mile intervals.

Certain items which do not fall into these categories, such as the air cleaner and drive chain are listed separately. Equally other items, such as the fuel and brake hoses, are only subject to a time interval for replacement. The symbol I denotes inspect, R denotes replace or change, and T denotes tighten.

Interval This should be judged by the odometer reading or months, whichever comes first	km Miles Months	Initial 1000 600 2	Minor 6000 4000 12	Major 12,000 7500 24	Minor 18,000 11,000 36	Major 24,000 15,000 48
Valve clearances		I	–	I	–	I
Spark plug(s)		–	I	R	I	R
Air cleaner element		Clean every 3000 km (2000 miles)				
Engine idle speed		I	I	I	I	I
Throttle cable play		I	I	I	I	I
Carburettor synchronisation		–	–	I	–	I
Fuel line		I	I	I	I	I
		Replace every four years				
Clutch (cable and lever freeplay)		I	I	I	I	I
Engine oil		R	R	R	R	R
Engine oil filter		R	–	R	–	R
Drive chain		I	I	I	I	I
		Clean and lubricate every 1000 km (600 miles)				
Brakes		I	I	I	I	I
Brake hose		–	I	I	I	I
		Replace every four years				
Brake fluid level		–	I	I	I	I
		Change every two years				
Tyres (pressures and condition)		–	I	I	I	I
Steering		I	–	I	–	I
Front forks		–	–	I	–	I
Rear suspension		–	–	I	–	I
Exhaust pipe and silencer bolts		T	–	T	–	T
Chassis nuts and bolts		T	T	T	T	T

4 Order of service

Deciding on what order to carry out the service will depend on whether the machine has a two-stroke or four-stroke engine, and in the case of a four-stroke whether the valves clearances require checking.

The following suggestions are for a major service on a four-stroke, multi-cylinder engined machine. It is assumed that the fuel tank, fairing panels etc. have been removed prior to the service.

A major service will often take a skilled mechanic at least four hours to complete. Leave yourself plenty of time or split the work across a couple of weekends, do the engine part one week and the chassis the following week. Make up a checklist (see Section 2) and tick the items off as you go.

Engine-related tasks:
1 With the engine cold, check and adjust valve clearances.
2 Clean and adjust or replace spark plugs.
3 Check fuel, vacuum and breather pipes for damage or leaks. Check the condition of their wire locking clips.
4 Adjust throttle cable and choke cable freeplay.
5 Fit vacuum gauges, start the engine and warm it up.
6 When warm, stop the engine and drain the old engine oil, fit new oil filter and pour new oil (correct type and quantity) into the engine.
7 Start the engine and adjust carburettor balance.
8 With balance correct, adjust tick over (idle speed). With the engine still running, turn the handlebars from lock to lock to ensure that steering movement does not cause engine speed to change.
9 Stop the engine, remove the vacuum gauges (refit take-off point caps, covers or hoses) and clean or replace air filter.
10 Leave the engine to settle for a few minutes then check and adjust the engine oil level.

Starting at the left-hand, rear of the machine and working forwards and around the motorcycle:
11 Check for play in rear wheel and swinging arm bearings, grease the swinging arm where grease nipples are fitted.
12 Check rear tyre pressure and inflate if necessary. Check tread depth and tyre condition.
13 Check condition of the rear wheel and the cush-drive rubbers.
14 Clean, lubricate and adjust the final drive chain tension and check condition of chain and sprockets.
15 Adjust wheel alignment.
16 Remove, grease and retighten rear suspension linkage bolts/nuts.
17 Strip, grease and re-assemble sidestand. Check, that sidestand switch works correctly.

18 Check that the centrestand retracts fully and if necessary strip and grease its pivot.
19 Strip, grease and re-assemble passenger footrests, rider footrests and gear lever pivot.
20 Drain the cooling system and refill with new coolant. Don't forget the expansion tank.
21 Lubricate the clutch cable and lever pivot, check cable condition and adjust cable freeplay.
22 Check front tyre pressure and inflate if necessary. Check tread depth and tyre condition.
23 Check condition of the front wheel and wheel bearings.
24 Remove, clean and refit the front brake caliper(s) and check the condition of the brake pads.
25 Check thickness, condition and run-out of front brake disc(s) and condition of brake hose(s).
26 Inspect front forks for damage and seals for signs of leaking.
27 Check the steering head bearings for slack or over tightness and adjust as necessary.

Working down the right hand side of the machine:
28 Lubricate the front brake lever pivot, check brake fluid level and top up as necessary.
29 If the service calls for brake fluid change, do it now for the front brakes.
30 Operate handlebar switches to check that all lights, turn signals, horn etc. work. Check headlamp alignment.
31 If the service did not call for the coolant to be changed, check the level in the reserve tank and top up as necessary.
32 Strip and clean the rear brake pedal pivot, adjust the pedal height and freeplay and check the operation of brake light switch.
33 Check the rear brake fluid level and top up as necessary. If the service calls for a fluid change, do it after you have cleaned the caliper and checked the disc and hoses.
34 Remove, clean and refit the rear brake caliper and check the condition of the brake pads.
35 Check the thickness, condition and run-out of the rear brake disc and condition of brake hose(s).
36 Prior to refitting the seat and road testing the machine, clean and retighten battery connections, carry out a charging voltage test then smear a small amount of petroleum jelly on each terminal.
37 Check condition and routing of battery breather pipe where fitted (maintenance free batteries don't have a breather pipe).
38 Refit all fairing panels, fuel tank etc. and road test the machine. When road testing check for smooth operation of the throttle, suspension, correct handling and brake operation. On completion of the road test, check that there are no coolant and oil leaks, leave the engine to cool for a few minutes then recheck the oil level.

5   Chassis nuts and bolts tightening

The manufacturer's service schedule will often state that the chassis nuts/bolts should be checked for tightness at regular intervals.

Do NOT use a torque wrench and socket to check if the nut or bolt is tight. The nut/bolt should be slightly loosened (about 1/4 turn) and then re-tightened to the correct setting using a torque wrench and appropriate socket. Do ONE nut/bolt AT A TIME to ensure that none are left loose.

The following table lists the important safety parts that should be checked for tightness, with a column for the actual torque setting specified by the manufacturer. Make up a similar list to suit your machine and fill in the torque settings as stated in your owners or workshop manual. Keep the list with the service data sheet described in Section 1.

Torque values are usually expressed in Nm (Newton-metre) units. You may also encounter kgf-m, lbf-ft and lbf-in units. If the units given do not correspond with the scale on your torque wrench you will need to convert the figure. See the 'Conversion factors' page at the end of this book for details.

* Certain items will require the removal of a split pin prior to checking tightness. Always fit a new split pin afterwards.

Item	Torque
Steering stem head bolt	
Front fork upper clamp bolt	
Front fork lower clamp bolt	
Front wheel spindle nut*	
Front wheel spindle pinch bolt (where used)	
Handlebar mounting bolts	
Front brake master cylinder mounting bolt	
Front brake caliper mounting bolts	
Front and rear brake disc mounting bolts	
Rear brake caliper mounting bolts	
Rear brake master cylinder mounting bolt	
Swinging arm pivot nut	
Rear shock absorber mounting bolts	
Rear suspension linkage pivot bolts/nuts	
Rear wheel spindle nut*	
Rear sprocket nuts	
Rear brake torque arm nut*	
Front and rear brake cam lever bolts (drum brakes)	
Exhaust system mounting bolts/nuts	
Footrest and stand mountings	

Chapter 3

Engine

Contents

1   Engine cycles

Two-stroke and four-stroke engine types are referred to in this chapter and described below. An understanding of their operating cycles will help when carrying out maintenance procedures, such as the valve clearances on a four-stroke engine, and aid fault finding when tracing running problems.

Two-stroke engine

The simple 'piston-ported' two-stroke engine is described below. In this basic form the two-stroke is not a particularly efficient design, but improved performance can be gained from the use of reed valve or disc valve induction and variable exhaust port timing devices.

Induction and compression stroke

The piston is nearing the top of its stroke and the fuel/air mixture above it (blue shaded area) is being compressed ready for combustion. As the piston has been rising the crankcase volume has been increasing, but since it is sealed a partial vacuum has been created. The piston has now passed the inlet port and fresh fuel/air mixture (indicated by the blue arrows) is drawn into the crankcase from the carburettor.

Ignition and exhaust stroke

The spark plug ignites the compressed mixture and the expanding gases force the piston downwards. The piston covers the transfer and inlet ports and begins to compress the fresh mixture trapped below it in the crankcase. As the top of the piston passes the exhaust port, the gases in the combustion chamber (indicated by the red arrows), which are still under some pressure (though most of the useful energy has been used to move the piston), rush out through the exhaust port.

The top of the piston then passes the transfer port, and the fresh mixture is now able to pass from the crankcase into the combustion chamber. Note that the transfer port directs the incoming mixture upwards, where it helps to displace the burnt gases. If this were not done, the incoming mixture would tend to rush (or 'short-circuit' as it is known) straight out of the exhaust port, wasting fuel and leaving some of the burnt mixture from the last power stroke in the cylinder.

The piston reaches the bottom of its stroke and begins to rise again. The transfer and exhaust ports close and the mixture in the combustion chamber is compressed. As the piston continues to rise, creating vacuum in the crankcase, the inlet port is uncovered and thus the cycle is completed and repeated.

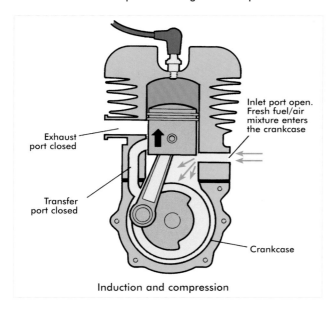

Exhaust port closed

Transfer port closed

Inlet port open. Fresh fuel/air mixture enters the crankcase

Crankcase

Induction and compression

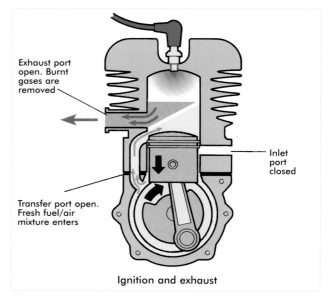

Exhaust port open. Burnt gases are removed

Transfer port open. Fresh fuel/air mixture enters

Inlet port closed

Ignition and exhaust

Four-stroke engine

Two revolutions of the crankshaft and four strokes of the piston complete one cycle of the four-stroke engine. While the four events 'induction, compression, ignition and exhaust' (or suck, squeeze, bang, blow as they are sometimes endearingly referred to) become inter-mixed over the cycle of a two-stroke engine, in a four-stroke engine each event is more defined, and in principal is assigned its own stroke in the cycle.

Induction stroke

+ The inlet valve is open and exhaust valve is closed.
+ Rotation of the crankshaft draws the piston downwards, towards the bottom of the cylinder, creating a low-pressure area above the piston.
+ The difference in the pressure above the piston, and atmospheric pressure, causes the air/fuel mixture to enter the cylinder.

Compression stroke

+ Both valves are closed.
+ Just after bottom dead centre (BDC), the inlet valve closes and the piston is driven back up the cylinder, compressing the charge (air/fuel mixture) to a predetermined value. This value is dependent upon the compression ratio of the engine.

Ignition (power) stroke

+ Both valves are closed
+ Just before the piston reaches top dead centre and final compression is achieved the mixture is ignited and a controlled burn takes place. As the piston travels over top dead centre the burning gases drive the piston down the bore.

+ Why is the ignition point before TDC? Although the cycle may be operating hundreds of times per second it still takes a length of time to burn all of the fresh charge. The burning of the charge, in what is a fixed space at TDC, raises the gas pressure to a very high value, which in turn is what drives the piston down the bore with great force. To obtain maximum power from each burn the engine designer wants the maximum pressure to occur just as the piston is at the end of its upper ineffective crank angle. To achieve this total burn the ignition must commence before TDC.

Exhaust stroke

+ The exhaust valve is open and the inlet valve is closed.
+ Just before the piston reaches the bottom of the stroke the exhaust valve opens, effectively signalling the end of the power stroke.
+ The pressure inside the combustion chamber is much higher than the pressure outside; thus, the burnt gases will start to leave, via the exhaust port, as soon as the valve opens.
+ The piston passes through BDC and starts its rise up the cylinder bore again. Although the burnt gases are leaving the cylinder, most of the energy has been used driving the piston down the bore therefore the rising piston pushes the remaining gas out of the cylinder.
+ Just before TDC, the inlet valve starts to open and there is a 'drag' effect on the fresh charge created by the exhaust gas leaving. This is the end of one cycle and the induction stroke of the next cycle begins.

> At an engine speed of 6000 revs/min the piston moves up and down 100 TIMES EVERY SECOND

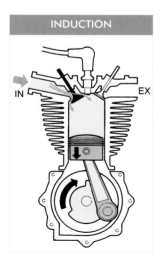

INDUCTION

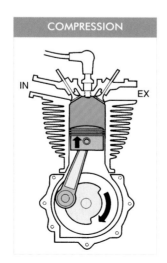

COMPRESSION

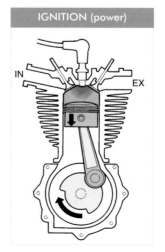

IGNITION (power)

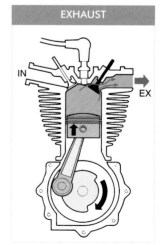

EXHAUST

2 Valve clearance check – four-stroke engines

The importance of checking the valve clearances regularly cannot be stressed highly enough.

If a valve clearance is **too large**, this can lead to a lot of noise at the top of the engine caused by the valve gear 'beating itself to death' and this hammering action leads to engine damage. Overly large clearances will also cause a reduction in power output. The valve opens later than it should and closes earlier, thus reducing the time the valve is open (duration). The reduction in inlet valve duration gives a corresponding reduction in the quantity of fuel/air that enters the cylinder. The exhaust valve, likewise, will not be open for as long as it should, resulting in poor scavenging and leading to contamination of the fresh charge. Consequently the rider will open the throttle that much more leading to a reduction in the fuel consumption figures and increasing the exhaust emissions.

Logic suggests that zero valve clearances should be the norm, but this is a false assumption. The maximum temperature of the burning gases, within the combustion chamber, is approximately the same as required to melt platinum. The exhaust gas temperature is approximately the same as that for the melting point of aluminium and it is only by good design of the engine and cooling system that the engine doesn't melt.

If a valve clearance is **too small**, the valve will not fully contact its seat once the engine reaches its operating temperature. Because almost all of the heat that goes into the head of the valve is transferred to the cylinder head, when the valve is closed, it is essential that the valve should be able to seat fully.

With an engine, doing 12,000 revs/min the crankshaft will be rotating 200 times per second and each valve is opening and closing 100 times per second. The four-stroke engine takes two revolutions of the crankshaft to complete each cycle therefore each valve has only 1/100th of a second to open and close and get rid of its heat before it all starts again. The exhaust valve takes the brunt of this, as it doesn't get a shot of cool incoming mixture like the inlet valve.

Refer to the machine's owners manual for the interval at which the valve clearances should be checked. An engine with 'screw and locknut' type valve adjustment will require checking more frequently than an engine with shim type valve adjustment. Typically, a manufacturer may specify an interval of every 3000 miles for a screw and locknut system, and intervals ranging from 8000 to 16,000 miles for a shim type system.

Refer to the appropriate valve clearance checking procedure in the following part of this section. The terms SOHC and DOHC relate to single overhead camshaft or double overhead camshaft engine types. Valve clearances are adjusted by a 'screw and locknut' mechanism or by a shim located either above or below the follower (bucket). Set aside sufficient time to carry out the valve clearance check, although checking and adjusting the clearances on a single cylinder 2-valve engine can be done fairly quickly it is a quite different matter on a four cylinder 16-valve engine, especially if replacement shims are required.

 Caution: The valve clearances must always be checked when the engine is cold.

Cylinder identification

In the case of a multi-cylinder engine mounted transversely in the frame, note that its cylinders are numbered from LEFT to RIGHT on the crankshaft - when sat on the motorcycle cylinder No. 1 is on the left. This is less obvious on a V-Twin engine due to the cylinder angles, but the same rule applies; cylinder No. 1 is the first cylinder from the left-hand end of the crankshaft and is usually angled to the front of the engine.

Where an engine has the crankshaft running in-line with the frame and wheels (e.g. Honda Gold Wing, Moto Guzzi or BMW) the cylinders are numbered from the front of the crankshaft.

Turning the engine

Most transverse engines normally run in a forward direction, but there are few which run backwards. Check the workshop manual for the correct direction of rotation.

When you are turning the crankshaft, to line up the camshafts for valve clearance checks, **never** rotate the crankshaft in the opposite direction to normal running; if you do, the cam chain tension will be transferred to the opposite side of the engine. This could cause the chain to 'jump' a tooth on the crankshaft sprocket, putting the crankshaft to camshaft timing out with disastrous results.

If you do pass the timing marks, continue to rotate the crankshaft, in the forward direction, and line up the timing marks again. Remember two revolutions of the crankshaft equal one revolution of the camshaft.

Note that removing the spark plug(s) or just slackening them by a few turns will make it much easier to turn the engine.

SOHC engine with screw and locknut type adjusters

Items required

✔ Set of feeler gauges
✔ Spanners, sockets, Allen keys as required
✔ Valve adjusting tool if square-head valve adjusters are fitted (see Chapter 1)
✔ Oil can filled with fresh engine oil
✔ Silicon grease
✔ The recommended valve clearance settings

Procedure

Before carrying out this procedure check that the engine is cold and that the ignition is turned OFF.

1 The inlet and the exhaust covers are on opposite sides of the engine. Both covers must be removed to gain access to the valve adjusters. There will be a rubber 'O' ring sealing each cover and this can sometimes cause the cover to stick to the engine casing. If this happens, ensure that **all** bolts are removed, and **gently** tap the top of the cover with a plastic hammer to break the seal.

2 This engine has two circular caps on the left-hand side. The centre one allows access to the crankshaft (to enable it to be manually rotated) and the upper one covers the timing marks.

Check the condition both of the rubber sealing rings, if in doubt renew them otherwise engine oil will weep out. Where no inspection caps are provided, the complete cover will have to be removed.

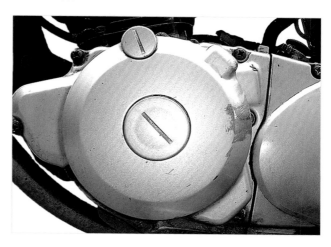

3 The valves **must** be adjusted with the piston at Top Dead Centre (TDC) on the **compression** stroke. The mark shown, when lined up with the index mark on the case will position the piston at TDC. Because a four-stroke engine takes **two** revolutions of the crankshaft to complete one cycle there will be **two** positions when the piston is at TDC.

4 To ensure that you adjust the valves at the correct position (TDC on the compression stroke), rotate the crankshaft in the normal direction of rotation whilst watching the **INLET** valve. Watch the valve open (go down) then close (come back up). Continue to rotate the engine until the index marks line up. If you rotate the crank past the marks **do not** turn the engine backwards, go round and do it again. Turning the engine backwards will cause the slack in the cam chain to be on the wrong side, which may allow the cam chain to 'jump' the cam sprocket changing the valve timing. If this happens the piston may hit a valve with disastrous results.

5 Which valve you adjust first doesn't matter, but you should slide an appropriate sized feeler gauge between the adjuster and the top of the valve. On this engine the specified inlet clearance is 0.05 to 0.09 mm, therefore a 0.05 mm gauge should fit whereas a 0.09 mm should not.

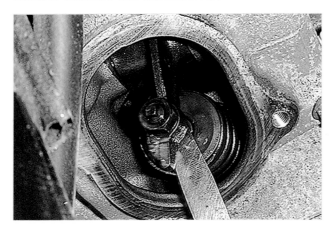

6 If adjustment is required, select a feeler gauge that is in the middle of the specified clearance range. In this instance, a gauge of 0.07 mm has been used for the inlet valve. Slacken the locknut, back off the adjuster (if necessary) and slide the gauge between the adjuster and valve.

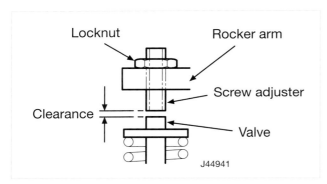

7 Turn the adjuster so that the gauge is a firm, but sliding fit between the adjuster and valve. Hold the adjuster and tighten the locknut. Repeat this process for the other valve, bearing in mind that the clearance for the exhaust valve will probably be larger than for the inlet valve. **Clean the gauge between uses.**

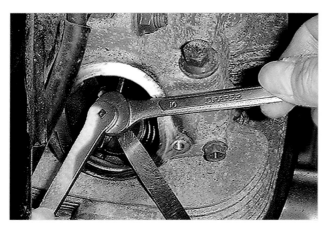

8 If working on a four-cylinder engine you can treat each cylinder as a separate engine, adjusting the inlet and exhaust valve with its respective piston at TDC on the compression stroke.

Alternatively, you can position cylinder No. 1 (left hand side) at TDC on the compression stroke and adjust the following valve clearances: inlet and exhaust valves of cylinder No. 1, inlet valve for cylinder No. 3 and exhaust valve for cylinder No. 2.

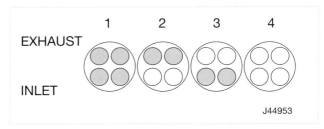

Then rotate the engine ONE complete turn and adjust the clearances for: inlet and exhaust valves for cylinder No. 4, inlet valve for cylinder No. 2 and exhaust valve for cylinder No. 3.

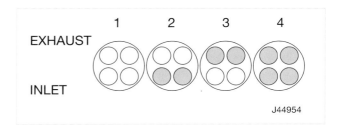

9 Before re-fitting the caps and covers, rotate the crankshaft **two** complete turns to bring the piston back to TDC on the compression stroke. Re-check the valve clearances and make certain that the locknuts are tight.

10 Smear a small amount of silicon grease or engine oil onto the cover O-rings to prevent them catching and tearing when the component is re-installed. Squirt a shot or two of clean engine oil between the adjuster and valve stem.

Clean the surfaces of the engine (where the covers will fit) and refit all covers. If the spark plug(s) was/were slackened to help rotate the engine, remember to tighten them.

DOHC engine with screw and locknut type adjusters

Items required

✔ Allen keys
✔ Variety of sockets and spanners
✔ Valve adjusting tool (see Chapter 1)
✔ Gasket sealant
✔ Oil can filled with fresh engine oil
✔ Parts tray to store screws etc.
✔ The recommended valve clearance settings

Procedure

Before carrying out this procedure check that the engine is cold and that the ignition is turned OFF.

1 Gain access to the top of the engine by removing the seat, fuel tank, airbox and any fairing panels. On liquid-cooled engines, it may be necessary to drain the coolant and remove the radiator for access – check with your manual.

2 On the engine photographed there are two external oil pipes, which must be released. Between the oil pipe and cylinder head cover will be some form of gasket, usually a rubber ring, make sure that it is in good condition. If uncertain – renew it on reassembly.

3 Slacken the cam cover screws in the order shown in your manual, about one turn is enough. The order will usually be from the **outside** inwards, in a diagonal sequence, as this will prevent the cover distorting. With all the screws loosened, remove and place them in your parts tray for safekeeping.

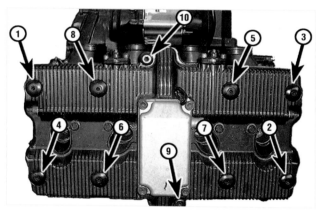

Watch out for any rubber sealing gaskets which may come off with the screws or stay stuck to the cam cover. Lift and slide out the cam cover. It may be a tight fit in the frame, so take your time and if it appears that the cover won't come out, step back and have a second look at it.

4 Take great care NOT to damage the rubber cam cover gasket. This machine also has four, separate, gaskets around the spark plug holes. Make certain that these are also removed. There is one (arrowed) on the right-hand side of the engine that has been purposely left in place as an example.

5 Move to the side of the engine that houses the ignition rotor and remove the screws holding the cover. This will allow access to the end of the crankshaft so that you can position the cams for the valve clearances to be inspected and adjusted. Put the screws in your parts tray and remove the cover and gasket; obtain a new gasket.

You may find that one of the cover screws has a sealing ring around it. If there is one, note which hole this screw fits into and, when re-assembling the parts fit it back here. The seal is important because it seals an oilway in the engine.

6 Behind the cover, you will find the ignition pulse coil (arrowed) and the ignition rotor.

7 Use a socket or ring spanner to turn the engine in the forward direction (normal running direction) until the timing mark on the rotor (usually a scribed line next to a 'T' mark) lines up with an index mark usually in the centre of the pulse coil. **Never** use the Allen headed screw in the centre to turn the crankshaft, use the large nut shape on the rotor. On the engine shown, with the rotor on the right-hand side, the forward direction is clockwise as you look at it. **Note:** *If there is also an 'F' mark on the rotor then this is for the ignition timing – ignore it for this task.*

8 To ensure that cylinder No. 1 is at TDC on the compression stroke, watch the inlet valve of that cylinder. As you rotate the crankshaft, the inlet valve(s) will open (go down) and then close (rise up). The next time that the 'T' mark aligns with its index mark, pistons 1 and 4 will at TDC. If you have the camshafts in the correct position for cylinders 1 and 4, their lobes will be away from the rockers, i.e. not depressing the valves.

9 Should you turn the crankshaft past the 'T' mark DO NOT, under ANY circumstances turn the engine backwards. This will cause the slack in the cam chain to be transferred to the wrong side of the engine, and may allow the chain to 'jump' a tooth on the crankshaft sprocket. This will immediately cause the crankshaft to camshaft relationship (cam timing) to be wrong. If this happens, the piston may hit a valve with disastrous results.

10 With the camshafts in this position (cylinder No. 1 at TDC on compression) the inlet and exhaust valves of cylinder No. 1

can be checked. If working on a four cylinder engine you can also check the exhaust valve of cylinder No. 2 and the inlet valve of cylinder No. 3.

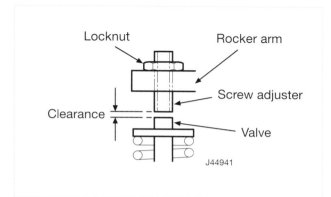

11 The feeler gauge MUST be inserted between the end of the valve and the tip of the adjuster screw. Where a forked rocker arm is used to operate two valves each valve must be measured and adjusted SEPARATELY. **Do not** place the feeler gauge between the rocker arm and the cam, as this will give a false clearance.

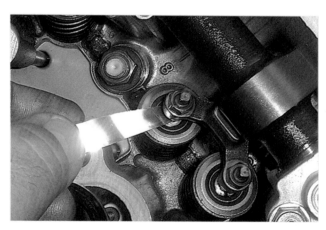

12 The manufacturer will specify a tolerance for the valve clearances. For example, those for the engine photographed are 0.10 to 0.15 mm inlet and 0.18 to 0.23 mm exhaust. To check that the clearance is within tolerance, a feeler gauge equal to the lower value MUST fit whereas a gauge equal to the higher value should NOT.

13 Measure the clearances of the valves identified in Step 10. Rather than just check and adjust those valves that are out of tolerance, it is better to adjust ALL valves.

14 To adjust the valve clearance, slacken the locknut by about 1/2 – 1 turn. If the clearance is below the minimum specified you will have to loosen the adjuster screw as well.

15 Select a feeler gauge that is equal in size to the midpoint of the tolerance and slide it between the end of the valve and the adjuster screw tip. On the engine photographed the gauge for the inlet would be 0.12 mm and 0.20 mm for the exhaust.

16 The engine photographed has 4 mm heads to the adjuster screws so use the special tool (see Chapter 1) to reposition the adjuster screw so that there is a firm but sliding grip on the feeler gauge. Do NOT use pliers, as they will slip. Note that some engines feature a slotted adjuster head which can be turned using a flat-bladed screwdriver.

17 Hold the adjuster screw in position and tighten the locknut. Recheck the clearance, as tightening the nut can sometimes change the setting. Re-adjust as necessary.

18 Now rotate the crankshaft one full turn (360°) and line up the timing marks again. This will position the pistons for cylinders 1 and 4 back at TDC but cylinder No. 4 will now be on the compression stroke. Repeat the adjustment process for the inlet and exhaust valves of cylinder No. 4, the inlet valve of cylinder No. 2 and the exhaust valve of cylinder No. 3.

19 Before you fit the cam cover, use an oil can filled with fresh engine oil to lubricate the cams, bearings, rocker arms and the ends of the valves. Check that all the adjuster screw locknuts are tight.

20 Apply a small amount of sealant (bonding agent) to the gasket grooves to hold the gasket in place. Its application is especially important on the four spark plug hole gaskets because it prevents oil leaks.

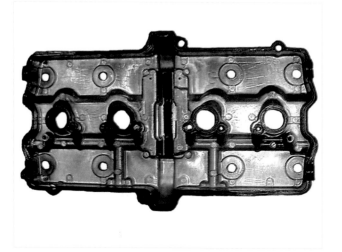

If the engine has four separate half-moon shaped plugs which locate in cut-outs in the cylinder head, also apply a smear of sealant to the plugs or cut-outs.

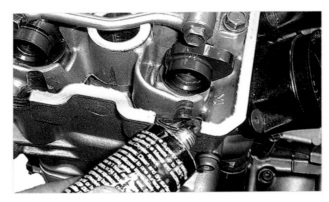

Smear sealant or bonding agent on the rubber seals for the cam cover bolts.

21 Fit all bolts, with their seals, into the cam cover then tighten each, finger-tight only. If an external oil pipe is fitted, place new gaskets on the flanges and fit the pipe to the cam cover. With all bolts secured finger-tight, tighten them evenly, starting from the centre and working outwards in a diagonal pattern (see numbered sequence).

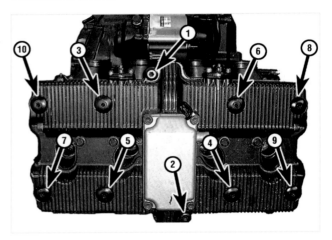

22 Fit a new gasket against the side of the engine and fit the ignition rotor cover. Fit the screws, and secure them finger-tight, then tighten each screw securely. Remember that there may be an 'O' ring fitted to one screw (see Step 5).

23 When all other jobs have been completed, run the engine and check that there are no oil leaks (if there are, did you clean off any old gasket from the cover and engine cases? Any old gasket left will cause a leak). Also check that there are no abnormal noises (e.g. rattles) coming from the top-end of the engine.

'Shim over bucket' type adjustment

Items required

✔ Appropriate screwdrivers, Allen keys or sockets
✔ Set of feeler gauges

✔ Micrometer 0 – 25 mm
✔ Oil can filled with clean engine oil
✔ Magnet on a stick – see tools chapter
✔ Clean cloth or kitchen paper
✔ Bucket depressing tool – which type depends upon the make of your machine
✔ For some engines you will need a new cam cover gasket – others have a re-useable rubber gasket – check before starting this task. If a rubber gasket is used, you will also need sealant
✔ Parts tray to store screws etc.
✔ The recommended valve clearance settings

Procedure

Before carrying out this procedure check that the engine is cold and that the ignition is turned OFF.

1 Remove the seat, fuel tank, airbox and any fairing panels necessary to gain access to the top of the engine.

2 Undo each cam cover bolt by about 1/2 a turn in the sequence shown in your manual. The order will usually be from the **outside** inwards, in a diagonal sequence, as this will prevent the cover distorting.

3 With each bolt slackened, remove all bolts and place them in the parts tray. Lift the cam cover and manoeuvre it out of the frame. Note that the rubber gasket will either be stuck to the cover or remain on the head. Take care not to tear the gasket on the cam chain or any sharp item.

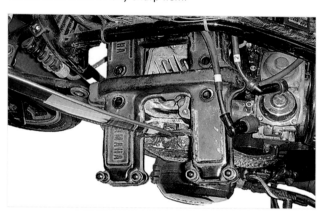

4 Depending on the design of the engine, the timing marks will either be on the generator rotor or the ignition rotor. On the engine shown below they are on the generator rotor. Remove the screws from the alternator cover and remove the cover.

The alternator stator (windings) is mounted inside the outer case and there will be some resistance to the cover coming off due to the magnetic effect of the rotor acting on the stator windings.

5 On the engine shown below the timing marks are on the ignition rotor. Remove the cap from the centre of the cover to access the end of the crankshaft.

Removal of the smaller cap above the crankshaft exposes the timing marks. The timing mark in the photo has been emphasised for clarity. To see yours more clearly highlight the mark with a small drop of white paint; use a small paintbrush or a dead matchstick pared to a point.

6 Using a spanner or a socket, rotate the crankshaft in the forward direction to line up the mark on the rotor (usually a scribed line with 'T' next to it) with the index mark on the casing. On a four cylinder engine this will position pistons 1 and 4 at Top Dead Centre (TDC).

7 To establish the compression stroke for cylinder No. 1, watch the inlet valve/cam for that cylinder as you rotate the crankshaft. The valve will open (move downwards) then move back upwards and close. Now look at the crankshaft and continue to rotate it in the forward direction. The NEXT time the rotor and crankcase index marks line up the piston will be at TDC on the compression stroke for that cylinder. If you go past the marks **never** turn the engine backwards – go round again.

8 With cylinder No. 1 on compression, its cam lobes should be positioned as shown below, with the lobes not depressing the valves. Note that on many engines slots in the camshaft ends or lines on the camshaft sprockets will line up with the cylinder head surface.

9 Use a feeler gauge to measure the clearance between the base circle of the cam and the shim for all the inlet and exhaust valves for cylinder No. 1 and note them down. On a four cylinder engine you can also measure the clearance for the exhaust valve(s) of cylinder No. 2 and inlet valve(s) of cylinder No. 3 with the crankshaft in this position.

Note these down as you measure them. At the end of this section is a typical chart to write down your measurements.

Before moving on to the next stage, double-check the clearances you have measured. Taking accurate readings is essential when calculating any replacement shims needed.

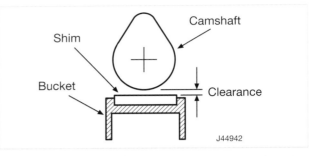

10 Now rotate the crankshaft (in the forward direction) one complete revolution (360°), realigning the index marks on the rotor. Now measure and record the clearances for the inlet and exhaust valves for cylinder No. 4, inlet for cylinder No. 2 and exhaust for cylinder No. 3. Re-check your measurements before moving onto the next stage.

11 Now compare the valve clearances recorded on your chart with those specified by the manufacturer, noting that inlet and exhaust clearances are usually different. Any measured clearances which fall outside of the specified range will require the shim to be changed on that valve.

12 To change a shim, rotate the crankshaft to position the selected piston at TDC on the compression stroke (see earlier). With the piston at TDC on the compression stroke all shims for that cylinder can be removed/replaced, but do them **one at a time**.

13 Use a small, flat-bladed screwdriver to turn the bucket so that its shim removal slot (arrowed) is positioned towards the middle of the engine.

14 Fit the valve-depressing tool so that it presses onto the edge of the bucket and **not** on the shim.

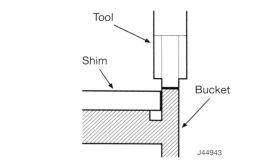

Note that you may have to hold the slot in the bucket with a screwdriver to prevent it rotating as you pull down on the handle depressing the bucket. The tool may slip off the bucket as you press down on the handle. The trick is to keep the tool and bucket at exactly 90° to each other and take your time. Make sure that the slot is still roughly central when the tool is fully down. You don't have to keep hold of the tool once it is down, as it will stay there by itself.

HINT

Before carrying out the next stage, it is advisable to place kitchen paper or a clean cloth into the top of the cam chain tunnel. If the shim should slip whilst you are removing or replacing it, and drops down the cam chain tunnel, you will have a total engine strip on your hands.

15 Use a small, flat-bladed screwdriver in the slot to prise up the shim.

With the shim lifted, use a small magnet-on-a-stick or a pair of tweezers to pull out the shim. Pull the shim clear of the bucket.

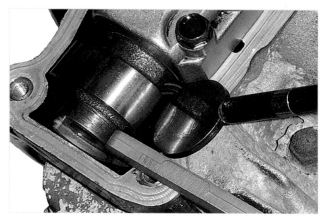

16 Measure the shim you have just removed and calculate the size of the shim you will need to replace it. Note the size etched on the shim, it isn't always there so be on the safe side and measure it anyway, and always in the centre of the shim, not the edges (see Chapter 1 for details of how to read a micrometer).

17 Using the shim size, measured valve clearance from your chart and the specified clearance, calculate the figure necessary to bring the clearance within tolerance. If the measured valve clearance is below the minimum specified then a **smaller** shim must be fitted. If the clearance is greater than the maximum specified then a **larger** shim must be fitted.

For example:

Clearance measured is 0.08 mm, manufacturer's specified valve clearance is 0.11 to 0.15 mm. Deduct clearance measured from minimum specification, i.e. 0.08 from 0.11 = 0.03 mm. Now measure the shim that has been removed and write down this figure (e.g. 2.75 mm).

In this example you would need to fit a shim that was at least 0.03 mm **smaller** than the original shim to bring the clearance within specification. Shims are usually available in increments of 0.05 mm; therefore using a 2.70 mm shim would make the clearance 0.13 mm, which is still within the tolerance.

18 It is unlikely that you will have a stock of shims with which to select the new size but note it anyway as most motorcycle dealers have shims in stock or can get them for you. You may be able to switch the shim with one of the others that needs replacing.

> ⚠ **Caution: Don't be tempted to use a shim from a different make of motorcycle just because the shim looks like it may fit. There can be minute differences in the diameters of some shims that the manufacturers use, and should the shim leave its bucket at any engine speed the resulting damage to your engine won't be a pretty sight.**

19 When refitting the existing shim or fitting the new one, always coat both sides with clean engine oil before placing it in its bucket.

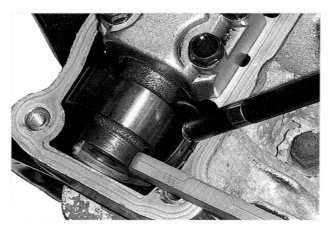

Using the magnet-on-a-stick or a pair of tweezers, slide the shim into place with its etched number facing **downwards**, otherwise the action of the cam, wiping across the shim, will cause any number etched on it to be worn off.

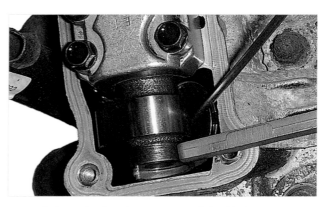

20 With the tool still in place, use a small, flat bladed screwdriver to push the shim fully home in its bucket. It is vitally important that the shim is completely seated in the bucket. With the shim in place, release the pressure by gently lifting the handle of the special tool and remove it completely. Remember to remove any cloth or paper you placed in the top of the cam chain tunnel.

21 Rotate the crankshaft two complete revolutions to bring the valve back to its previous position and recheck the valve clearance. This process squeezes the excess oil out of the shim to bucket seating, ensures that the shim is fully home in its seat and confirms that your calculations were correct.

22 Now position the next cylinder at TDC on the compression stroke to repeat the process on any other shims which need changing.

23 Coat the cams and shims with fresh engine oil before refitting the cam cover gasket. If necessary, carefully use a scraper to clean the gasket surface. Any bits of old gasket left on the gasket face will cause the joint to leak.

24 Smear sealant on any rubber gaskets that may be around the cam cover bolts and ensure that the gaskets are in good condition; if in doubt renew them. Finally, fit the cam cover gasket in place. If it is a rubber one a small amount of sealant will help to hold it in place in the cover. If it is of the paper type then it lays on the cylinder head and will NOT need any sealant, the coating on the gasket does it all. Fit the cam cover and check that the gasket is seated properly. Tighten the cover bolts in a diagonal sequence starting from the centre and working outwards.

25 Smear sealant on the alternator rotor cover or ignition rotor cover rubber seals, or fit a new gasket if of the paper type. Fit the covers.

26 With everything put back together run the engine and check that there are no oil leaks or top-end rattles.

Valve clearance chart

Note: *The layout of this chart corresponds to a 16-valve four cylinder engine. Similar charts can be drawn for engines with a different number of cylinders/valves or different engine configurations. It can be used on an engine with shim type valve adjustment to record measured valve clearances, existing shim thickness and then following calculation, also the required replacement shim thickness.*

a) Measure the clearance for EACH valve and record the figure in the appropriate circle.
b) Note which valve clearances are outside of the manufacturer's specified tolerance.
c) Remove the shim and record its size (thickness) on the chart where marked 'Shim fitted'.
d) Calculate the size of replacement shim needed to bring the clearance within the specification (see text). Record this figure on the chart where marked 'Replacement'.

Valve clearances

Exhaust ....

Inlet J44944

Shim fitted   ....
Replacement   ....

      CYLINDER 1   CYLINDER 2   CYLINDER 3   CYLINDER 4

EXHAUST   ◯ ◯   ◯ ◯   ◯ ◯   ◯ ◯

INLET   ◯ ◯   ◯ ◯   ◯ ◯   ◯ ◯

Shim fitted   ....
Replacement   ....

'Shim under bucket' type adjustment

Shim changing on this type of engine isn't a job for the amateur mechanic as it requires removal of the camshafts. You can, however, measure the clearances quite easily and pass this information to your dealer who will remove the camshafts and change the shims. For the skilled mechanic, the camshafts can be removed following the procedure in the workshop manual.

Items required

✔ Sockets, spanners and Allen keys as required
✔ Feeler gauges
✔ Gasket sealant
✔ Oil can filled with fresh engine oil
✔ Parts tray to store screws etc.
✔ The recommended valve clearance settings

Procedure

Before carrying out this procedure check that the engine is cold and that the ignition is turned OFF.

1 Remove the fuel tank, airbox and any fairing panels necessary to gain access to the cam cover.

2 Remove the cam cover bolts in a diagonal sequence, starting from the outside and working inwards. Lift and slide the cam cover off the engine taking care to ensure that the gasket is not damaged. If the gasket sticks to part of the cylinder head, do not pull it off. Slide a thin feeler gauge between the gasket and the head and ease the gasket away.

3 This engine has two caps on the right-hand side of the engine. Removal of the large cap exposes the bolt head used to rotate the crankshaft, the smaller cap covers the timing marks.

Use a socket through the engine cover and rotate the engine in the forward direction until the timing marks line up. The timing marks will take the form of a scribed line on the ignition rotor (usually next to a 'T' mark) and a static index mark on the edge of the inspection hole.

4 To set cylinder No. 1 at TDC on its compression stroke, watch the inlet valve/cam for that cylinder as you rotate the crankshaft. The valve will open (move downwards) then move back upwards and close. Now look at the crankshaft and continue to rotate it in the forward direction. The next time that the rotor and crankcase index marks line up the piston will be at TDC on the compression stroke and the cam lobes will be away from the valves as shown below.

5 If you do go past the marks, never turn the engine backwards. Should you turn the engine backwards this will cause the slack in the cam chain to be transferred to the wrong side of the engine, and may allow the chain to 'jump' a tooth on the crankshaft sprocket. This will immediately cause the crankshaft to camshaft relationship (cam timing) to be wrong. With the result that a piston could contact a valve with disastrous results.

6 Starting with the inlet valve(s) of cylinder No. 1 use feeler gauges until you find one that gives a firm, but sliding fit between the cam base circle and the bucket. Record the measured clearance for each valve – make up a chart similar to that on the previous page so that the valves can be easily identified. This engine has four valves per cylinder; therefore, BOTH inlet valves must be measured and recorded. Move to the exhaust valves of cylinder No. 1 and measure and record the clearances of BOTH valves.

7 With the cams still in this position measure and record, the valve clearances for both exhaust valves of cylinder No. 2 and both inlet valves of cylinder No. 3.

Before moving on to the next stage, double-check the clearances you have measured. Taking accurate readings is essential when calculating any replacement shims needed.

8 Rotate the engine in the forward direction one full turn (360°) so that the index marks align once again (see Step 3). Now measure and record the clearances for the other valves – inlet and exhaust valves for cylinder No. 4, the inlet valves for cylinder No. 2 and the exhaust valves for cylinder No. 3. Re-check your measurements before moving onto the next stage.

9 Now compare the valve clearances recorded on your chart with those specified by the manufacturer, noting that inlet and exhaust clearances are usually different. Any measured clearances which fall outside of the specified range will require the shim to be changed on that valve.

10 Because the shims are located between the end of the valve and the underside of the bucket (arrowed), the camshafts must be removed to access them. If you have a workshop manual, follow the procedure for changing the shims, otherwise entrust this work to a dealer. It is not a difficult task but care must be taken at all stages of the job. With your recorded clearances, the job will be easier, quicker and may even cost less. Recheck the valve clearances after the shims have been changed.

✦ Take care when removing the bucket – the shim will often stick to its underside.
✦ It is imperative that each bucket is returned to its original bore.
✦ Coat the shim and bucket with clean engine oil.

11 The cam cover usually has a one-piece rubber main gasket and four separate spark plug hole gaskets. Use a smear of sealing compound in the cover grooves and fit the gasket into the cover.

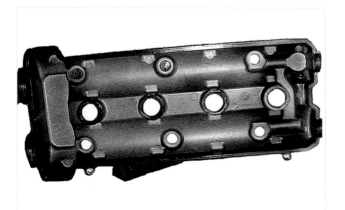

12 Before replacing the cam cover, lubricate the cams and bearing surfaces with fresh engine oil.

13 Place a smear of sealing compound onto the cut-outs in the cylinder head or onto the camshaft end plugs set in the rubber gasket. The sealing compound complete with the rubber gasket will prevent any oil leaks.

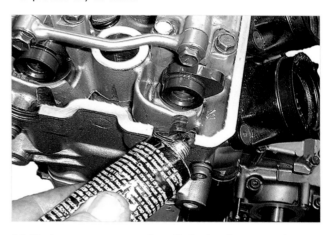

14 Fit the cam cover onto the cylinder head ensuring that the gasket remains in place and the end plugs are in their grooves.

Fit the rubber gaskets onto the cam cover bolts and smear them with sealant.

Fit all the cam cover bolts and tighten them finger-tight only at this stage. When all are seated, tighten them in a diagonal sequence, starting with the centre bolts and working outwards.

15 Check the condition of the O-rings on the caps and if in doubt, fit a new ones. Use a small amount of clean engine oil, grease or sealing compound on the O-ring to act as a lubricant and fit and tighten the caps.

16 With everything reassembled, run the engine and check that there are no oil leaks or rattles from the top-end.

3 Air filters

Air filter cleaning and eventual renewal is one of the most important maintenance jobs, second only to changing the engine oil and filter.

If the air filter is excessively dirty, clogged or over oiled (foam type) the engine will not be able to 'breathe' sufficiently and this will lead to a loss of power, increased fuel consumption, poor emissions and black, sooty deposits on the engine internals. This is often seen as a sooty deposits on the firing end of the spark plug. Always adhere to the manufacturer's service intervals for cleaning and renewal (usually clean every 2000 miles and renew every 8000 miles). This should be done more often when riding in dusty conditions.

Running the engine without an air filter, or with a split or damaged filter is not advised. This will allow the engine to suck in minute pieces of dirt and grit, which is very hard and sharp and is guaranteed to wreck your engine.

Air filter elements are of the paper or foam type and the method of cleaning them is quite different. The following procedures describe several typical fitments of the two element types.

Paper air filters

1 Gain access to the airbox and remove the securing mechanism, in this case a single screw (arrowed). On the motorcycle photographed, the airbox is under the fuel tank. Take care when removing the tank, ensure that the fuel is switched off and note where various fuel and air pipes are connected. If necessary make a sketch so that you will know where to reconnect the pipes when it is time to refit the tank.

Removal of the cover will allow access to the air filter itself and it is just a case of lifting the filter out of the airbox. As you remove it, have a look to see if it should be fitted in a particular manner. Take a good look at the inside of the cover to check the condition of the seal – a failed seal will allow unfiltered air to enter the airbox.

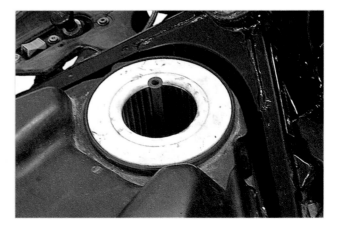

The filter will often have some indication (e.g. TOP) printed on one end, or the ends will be different in some way. With this type of filter there is a foam-sealing ring incorporated in the top and bottom. The filter on the right is a new one whereas that on the left has been in the machine far too long. Don't let your filter get into this state.

If you have access to an air supply, not from a garage forecourt, blowing on the OUTSIDE of the element will clean the filter – **never** blow from the inside outwards. Do not wash the element.

When fitting the new filter ensure that it is the correct way up and is seated firmly within the filter housing. Do NOT use oil on this type of filter as it is designed to be used dry.

Smear silicon grease around the lip of the cover before you refit it unless it has a foam type seal. In which case, check that the foam is in good condition. The use of silicon grease on the lips of the case will help to ensure that air enters ONLY through the filter.

2 On this model the airbox is located under the fuel tank. The seat must be removed to allow the fuel tank to pivot out of the way.

Note the four clips (two on each side of the case) that hold the top of the airbox in place. Use a small, flat-bladed screwdriver to prise the clips away from the airbox.

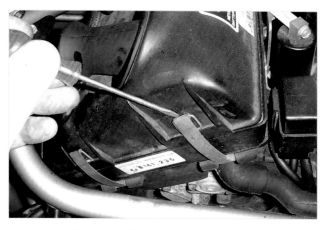

Push the airbox cover forward then lift it away to expose the flat paper filter.

Note the difference between the new filter (right) and old filter (left). In this case the filter requires renewal, but if the element is suitable for reuse, tap it on a hard surface to dislodge any particles of dust and dirt. Do not wash the element.

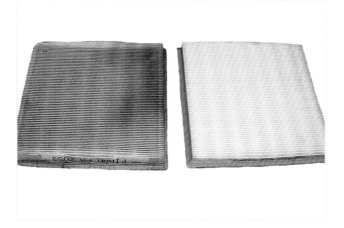

Fit the new filter into the airbox ensuring that it is fitted with the paper elements uppermost. Before you fit the cover make sure that the filter is fully seated and that the cover sealing ring is in good condition – use a smear of silicon grease on the cover edges.

After refitting the cover, fit the hinged ends of each clip into its respective slot and press on the centre of the spring strip. This will cause the spring to 'snap' into place. Make certain that all four are fully home.

3 Motorcycles with an upright engine (as opposed to those with the engine tilted forward in a sports style) will usually have the airbox located under the seat or behind a sidepanel. Lifting the seat will expose a cover such as this one. Note the arrow and the word 'front' on the cover.

Lift off the cover and the air filter can be seen. Pull up the clip (arrowed) at the rear and the filter can be lifted out. Before you pull it out note which way round it is fitted and fit the new filter in the same way. Apply silicon grease to the lip of the airbox before you refit the cover.

Foam air filters

1 This sports motorcycle has its airbox under the fuel tank, which must be removed to gain access. The seat and some of the bodywork must also be removed to allow removal of the fuel tank.

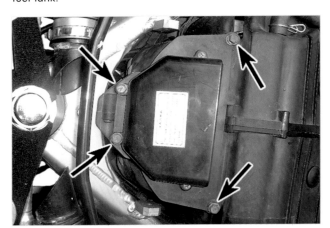

With the tank removed, undo the airbox cover (four screws) and lift off the cover.

Removal of these two nuts will allow the air filter and its carrier to be removed for cleaning.

Remove the foam air filter from the carrier. You will find it dirty and oily – this is normal, provided it has not been over oiled (see later). The oil coating on the filter's individual cells traps particles of dust etc. preventing it passing into the engine.

Get yourself a bucket of warm soapy water (hand hot) and wash the filter. Use a 'stroking motion' to clean the oil and grease from the filter then squeeze the filter between the palms of your hand to extract the maximum amount of liquid. **Do not** wring or twist the filter, as this will damage its individual cells.

Dunk the filter into clean water to rinse off the soapy residue and repeat this process until all the soap is gone. Two or three 'dunks' is usually sufficient. Squeeze the filter as dry as you can get it then hang it up to dry or use clean kitchen paper or cloth to pat it dry.

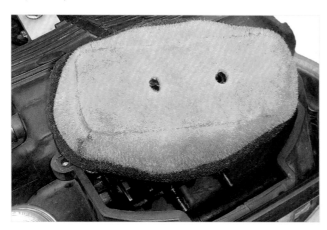

The filter shown is made from two pieces of foam, and the joint must be checked for condition. If it has started to split at the seams **carefully** apply an adhesive to close any open seams. Remember that air must only be allowed to enter the engine via the filter.

Either coat the filter with a propriety brand of dedicated foam filter oil or use the type of oil recommended by the manufacturer of your machine. How much oil to use? Put about 1/2 a cup full of oil onto the filter and place it into a clear plastic bag. Squeeze the filter/bag to evenly distribute the oil,

then holding the top squeeze downwards to expel the excess. Once done the filter should feel SLIGHTLY oily, not soaked with oil.

Before you refit the cover, check that its sealing ring is in good condition and apply a smear of silicon grease to the ring.

2 The foam air filter on this two-stroke engine machine is housed in a canister under the fuel tank.

To gain access undo the two screws and remove the cover.

The foam filter is mounted on a plastic carrier. Remove the unit, take off the foam filter and treat as described in Step 1.

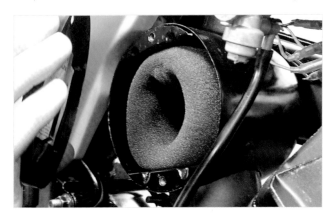

3 This type of foam air filter is held between two plates, which slide into grooves in the upper and lower airbox sections. Cleaning and re-oiling of the filter is the same as described previously. Its purpose here is to illustrate that there is a faint arrow mark on each plate. When re-fitting this type the arrows must face inward.

When re-fitting the outer cover ensure that the edge of the airbox fits neatly into the slot in the cover.
A smear of silicon grease, worked into the slot with a small screwdriver will help to exclude water.

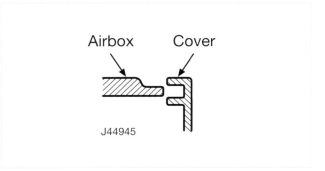

J44945

4 The airbox on this machine is located behind the right-hand side panel.

Remove the two screws (arrowed) and pull off the cover.

The air filter is retained by a plastic frame, which pulls out. Pull out the air filter and treat as described previously. Apply a smear of silicon grease to the cover slot on refitting.

| 4 | Liquid cooling system |

Motorcycles fitted with a liquid cooling system will have a radiator with its pressure cap and associated hoses, a coolant reservoir, an engine-driven water pump, and a thermostat. The electrical side of the system consists of a thermo-switch which operates the cooling fan motor, and a thermal resister which controls the temperature gauge or a warning light.

Coolant safety warnings

✦ The anti-freeze/distilled water solution is harmful if swallowed so keep it away from children. If swallowed, DO NOT induce vomiting, instead seek IMMEDIATE medical aid and take the anti-freeze container with you so that the doctor can see what it consists of. This applies equally to pets, which might be attracted by its sweet smell and drink it.

✦ Use a 50/50 mix of antifreeze and distilled (de-ionised) water for topping up and coolant changing. This will protect the engine down to approximately -36°C. If your machine will be subjected to temperatures that are lower than this then the concentration can be increased to 60% antifreeze to 40% distilled water. Never let the coolant density fall below 50% or exceed 60%.

✦ Do NOT use tap water, the thawed ice from a refrigerator or boiled water from a kettle etc. as this contains chemicals that can 'fur' up the coolant passages in the engine and radiator, reducing its efficiency – use distilled water only.

✦ When changing the coolant, do NOT pour the old coolant down surface or domestic drains, instead pour it into an old container and take it to your local re-cycling centre.

✦ Always wash your hands after handling anti-freeze or coolant.

Coolant level check

The coolant level in the reservoir tank should ideally be checked before EVERY journey.

1 The coolant reservoir is often located under the side panels, seat or bodywork, and on faired machines is often located inboard of the fairing side sections.

2 Check the level with the motorcycle held upright, not on its sidestand. The coolant level should lie between the two level markings on the side of the tank, either FULL and LOW, MAX and MIN or UPPER and LOWER. To top up, remove the reservoir cap, and add the correct mix of anti-freeze/distilled water – do not use distilled water only because this will dilute the anti-freeze strength.

3 If you need to top up the coolant every few days there is a problem. This could be a loose or split radiator hose or even a split radiator. Check and repair/renew **immediately**, because if you run the system out of coolant the engine will overheat causing it to seize. This will require a very expensive engine rebuild and could be all because of a small weep from a loose hose connection.

4 At the same time as the coolant level is checked, make a quick visual inspection of the reservoir tank, cap and radiator hoses – there should be no sign of leaks.

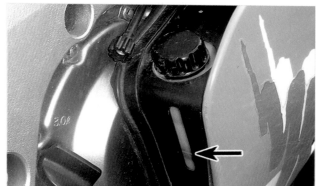

Coolant density check

⚠ **Warning: This task must only be undertaken when the engine is cold.**

⚠ **Warning: The radiator cap pressurises the cooling system so that the coolant temperature can exceed 100°C (usually 107°C). If the cap is removed when the engine is hot, you will have scalding water exploding at you at 107°C, which is likely to cause a serious injury.**

A coolant density check will show how much protection the coolant will give from freezing. It is often advised as a service item, say every 8000 miles or 12 months, whichever comes first, or can be carried out just before the cold season. An anti-freeze tester or coolant hydrometer will be required to measure coolant density (see Chapter 1).

1 Take the coolant sample at the radiator by removing the pressure cap – see above **Warning**. The pressure cap is often hidden under a cover on faired machines or may be exposed and easily visible on naked machines.

Remove the radiator cap by turning it anticlockwise against its spring pressure until it 'clicks' and releases. Continue to turn the cap and lift it clear of the radiator.

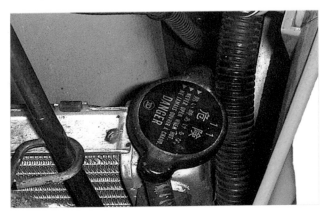

2 Squeeze and hold the bulb of the tester, then insert its pipe end into the radiator. **Slowly** release the pressure on the bulb end allowing coolant to enter the glass tube.

3 Draw up only enough coolant so that the internal float is stable within the coolant. If you draw up too much coolant, the float will jam against the top of the glass tube and give a false reading. Note that some radiators are very small and it is not possible to draw sufficient coolant into the glass in one go. If this is the case, it will be necessary to drain some of the coolant (from the water pump or lower hose) into a clean jug and use this coolant to measure the density.

4 Reading the scale will tell you the protection that the coolant will give. This tester shown is marked in degrees C below freezing, others will have different scales. Check the instructions for the tester you have.

As a 'rule of thumb' the higher the float rides in the coolant the more dense the liquid and the greater its protection. When you have noted the reading, return the coolant to the radiator and refit the radiator cap. Make sure that the cap is fully 'home' before running the engine.

⚠ **Warning: Always lower your head to read the scale rather than lifting the tester up to your face – coolant is harmful if it gets into your eyes.**

Radiator check

Coolant enters the radiator via the top hose (often from the thermostat housing), flows through the radiator's internal pipes where it is cooled by the passing airflow, and then exits via the bottom hose where it passes to the water pump.

1 Road dirt, grass, dead insects and other debris should be cleaned from the radiator fins. The use of a soft brush and plenty of water usually does the trick.

2 Fins that are bent down or dented can be straightened by careful use of a small, flat-bladed screwdriver.

3 Any hose that is cracked or flattened must be renewed. Check the hose joints for signs of leakage; tightening the joints may solve any problems, but if the hose or clamp are distorted it is preferable to renew them.

Coolant change

The coolant should be changed and the hoses renewed in accordance with the maintenance schedule. This is often specified every two years and every four years respectively.

 Warning: This task must only be done when the engine is COLD. If the radiator cap is removed when the engine is hot, there is a very real probability that you will be scalded as it is released. Cover the cap with a heavy cloth and turn it anti-clockwise to release it.

Items required

- ✔ Drain bowl, funnel and clean jug
- ✔ Anti-freeze (an ethylene glycol type is usually recommended) and distilled water OR pre-mixed coolant
- ✔ Variety of sockets, spanners and screwdrivers

Procedure

1 Remove the seat, fuel tank and any bodypanels necessary to gain access to the radiator pressure cap and coolant reservoir.

Remove the pressure cap from the radiator (see **Warning**). This will vent the system and help the coolant flow quickly when draining the system.

2 Locate the water pump. Many four-stroke multi-cylinder engines have the pump mounted on the lower left-hand side of the engine. Place a clean drain bowl under the pump. Where a drain screw (arrowed) is built into the pump, remove the screw and allow the old coolant to flow out. The screw will have a sealing washer fitted; if its condition is in doubt renew it.

If the pump does not have a drain screw, the bottom hose will have to be removed to allow the coolant to drain.

This two-stroke engine has its water pump on the right-hand side of the engine. The drain screw (arrowed) uses a copper sealing washer – fit a new one if its condition is in doubt.

3 When the coolant has fully drained, refit and tighten the drain screw (complete with its sealing washer) or refit the bottom hose.

4 Some engines also have drain screws set in the cylinder barrel casting, thus allowing all old coolant to drain fully from the engine's coolant passages. Where fitted, remove the screw to allow any residual coolant to drain. Refit the screw using a new sealing washer if the old one is damaged.

5 Make up a mixture of anti-freeze and distilled water (usually 50/50 mix) which is of sufficient quantity for the system and

which leaves a small quantity for topping up. The machine's owners manual may specify the quantity required, or you can measure the amount drained to get an idea of the quantity of fresh coolant required. Note that pre-mixed coolant can be purchased for motorcycle use if desired.

6 Pour the coolant slowly into the radiator to avoid trapping air. Squeezing the hoses as you pour the solution in will help to expel any air trapped in the system. Fill the system until the coolant comes up to the bottom of the filler neck. Fit the radiator cap and make sure that it is fully closed.

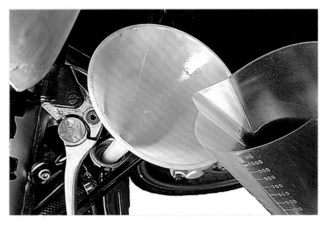

7 Drain the old coolant from the reservoir tank using either a large syringe and a length of plastic hose to draw it out, or unbolt the reservoir and tip the coolant in the drain tray.

Refill the reservoir tank with fresh coolant and make sure that the level comes to the upper mark. Refit the reservoir cap.

8 Start the engine and allow it to reach its operating temperature. Check for any leaks and stop the engine immediately if any are found.

9 When the engine has reached its operating temperature (the temperature gauge needle moves to its normal position) stop the engine and allow it to cool down. When it has cooled, check the level in the reservoir and top up as necessary.

5   Fuel system

> **Warning: Petrol (gasoline) is extremely flammable, so take extra precautions when you work on any part of the fuel system. Don't smoke or allow open flames or bare light bulbs near the work area, and don't work in a garage where a natural gas-type appliance is present. If you spill any fuel on your skin, rinse it off immediately with soap and water. It is strongly advised that you wear safety glasses when working with fuel and that you have a suitable fire extinguisher within easy reach of the work area.**

Carburettor fuel level

It is unlikely, until many thousands of miles have been covered, for the maximum fuel level within the carburettor float chamber to change from standard (unless someone has been tampering with the float height or the fuel jet/needle is faulty). This simple test will determine whether further examination is necessary and will aid in the diagnosis of engine problems.

Items required

✔ Length of clear plastic fuel pipe to fit the spigot on the float bowl
✔ Appropriate screwdriver
✔ Fuel level specification

Procedure

1 Make sure the motorcycle is positioned upright for this check, ideally on its centrestand (or a paddock stand) on level ground; do not carry this out with the machine on its sidestand.

2 Connect the clear plastic pipe to the carburettor float bowl drain spigot and hold the pipe against the carburettor body as shown.

HINT

Warming the end of the pipe in hot, but NOT boiling, water for a few minutes will soften it and make fitting easier.

3 Locate the mark on the float bowl or carburettor body (arrowed); it often helps to highlight this mark with a felt tip pen as well. Now make a reference line on the pipe with a black felt tip pen at a point approximately 10 mm above the float bowl or carburettor mark.

4 Ensure the fuel tap is switched on. If you have a vacuum operated fuel tap switch it to prime (PRI) which manually opens the fuel tap. Note that the ignition should be OFF during this test. Holding the pipe in position, undo the drain screw (approximately 1 to 1 1/2 turns) until fuel flows in the pipe.

5 Wait for the fuel level to stabilise, then slowly lower the pipe until its reference line aligns with the float bowl/carburettor mark. Do not lower the pipe below this mark and then bring it back up because the reading will be inaccurate. Use a ruler to measure the distance between the reference line on the pipe and the fuel level in the pipe. Close the drain screw and repeat this for all carburettors.

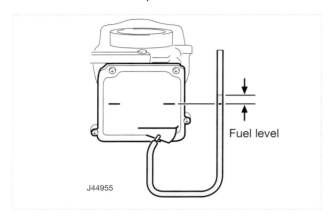

J44955

Fuel level

6 Compare the measurements taken with the fuel level specified by the manufacturer. This will typically be specified as a figure ± 1 mm (e.g. 5 ± 1 mm, which is between 4 to 6 mm), above or below the mark on the float bowl or carburettor. If the fuel level is incorrect on any carburettor, the float height should be adjusted for that carburettor.

HINT

Once the gauge has been placed alongside the carburettor and the fuel has entered the pipe do not move the pipe position otherwise the reading will be inaccurate. If this happens, tighten the drain screw, then drain the fuel from the gauge and start again.

7 On engines where the carburettor(s) is/are mounted upright, the fuel level is often specified in terms of a distance below the gasket face, i.e. the joint between the carburettor body and float bowl.

A plastic pipe can be connected as described previously and held upright against the side of the carburettor. Mark a line level with the gasket face and another the specified distance below the gasket face (in this case 3.5 mm). With the pipe held in this position, the fuel level should align with the lower mark when the drain screw is opened.

⚠️ **Warning: Remember that the fuel in the pipe is highly volatile. When removing the pipe from the drain spigot use a cloth, kitchen paper or a small container to catch the fuel and dispose of it safely.**

Carburettor float height

If the fuel level is incorrect the float height must be checked and adjusted. This procedure requires the removal of the carburettor. The following procedure is based on a slide carburettor fitted to a single cylinder engine; refer to the workshop manual for your machine for specific details.

Carburettor removal

1 Switch the fuel tap OFF and remove the fuel tank. Check the condition of the pipe and clips; if the clips are corroded or missing renew them on the rebuild.

2 Connect a pipe to the spigot on the float bowl and open the drain screw to drain the fuel from the float bowl. Tighten the drain screw.

3 Release the top of the carburettor and lift out the throttle slide. The slide can be left attached to the throttle cable.

4 If there is a cable-operated choke connected to the carburettor body, disconnect the cable from the choke plunger. Similarly if a carburettor heater is fitted, disconnect its wiring.

5 On two-stroke engines, detach the oil pipe from its stub on the carburettor body and place it out of the way.

6 Slacken the inlet stub mounting clip (carburettor side) and the air filter-to-carburettor pipe clip. It is not necessary, nor advisable to remove the clip screws completely.

With the clips loose, the carburettor can be pulled out of its rubber stubs. If you have undone the clip screws until they are almost out, you shouldn't have too much trouble removing the carburettor.

Check and adjustment

7 With the carburettor off, lay it on a clean cloth or paper and undo the float bowl screws (arrowed). Do not disturb the pilot screw (item A).

Lift the float bowl off the carburettor body, taking care not to damage the gasket. If it is damaged, it must be renewed or the carburettor will leak.

8 Hold the carburettor body upside-down in one hand and angle it so that it is approximately 45° away from you. This will allow the float tang to rest on the float needle's spring-loaded tip without putting pressure on it, thus allowing an accurate measurement to be taken.

Measure the distance from the gasket seat of the carburettor body to the top of the float and compare it with the manufacturers specification. Repeat this for the other float. **Note:** *If the gasket is still on the body allow 1 mm for the thickness of the gasket. Most manufacturers allow a float height tolerance of ± 1 mm.*

9 If the float height is within specification then there is some other fault causing the high fuel level. If the float height is out of tolerance, it will require adjusting. Most, but not all, floats have a small tang that sets the height of the float.

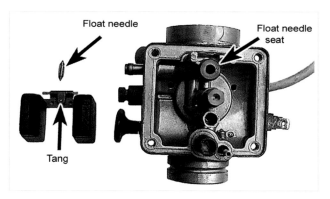

Float needle   Float needle seat

Tang

Remove the pivot pin to free the float, then very carefully bend the brass tang by a very small amount; if the float tang is plastic it cannot be adjusted. Refit the float and recheck the float height.

If the float height is now worse, you have bent the tang the wrong way, in which case remove the float and try again. Take your time and be GENTLE, a very small adjustment of the tang will result in a large change to the float height.

> ⚠ **Caution: In some cases, the float pivot pin is a shrink fit in the carburettor body. If this is the case, DO NOT try to drive the pin out with a drift and hammer, you will only succeed in breaking the carburettor body, which is very expensive. Instead, reassemble the carburettor and take it to your local dealer who will have the expertise to make the necessary adjustments.**

10 The float needle's tapered face (arrowed) and its seat in the body of the carburettor will wear during its working life and allow fuel to flow even if the float height is correct.

To check the sealing of the float needle and seat, refit the float and fit a CLEAN length of pipe to the fuel inlet stub. Hold the carburettor so that the float closes the needle against its seat. Take a breath and blow through the pipe as shown. If you can hear air escaping, the float needle and seat are worn or the gasket is damaged, both should be renewed.

Carburettor installation

11 Reassemble the carburettor using new gaskets where necessary. Install the carburettor in the inlet stub and air filter pipe, making sure it aligns with any marks or spigots on the inlet stubs, then tighten the mounting clip screws. Don't over-tighten the screws, be guided by the corrosion marks on the screws and match the original screw positions. If too tight, the clips will cut into the rubber pipes with the possibility of air leaks.

12 Note that the cut-away (A) in the throttle slide must face the air filter when you fit it into the carburettor. Take care that the jet needle (B) enters the needle jet smoothly and that the throttle slide is seated in the bottom of the carburettor before securing the carburettor top.

Fuel taps and fuel strainers

The fuel tap will either be a gravity-fed manual operation type with ON, RES and OFF positions, or a vacuum-operated type with ON, RES and PRI positions. Both types of tap will have a hose from the tap union to the carburettor or fuel pump, but the vacuum tap also has a small-bore vacuum hose to the engine's inlet stub.

Engine vacuum acts on a diaphragm in the back of the vacuum tap to open the tap valve and allow fuel to flow. When the engine is stopped the tap is closed by an internal spring. Its PRI position manually turns the tap on without the need to have the engine running and is used mainly to fill the carburettor float bowls if they have been drained at any time. **Do not** leave the tap in the PRI position when not using the machine. It is not unheard of for fuel to pass the float needle (in the carburettor), flow into the engine, pass the piston rings and dilute the engine oil. With the crankcases venting into the airbox, richening of the mixture can occur when hot.

Fuel tap filter

1 All fuel taps incorporate some form of fuel strainer. A gauze strainer fits over the inner part of the fuel tap which extends into the fuel tank. The manual tap shown has a gauze strainer (A) over the fuel inlet and reserve pipes and a detachable sediment bowl (B) on the underside of the tap.

2 On manual taps which have a detachable sediment bowl (not all have them), turn the tap OFF and unscrew the bowl. Clean

any sediment from the inside of the bowl and if a circular gauze filter is fitted inside the tap body clean it using a soft brush. Check that the O-ring is in good condition and renew it if necessary. Smear silicon grease onto the threads of the sediment bowl before reinstalling it. Turn the fuel tap ON and check that there is no signs of leakage.

3 To access the gauze filter inside the fuel tank it will be necessary to remove the fuel tank and then the fuel tap assembly. **Do not** do this with a full tank of fuel – drain the tank completely beforehand.

With the fuel tank laid on its side, on cloth or cardboard, undo the screws securing the fuel tap and remove it.

Gently clean the mesh of the filter (a clean, old toothbrush is ideal). If the mesh is damaged or torn it must be renewed. On some models the mesh can be detached from the tap for renewal.

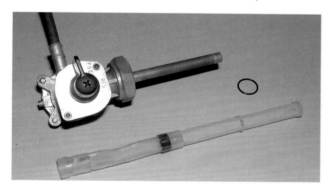

When refitting the fuel tap, check that the O-ring seal between the tap and tank is in good condition – it is advisable to renew it anyway. Smear silicon grease over the O-ring. Use new sealing washers on the tap retaining screws and apply one drop of locking agent on their threads before fitting and tightening them. When the tank has been refitted and refilled, check that there are no leaks from the fuel tap.

In-line fuel filter

1 Additional fuel filters are often fitted in the fuel hose between the tap and carburettor and at the hose union on the carburettor. The carburettor shown below has an in-line filter (A) and a gauze filter at the hose union (B).

2 Make sure that the fuel tap is switched OFF before removing any parts. Where a vacuum tap is fitted, the tap lever must be in the ON or RES positions.

The in-line filter is usually of the paper type. It cannot be cleaned and is simply renewed at the specified interval or if it is obviously dirty (it has a transparent case so you can check its condition easily). Note that residual fuel in the hoses will be released when the filter hoses are freed; have a rag handy to catch the fuel or clamp the hoses each side of the filter to prevent fuel escaping. Release the hose clips and remove the filter.

Note that the new filter must be fitted so that the arrow on its casing points in the direction of fuel flow, i.e. towards the carburettor. Reconnect the hoses and secure them with the clips. If the clips are corroded or distorted, renew them – they are quite cheap.

3 Filters at the hose unions are less common than in-line filters, but where fitted, can be cleaned with a soft brush (an old soft bristled toothbrush is ideal) or with a gentle puff of air (not from an air line). The photo below shows a simple insert type gauze filter fitted inside the fuel hose union on the carburettor.

Throttle freeplay

Throttle cable freeplay should be checked and adjusted at every service. If there is too much freeplay the throttle will feel 'sloppy', too little freeplay will not allow the throttle valve to close fully and there is a possibility of the engine speed increasing when the handlebars are turned.

Refer to the machine's owners manual for the specified freeplay measurement. It will either be expressed in terms of throttle grip rotation or as linear freeplay in the cable.

Measured as throttle grip rotation

The manufacturers will quote two figures for throttle freeplay, such as 2 to 6 mm. These figures equate to the minimum and maximum distance that the throttle grip will turn before the cable slack is taken up.

1 Stick a piece of masking tape on the switch unit and mark three lines on it. The first line is the datum line, the second 2 mm away and the third a further 6 mm away. Stick a second piece of masking tape on the closed throttle grip and mark it with a single line which matches up with the datum (first) line on the switch unit.

With the engine running, gently open the throttle grip and note the positioning of the marks when freeplay is taken up and engine speed starts to increase. If the throttle grip mark lies between the minimum and maximum lines, all is OK and no adjustment is required.

2 If adjustment is required, slacken the cable adjuster locking nut and turn the adjuster to increase or decrease the freeplay as necessary.

Hold the adjuster with one spanner and secure the locknut with another spanner when finished. Blip the throttle and check that it 'snaps' back fully when released.

3 With some experience, it is possible to gauge the point when freeplay is taken up without running the engine.

4 Many engines use two cables to operate the carburettors; one is an opening (pull) cable and the other a closing (push) cable. The principles of cable freeplay adjustment are the same as above. Coarse adjustment can be made at the carburettor end, although this is rarely necessary unless all adjustment range at the throttle grip end has been taken up.

5 The important point to note when adjusting 'push-pull' cables is that the throttle pulley stops against the idle speed adjusting screw with the throttle closed and stops against the carburettor stopper when fully open.

Measured as linear freeplay

The manufacturer may specify a freeplay measurement of say 0.5 to 1.0 mm, measured in terms of in-line play in the cable.

6 Pull any rubber cover away from the adjuster and gently pull on the cable to measure the amount of freeplay. Hold a rule alongside the adjuster so that you can measure the amount the metal cap of the outer cable moves out of the adjuster.

7 If adjustment is required, undo the locknut (A) and turn the adjuster (B) until the specified freeplay is obtained. Don't forget to tighten the locknut when finished and refit the rubber cover.

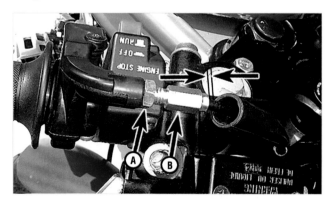

8 Where there is also an adjuster at the carburettor end of the cable this is used for coarse adjustment. All minor adjustment is made using the adjuster at the throttle grip end of the cable.

Engine idle speed

Engine idle speed (tickover speed) should be adjusted after adjusting throttle cable freeplay and if it is obviously too high or too low. Idle speed is adjusted using the idle adjuster screw or knob, often called the throttle stop screw.

Idle speed adjuster locations

On older multi-cylinder engines the idle speed adjuster is usually situated between the carburettors; between carburettors 2 and 3 on a four cylinder engine. The adjuster is accessed from below the carburettor bank. One idle screw adjusts all carburettors.

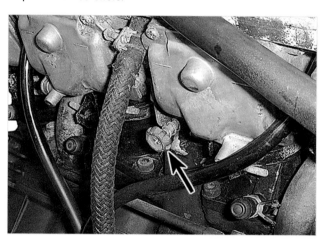

On modern multi-cylinder engines the idle speed adjuster is mounted on one side of the carburettors. Again, one screw adjusts all carburettors.

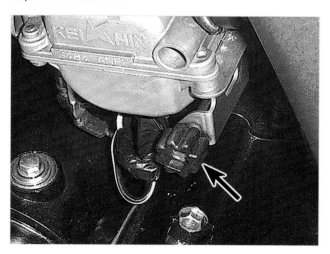

On single cylinder engines with a slide carburettor the idle speed screw is set in the throttle body. Do not confuse the idle speed screw with the pilot screw (see **Hint**).

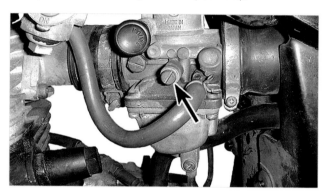

HINT

The engine idle speed screw (A) is the one that is directly beneath the throttle slide. Do not disturb the pilot screw (B), this is usually set at the factory and should be left alone. As a point of interest, if the pilot screw is close to the engine, as shown, it controls fuel and air. If it is near the air intake, it controls the amount of air into the pilot system.

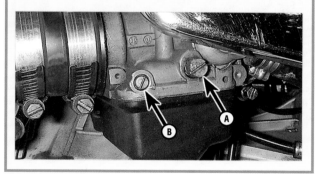

Idle speed adjusting procedure

1 Refer to the machine's owners handbook or workshop manual for the idle speed specification.

2 Run the engine until it is at its normal operating temperature and the choke is off.

3 Turn the adjuster until the correct engine idle speed is achieved. Where you have to reach under the carburettors to access the adjuster, take care not to burn your hand – the engine cases will be hot.

Carburettor balance (synchronisation)

Most multi-cylinder four-stroke motorcycles have one carburettor per cylinder. To maintain optimum engine performance and fuel consumption yet minimum exhaust emissions it is necessary to check and balance the air flow through the inlet tracts. This is commonly called 'balancing the carbs' and should be carried out in accordance with the service schedule, typically at every major service (8000 miles).

Note that the procedure for balancing the carburettors of multi-cylinder two-stroke engines differs from that described here, and involves checking the position of reference marks on the throttle slides.

Items required

✔ Remote fuel supply (tank, connecting hoses, tap and fuel)
✔ Carburettor balancing kit with adapters (vacuum gauge set or manometer)
✔ Appropriate screwdriver, spanners or adjusting tool to fit the adjuster screws
✔ Parts tray to store screws etc.

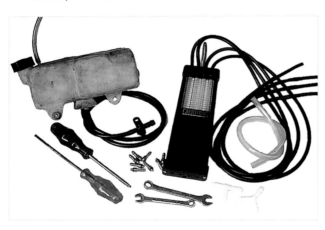

Procedure

1 Before carrying out this procedure, ensure that the engine has the correct amount of oil, and coolant if liquid cooled. Remove the fuel tank. Check and adjust the valve clearances and spark plug gaps.

2 Check the location of the vacuum take-off points (see Step 3) and the balance screws (see Step 7) and whether the airbox will have to be removed to access them. This will be necessary on most sports motorcycles with inclined engines.

As an example, on the machine photographed remove the four screws (arrowed) to gain access to the air filter. Remove the air filter.

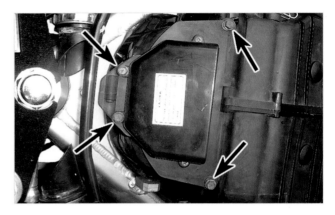

Remove the airbox retaining screws, noting that some may be hidden under rubber plugs (arrowed) and place all screws in your parts tray. There may be one or more breather or drain hoses attached to the airbox; squeeze the clip securing the hose and remove the hose from its stub.

Once the airbox has been removed, it will be necessary to remove the carburettor intake cover to gain access to the adjusters and vacuum take-off points. Undoing the eight screws will allow the plate and bell-mouths to be removed.

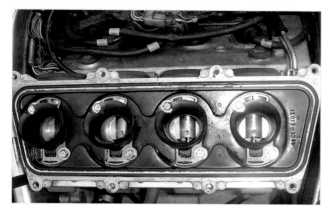

3 The vacuum take-off points are located in the inlet stubs, between the carburettors and engine. They will either take the form of spigots sealed with caps, or screws with washers which thread into the inlet stubs. Note that one take-off point will often have the fuel tap vacuum pipe connected to it.

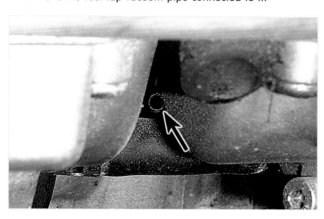

Where the spigot type of take-off point is fitted, remove the caps and where fitted, the vacuum pipe. Note that the caps often come off easier if you give them a twist at the same time as you are pulling.

Where the screw type take-off point is fitted, remove the screw and its aluminium sealing washer from each inlet stub.

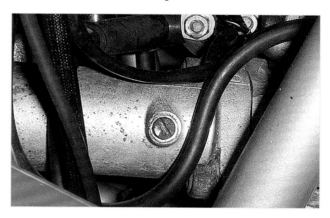

Thread in the adapters supplied with the balancer kit, making sure that their O-rings are in place and are in good condition. The two adapters shown may look identical but closer examination will show that one has a smaller thread diameter. Which adapter you use will be determined by the machine manufacturer. Tighten the adapters finger-tight only; do NOT use pliers or other tools to tighten the adapters – they are made of brass and excessive force will break them.

4 Fit the pipes from the balancer kit to each take-off point.

When fitting the balancer kit pipes push the left-hand pipe onto the take-off for cylinder No. 1 (left-hand side). Pipe No. 2 fits to cylinder No. 2 and so on until all pipes are fitted. This ensures that you can match the gauge reading with the appropriate cylinder. Modify the procedure if working on a vee or flat engine configuration.

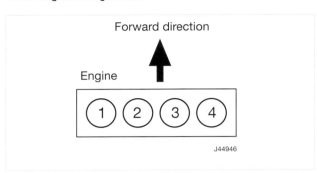

Forward direction

Engine

1 2 3 4

J44946

Push the balancer pipes onto the spigot as far as the pipe will go and make sure they form an air-tight seal, otherwise a false reading will result.

5 With the pipes fitted to the take-off points, position the balancer gauge where it can easily be seen. To operate effectively most balancer systems should be upright. Make sure that the gauges are secure as the engine vibrations may cause them to fall off the machine. The manometer shown below can be hung over one of the handlebar ends.

The vacuum gauge set is best positioned across the steering head or handlebar/instrument area.

6 Fill the remote fuel tank about 1/2 to 3/4 full of fuel, connect the fuel pipe THEN turn the fuel tap on (arrowed). This machine

has only one fuel pipe whereas yours may have two pipes. If this is the case, you will need to use a 'T' or 'Y' piece to connect the pipes. See Chapter 1 for the remote fuel tank and fittings.

It is vitally important that there are no fuel leaks from the remote tank, hoses and tap and that the hose connection to the carburettors is good. Secure the hose will a wire clip if necessary.

7 Before starting the engine take a minute to find the adjusters (or synchronising screws as they are often called). Do it now while the engine is cold, trying to find them when the engine is hot can cause burns. They may be screws with springs under them (arrowed), or on older designs screws with locknuts.

The screw on the left (A) is the balance adjuster. Be careful not to mistakenly adjust the pilot screw (B).

The two adjusters with locknuts (arrowed) on this late 70's Honda Four control balance on cylinders 1 and 2. Between each pair of adjusters is a locking strip that must have the locking 'ears' flattened and the locknuts slackened before adjustment can take place.

8 Start the engine and allow it to reach normal operating temperature and ensure the choke is OFF. Check the idle speed and adjust it if necessary. Some manufacturers state that the carburettors should be balanced at idle speed, others at a fast tickover e.g. 1750 revs/min. Check your workshop manual to see at what engine speed your carburettors are adjusted and set the engine idle speed accordingly.

9 Inspect the vacuum gauges to see if the carburettors are balanced. If perfectly balanced, the manometer rod levels or vacuum gauge needle positions on the dials should be the same for all cylinders – the actual gauge reading is less important. If using vacuum gauges note that needle flutter can be reduced by the damping on the gauges, although there must be a small amount of flutter.

The manometer reading shown below indicates that the carburettor balance of this four cylinder engine is not too bad but they can certainly be brought closer together.

10 Make small adjustments to the adjuster screws to bring the carburettors into balance. On the straight four cylinder arrangement shown below, the carburettors should be adjusted in the following sequence:

✦ Adjuster A – this balances cylinder No. 1 to cylinder No. 2. Gauge rods 1 and 2 should be level
✦ Adjuster B – this balances cylinder No. 3 to cylinder No. 4. Gauge rods 3 and 4 should be level
✦ Adjuster C – this balances cylinders Nos. 1 and 2 to cylinders Nos. 3 and 4. All gauge rods should be level

The arrangement for adjusting the carburettors of different engine configurations, such as on a vee-four engine, will differ. Reference should be made to the workshop manual for details.

11 Allow the engine to settle between adjustments and reset the idle speed if necessary. If the engine overheats, stop it and allow it to cool before resuming the balance procedure.

12 Finally, snap the throttle open then closed – the gauge rods should drop together then rise together then settle back to the normal position. When balanced, adjust the engine idle speed, stop the engine and remove the balancer kit.

13 Refit the vacuum screws or caps when complete, noting that an air-tight seal is essential. Where screws are fitted, ensure that their washers are in place, otherwise the engine will run lean and serious engine damage will occur. Don't forget to reconnect the fuel tap vacuum hose, where applicable.

6   Oil and oil filters

Technical – four-stroke oil

Oil is the lifeblood of an engine – it has the job of keeping moving components apart as well as acting as a coolant. It also prevents corrosion, reduces mechanical noise, removes the by-products of combustion, seals the piston rings to the cylinder and cushions the bearings. On most four-stroke engines the engine oil also lubricates the gearbox and clutch.

The oil needs to be free flowing at low engine temperatures yet still be sufficiently thick at very high engine temperatures. An SAE 10W oil is free flowing at low temperatures (e.g. start-up) but becomes too thin to bear the loads imposed on it as the engine reaches its normal operating temperature. Conversely an SAE 40W oil would be too thick for cold starting but is free flowing at normal engine operating temperature. To this end, the base oil used contains various additives to improve its characteristics.

The SAE (Society of Automotive Engineers) rating classifies engine oils into viscosity ranges (numbers) at prescribed temperatures. Multi-grade oil is not a combination of different grades of oil, but base oil with viscosity index improvers added. These additives reduce the extent to which oil thins as its temperature rises. An example would be a 10W/40 multi-grade oil, which has a viscosity within the range for SAE 40W oil at 100°C but when its temperature is lowered to -18°C will be sufficiently thin to be in the range for SAE 10W oil.

The API (American Petroleum Institute) code is an oil performance standard ranging from SA to SL. The 'S' relates to spark ignition engines, as opposed to diesel engines, and the letters A through to L rate oil performance with L being the highest currently available. Most motorcycle manufacturers recommend the use of an SE, SF or SG quality oil, which is a high quality oil suitable for most automotive applications. Note that many of the low friction SH or SJ engine oils packaged for car use will cause clutch slip in a motorcycle engine – always purchase engine oils packaged for motorcycle use.

There are now new JASO (Japanese Automotive Standards Organisation) standards for four-stroke engine oils. JASO has two classifications for oil performance – MA and MB; look for the MA classification on the oil container which denotes that the oil does not contain friction modifiers and is thus designed for motorcycle use. Motorcycles with a dry clutch (Moto-Guzzi, BMW etc.) may need to use an MB classification of oil.

The main oil additives are as follows:

Oxidation inhibitors

Mineral oils form hard deposits on the hotter parts of the engine (under the piston crown) and varnish like deposits on the cooler parts. Anti-oxidants are added to reduce this but the products of oxidation can be carried in the oil and form a sludge that would block oil ways etc.

Dispersants and Detergents

Dispersants keep the varnishes etc. in suspension in the oil, thus preventing the formation of sludge and the detergents deal with the high temperature deposits.

Anti-foam and corrosion additives

The antifoam additive keeps the oil from frothing too much, which would cause serious damage to the bearings etc. and the corrosion inhibitors react with the acidic products of oxidation.

Friction reducers

These are used exclusively in oils designed for cars. Almost every car has a 'dry' clutch that is not cooled by oil. Most motorcycles have 'wet' clutches where the engine/gearbox oil acts to cool the clutch plates as well as act as a cushion during clutch engagement. If you use car oil in a motorcycle, you will experience major clutch slip due to this additive. Only use oil that is specified for motorcycle applications.

Extreme pressure additives

With the high, relative contact pressures found in a shaft final drive unit the oil film between the surfaces of the gears can be ruptured. When this happens the additive forms a protective coating on the surfaces acting as a 'dry' lubricant. These oils are known as EP or Hypoid oils and are normally of 75W or higher.

> **HINT**
>
> No matter how good the oil used, it will not last forever. If you do nothing else, changing the oil and filter at the manufacturers recommended intervals is essential.

Technical – two-stroke oil

The majority of two-stroke road motorcycles use oil from a separate oil tank for engine lubrication while the transmission is lubricated in a separate gearbox. The gearbox oil is usually a light or medium weight oil. The engine oil is fed to a pump and then injected into the inlet tract where it joins the fuel/air mix from the carburettor. There are two major considerations:

Ensure that the oil tank is kept topped up. If you run the tank dry the least that will happen is an engine 'heat seizure' where the engine 'nips up' or at the worst, a complete and total engine seizure which will be very expensive to repair and may even cause an accident. Make a point of checking the oil level in the tank at the same time as you fill up with fuel.

Use two-stroke oil packaged for injector systems which meets JASO FB standard or greater. Do not use two-stroke oil which is packaged for premix systems only, this is generally for 'Off-road' motorcycle use, agricultural machinery, lawnmowers and marine two-strokes etc., and is a much thicker oil.

HINT

Certain highly tuned two-stroke machines used on the road MUST use fully synthetic two-stroke oil for engine lubrication. If ordinary two-stroke oil is used, there is a distinct probability that rapid engine wear will occur. The cost of the engine rebuild will negate the modest savings made by using cheaper oil.

Engine/gearbox oil level check – four-stroke engine

If your engine develops an oil leak the first indication may be a seized engine or gearbox, or you may even have an accident. Take a few minutes before **every** journey to check, and if necessary, top up the engine oil level. The machine must be upright when the level is checked.

Oil level window

1 The sight-glass is probably the most common form of level check used on four-stroke engines. It is usually found in the lower part of the clutch cover, below the oil filler hole.

2 Place the machine on its centrestand or hold it upright and look at the oil level through the sight-glass. If it is correct, the oil will be level with the upper mark as shown. If the level is low, add oil through the filler hole, until the level is correct.

3 It will take a few minutes for the level to rise after you have added fresh oil, so add a small amount and wait for the level to stabilise. If necessary add a little more until the level is correct. Do NOT exceed the maximum level marking.

4 Check the condition of the O-ring on the filler cap before screwing it back into the cover.

Oil level dipstick

5 The combined filler cap/dipstick will be fitted to small capacity models and often older motorcycles. It is usually located in the clutch cover.

6 Place the machine on its centrestand or hold it upright. Clean around the filler cap area, then unscrew the dipstick and clean the measuring end with a piece of soft paper (kitchen towel is ideal).

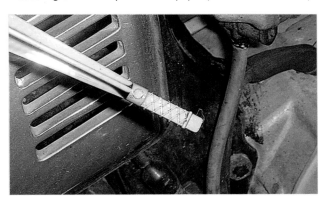

7 Install the dipstick, but **do not** screw it back into the cover. Rest the first part of its screw thread on the cover aperture.

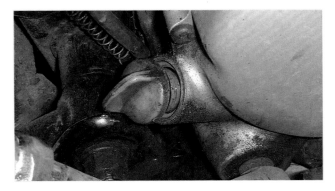

8 Leave the dipstick in the cover for a few seconds then remove it and check the level of oil on the measured end. The oil level should be up to, but NOT exceeding the upper level mark.

9 If, as shown in the photograph, the oil level is between the upper and lower marks add oil, via the filler hole, until the level is correct. Recheck the level by repeating the checking process. Clean the dipstick before each check. It will take a few minutes for the level to rise after you have added fresh oil, so add a small amount and wait for the level to stabilise. If necessary add a little more until the level is correct.

10 Check the condition of the O-ring on the filler cap/dipstick before screwing it back into the cover.

Separate gearbox oil level check

Where the gearbox oil is separate, such as on an engine of pre-unit construction, the gearshafts are lubricated by 'splash' from the reservoir of oil in the gearbox housing. Unless there is obvious sign of oil leakage, the oil level should not go down, and therefore need only be checked at the service interval specified by the manufacturer.

11 Before checking the oil level position the motorcycle on its centrestand or hold it upright.

12 On the motorcycle photographed, the combined filler/level plug should first be removed.

13 Add oil slowly until it starts to trickle out of the level hole, then refit the plug.

Engine oil level check – two-stroke engine

Because the engine oil is burnt in the combustion chamber (total loss system), the oil level will go down in accordance with use of the motorcycle in the same way as the fuel. It is therefore necessary to keep an eye on the level of oil in the tank. Get into the habit of checking and topping up the oil tank weekly or whenever you top up with fuel – **do not** rely solely on the oil level warning light.

1 The oil tank on this machine is sited behind a sidepanel. The oil level can be seen through the body of the tank. To top up, first clean around the cap then unscrew it. Add two-stroke oil to the upper limit only – usually up to the base of the filler neck. **Do not** overfill – if air cannot get in oil will not get out.

2 On most scooters the oil tank is located under the seat, with its filler cap alongside the fuel filler. Lift the seat then remove the cap.

With the cap removed, this is what you will see. On this machine, the bar across the filler hole is the oil level. Your machine will have something similar.

3 To top up, place a clean funnel into the filler hole and add good quality two-stroke oil until the level is correct. Note that many two-stroke oil bottles now incorporate a filler spout which makes topping up much easier.

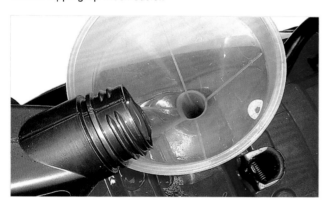

Add oil until the upper level is reached. This is easier said than done and it is probable that you will overfill the tank unless care is taken.

If you do overfill the tank, use a small, plastic syringe (available from chemists) to draw out the excess and put it back in the bottle. Don't forget to clean off any spillage and refit the cap before closing the seat.

Engine oil pump setting – two-stroke engine

Two-stroke engines must have their oil pump setting checked at each service. This machine uses a cable operated lever arm to change the amount of oil pumped relative to the throttle position. It is important that the throttle cable is adjusted prior to checking the oil pump setting (see Section 5 of this Chapter).

The accompanying photograph shows an arrangement where the throttle is held open to check the oil pump setting. On other machines, the setting may be checked with the throttle closed. Also the oil pump lever or pulley may contain several different markings – check the workshop manual for your machine to establish the correct procedure.

1 This setting should be checked with the throttle grip held fully open (engine **not** running). The line on the arm (D) must be parallel to the angled casting.

2 If it is not in alignment, slacken locknut (A) and turn nut (B) until the line is parallel to the casting.

3 Open and close the throttle and recheck the setting with the throttle fully open. Tighten the locknut (B) when the setting is correct.

4 Also check the condition of the pipe clips (C), and renew any that are missing or showing signs of fatigue.

Gearbox oil level check – two-stroke engine

The two-stroke gearbox is lubricated separately from the engine. The gear oil 'splash' feeds the gears and shafts and is contained within the crankcases. It should not need regular topping up, but its level should be checked and the oil changed at the manufacturer's service intervals. The oil level will only fall if:

+ The clutch side crankshaft oil seal has failed, causing the gearbox oil to be drawn into the crankcase. The engine will produce a lot more smoke and the spark plug will be excessively oily.
+ The gearchange shaft seal or gearbox output seal (by the rear sprocket) has failed allowing gearbox oil to leak over the drive chain.
+ The engine cases have cracked allowing oil to leak onto the ground.
+ Leakage from the clutch cover joint, possibly due to a failed gasket.

Many engines have a level screw and washer like the one shown.

Engine oil and filter change – four-stoke engine with spin-on filter

Most motorcycles use the 'spin-on' type oil filter. The filter is a throw away item and cannot be cleaned or dismantled for access to the element. Always purchase a new filter which is specifically designed for your model of motorcycle. The wide range of spin-on filters may look similar but their capacity; thread specification and filtering characteristics differ. Fitting a filter that is NOT specified for your machine may cause serious engine damage.

Items required

✔ Sufficient oil of the recommended viscosity and type.
✔ New oil filter and sump drain plug washer
✔ Variety of sockets, filter tool (see Chapter 1) or chain wrench and a torque wrench
✔ Drain bowl, jug and funnel
✔ Clean cloth or kitchen paper

Procedure

1 Most manufacturers will recommend that the engine oil should be drained when the oil is HOT. Run the engine for a few minutes until the oil is hot then switch it off. This will allow the oil to flow freely when the sump drain plug is removed, and ensure that any sludge and carbon is swept off the engine's internals and into the oil.

2 Clean around the filler cap and remove it. Removal of the filler will vent the crankcase whilst the oil is draining and will serve as a reminder that there is no oil in the engine.

3 Clean around the sump drain plug BEFORE you undo it. Place a container or bowl under the engine and remove the sump plug and washer.

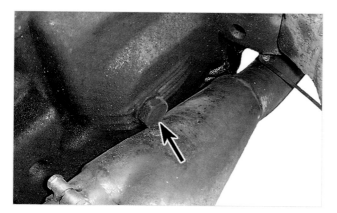

Allow the oil to drain fully from the engine. As this will take a few minutes, you can usefully employ this time by doing simple tasks, such as checking the tyre pressures.

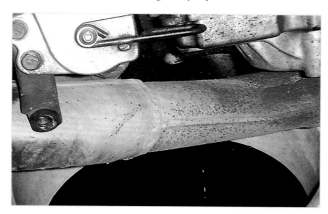

Caution: Be careful not to mistakenly remove oil galley plugs (arrowed) instead of the drain plug. Make sure you positively identify the oil drain plug – it will usually be situated in the lowest part of the sump – see your workshop manual for the exact location.

Warning: Take care when removing the sump drain plug as the oil will be HOT.

4 Move the drain bowl underneath the oil filter. Use a chain wrench or filter adapter tool to break the seal of the oil filter. With the seal broken, remove the tool and spin the filter off by hand. Take care you do not burn yourself on the hot exhaust.

A chain wrench is required on this machine as the filter is very close to the exhaust downpipes. Place the chain as close to the filter rim as possible (see photo) to prevent the filter from ripping and leaving the rim in situ.

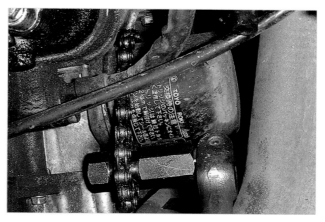

This machine has sufficient room to use a filter adapter tool to break the seal of the filter. The tool fits over the flats on the end of the filter and a spanner or socket wrench can be used to undo it.

HINT

RESIST the temptation to drive a screwdriver through the oil filter and twist it off. In almost every case, the filter body will be torn off the rim leaving this part stuck on the engine. Not only will it be very difficult, and time consuming to remove but could also be expensive and you may even do damage to yourself or the machine.

Note the use a piece of cardboard as a chute to direct the oil away from the exhaust downpipes. The cardboard will prevent oil getting onto your exhaust system, which would create an unpleasant amount of smoke when the exhaust heats up.

5 With the oil drained and the filter removed, refit the sump plug using a new washer, and tighten it to the recommended torque setting. Doing this now will prevent you forgetting later. There is nothing more frustrating than starting to refill the engine oil only to see fresh oil pouring all over the floor!

6 Before you fit the new filter lubricate its rubber sealing ring. Using fresh engine oil or multi-purpose grease on the ring will prevent it snagging and becoming damaged when it is tightened. If you fit it dry and it tears you will have an oil leak.

7 Apply a few drops of clean engine oil to the threads of the new filter. Ensure that the area around the oil filter mounting is

clean and spin the filter on by hand until you feel its sealing ring contact the mounting. Check your workshop manual for the required tightening method. This will either be expressed as a torque setting or as a number of turns (often two full turns). Use the filter adapter tool to tighten the filter, but do not overtighten it. **Do not** use a chain wrench to tighten the new filter; if you do, you are likely to damage the filter body.

8 Place a clean funnel into the filler hole and pour the correct amount of oil into the engine. Most manufacturers will quote three figures for the necessary amount of oil required. The quantity you will need will be either 'oil change only' or 'oil and filter change'.

✦ After an engine overhaul
✦ Oil change only
✦ Oil and filter change

9 Check the oil level as described earlier in this section. Note that it is imperative that the oil level is checked with the motorcycle upright, either on its centrestand or held upright.

10 Start the engine and allow it to run for a few minutes at idle speed. Whilst the engine is running check that there is no oil leakage from around the filter and sump drain plug, and that the oil pressure warning light goes out within a couple of seconds. If the warning light stays on, switch off the engine immediately and investigate the cause (see **Hint**). **Note:** *Certain models (with Yamaha engines) often have a an oil level warning light instead of an oil pressure light. If the oil level is correct, the light should go out a few seconds after the engine is started.*

11 If all is well, switch off the engine and wait for one or two minutes to allow the oil to settle. The level will have fallen and this is due to the filter having been filled and oil finding its way into various parts of the engine. Remove the filler cap and add small quantities of oil SLOWLY until the oil level reaches the upper limit.

> **HINT**
>
> If the oil warning light is taking longer to go out than usual, this is a good indication that the oil filter is blocked and needs changing. All systems have an oil bypass device built into the filter or filter housing bolt so that if the filter becomes blocked (because it hasn't been changed regularly) the pressure in the oil will activate the bypass valve allowing unfiltered oil to flow, bypassing the filter. Unfiltered oil is better than no oil.

> **HINT**
>
> If, having changed the oil and filter, the oil pressure warning light does not go out, stop the engine immediately. This will probably be caused by air being trapped in the filter stopping the oil flowing. This is a very rare situation but there are two possible ways to cure this:
>
> ✦ Remove the filter and fill it with oil before replacing it. If this has happened when you first changed the oil, you will need to fill the filter every time you change it.
>
> ✦ Place a rag under the filter and unscrew it by about 1 turn then start the engine. When oil flows from the filter joint (after a second or two), tighten the filter by hand then switch off the engine. Tighten the filter fully, start the engine and check that the oil pressure light goes out.

Engine oil and filter change – four-stoke engine with cartridge filter

Items required

✔ Sufficient oil of the recommended viscosity
✔ New oil filter and sump plug washer/O-ring
✔ Variety of sockets, spanners and a torque wrench
✔ Drain bowl, jug and funnel
✔ Clean cloth or kitchen paper

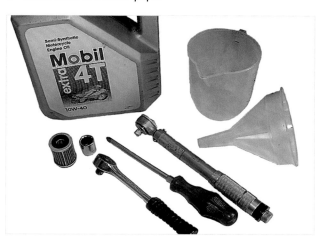

Procedure

1 Check that the engine has sufficient oil, then start it and allow it to run for a few minutes to warm the oil. Stop the engine.

2 Place a bowl or container under the machine. Remove the filler cap to vent the crankcase and to act as a reminder that there is no oil in the engine.

3 Remove the drain plug to allow the old oil to run out into the drain bowl. Take care because the oil will be HOT.

This machine has its engine oil drain plug on the lower, left hand side of the crankcase behind the gearchange lever. Pushing the gear lever down will allow the use of a six-sided socket and wrench or 'T' bar socket to undo the engine oil drain

plug. Note that it is very easy to damage the head if a 12-point socket or spanner is used – a six-sided socket will grip on the flats and not on the corners, thus protecting the head. If it has already been damaged by a previous owner, it may be extremely difficult to remove and a new drain plug should be obtained.

Some engines have a spring and coarse filter fitted behind the drain plug. Note the positioning of these items for correct refitting and remove them for cleaning. While the oil is draining into the bowl use an old toothbrush to clean the filter. Once the oil has drained fully fit the spring onto the filter and replace it in the engine.

4 Renew the O-ring or washer, on the drain plug. If an O-ring is fitted, lubricate it with clean engine oil. Refit the drain plug and tighten it to the manufacturer's specified torque setting.

5 On the model photographed, the main filter is on the opposite side of the engine, under this cover. Removal of the lower screw (arrowed) allows the filter cavity to drain, so make sure that you have placed the bowl under this cover BEFORE you undo any screws. With all three screws removed, the cover can be removed. If it is stuck in place, tap it gently with a rubber hammer to loosen its grip.

6 With the cover removed, the old filter can be pulled out. Note which way round the old filter was fitted. Some filters have the word 'OUTSIDE' stamped on one end.

The filter on the left is new whereas the one on the right had been in the engine for 8000 miles. Considering that the filter protects your engine from all sorts of contaminants picked up by the oil this is NOT an area where cost cutting should occur – always renew the filter at the recommended service interval.

7 Clean the filter housing in the crankcase and the inside of the cover before installing the new filter. This engine has two O-rings, the larger cover ring and a smaller one fitted in the engine case. Make sure that they are both in good condition, if

in doubt, renew them. Apply a smear of grease or clean engine oil to the O-rings before fitting the cover. Note the small slot in the engine case, which lines up with a corresponding slot in the cover. Your machine may have something similar, always examine each item as you remove it to see if there is a particular way it must be refitted.

8 Place a clean funnel into the oil filler hole in the clutch cover. Fill a clean jug with the correct quantity of oil and slowly pour the oil into the engine. The manufacturer will usually quote three quantities of oil to use.
+ After an engine overhaul
+ Oil change only
+ Oil and filter change

9 Check the oil level as described earlier in this section. Note that it is imperative that the oil level is checked with the motorcycle upright, either on its centrestand or held upright.

10 Start the engine, run it for a few minutes and check that there are no oil leaks. Stop the engine and wait for a few minutes to allow the oil level to settle. Recheck the oil level and add small quantities of oil until the level reaches the upper mark.

Gearbox oil change – two-stroke engine

The gearbox oil should be changed at the manufacturer's specified service interval. The gearbox is lubricated by 'splash feed' (no oil pump) so there will be no filter to renew.

Items required

✔ Sufficient oil of the correct viscosity
✔ Jug, funnel and drain bowl
✔ Sockets, spanners, screwdriver and torque wrench
✔ New drain plug washer
✔ Clean cloth or kitchen paper

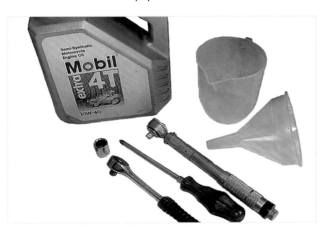

Procedure

1 Position the machine upright on its centrestand or a paddock stand. Clean around the filler cap before unscrewing it. This will prevent any dirt falling into the transmission. Check the condition of the cap O-ring and renew it if there is any doubt about its condition.

2 Locate the drain plug, which may be underneath the engine or to the side as on this motorcycle.

3 Place a drain bowl under the engine, undo the drain plug and allow the oil to drain. It will take some time to drain the oil as, unlike a four-stroke, running a two-stroke engine will not warm up the gearbox oil significantly. Whilst the transmission oil is draining, other tasks can be undertaken such as checking and setting the engine oil pump.

4 Most two-stroke transmissions use a level screw mounted in the clutch cover case to check the oil level. Remove this screw and check the condition of its sealing washer. If there is any doubt about its condition, renew it.

5 When the oil has finally drained from the transmission, use a new washer and refit the drain plug. Tighten the drain plug to the manufacturer's specified torque setting.

6 Measure out the specified amount and type of oil recommended for the machine, keep the machine upright and pour the new oil slowly into the transmission case via the filler hole. On many machines you will find the gearbox oil quantity cast into the clutch cover.

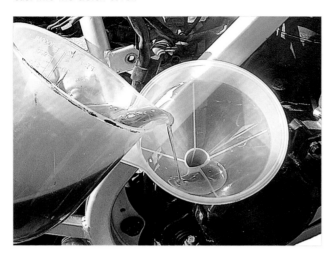

7 Slide the drain bowl under the engine so that it is directly below the level screw hole. It will take a few minutes for the oil to find its way into all the cavities in the gearbox, so be patient. You should eventually see the oil trickle from the level screw hole.

8 When the oil stops running from the level screw hole, fit and tighten the level screw. Refit the filler cap.

Scooter transmission

Some scooters have no means of draining the transmission oil; they have a level/filler plug only and the lubricant is intended to last the life of the machine, except where the transmission is overhauled and fresh oil used on the rebuild. Other scooters have a drain plug at the base of the transmission case to allow the oil to be changed at the manufacturer's specified interval.

1 To check the oil level, first clean the area around the level/filler plug and remove the plug.

2 Hold a cloth under the hole and add oil until it starts to come out of the hole. The total amount of oil in the transmission is usually very small; the scooter photographed uses 120 ml of SAE 80W/90 gear oil. Some oil companies package scooter transmission oil in exact quantities in tube form. Otherwise the oil can be added using a piece of plastic pipe and funnel or an oil can with a flexible spout.

3 Once the oil stops draining from the hole check the condition of the level/filler plug washer (renew the washer if necessary) and refit the plug.

Gearbox oil change – four-stroke engine

Although the majority of four-strokes use the engine oil to lubricate the gearbox, there are a few designs (e.g. BMW and Moto Guzzi) where the gearbox has a separate oil supply. A gear oil is usually specified and the service intervals for checking the oil level and changing the oil differ from those for the engine oil.

Items required

✔ Sufficient oil of the correct type and viscosity. Many machines use a hypoid gear oil of SAE 80, SAE90 or SAE80W/90 viscosity
✔ Drain bowl, jug and funnel
✔ Appropriate sockets, Allen sockets and torque wrench
✔ New drain plug washer and filler/level plug washer

Procedure

1 Ride the motorcycle for 3 or 4 miles to warm the gearbox oil prior to draining it.

2 With the motorcycle on its centrestand or a paddock stand, place a drain bowl under the gearbox and remove the drain bolt. Allow the gear oil to drain from the gearbox. This will take

some time, as the oil may still be cold. Whilst the oil is draining, carry on with other service tasks such as checking the tyre pressures.

3 When the oil has drained fully, fit a new washer and refit the drain plug. Tighten the drain plug to its correct torque setting.

4 On this motorcycle the combined filler/level plug is on the right-hand side of the gearbox and has an Allen socket head. Remove the plug and carefully add oil until it starts to flow from the hole.

5 Wait a few moments until the flow has stopped then fit a new washer and refit the filler/level plug.

Shaft final drive oil change

Although shaft drive systems are considered 'maintenance-free' it is necessary to check the oil level in the final drive box and change the oil periodically. A gear oil is specified for this purpose, usually of the EP (Extreme Pressure) type due to the shearing forces between the spiral bevel gears.

1 Place the motorcycle on its centrestand or support it on a paddock stand.

2 Place a drain bowl under the final drive box and remove the drain bolt (arrowed).

It will take some time for the oil to drain so it may be useful to do some other service tasks while this is happening. Remove the level/filler bolt (arrowed) to vent the box and help the oil to drain.

3 When the oil has drained fully, fit a new washer to the drain bolt and tighten it to the manufacturer's specified torque.

4 Add oil via the filler/level hole until oil starts to flow from it. When the flow stops, fit a new washer to the filler/level bolt and tighten it.

5 All systems have some form of breather incorporated, either removable (arrowed), non-serviceable or simply a small hole in the bevel box. Whatever type is fitted, ensure it is clean.

7   Clutch

Note: *This section applies to cable-operated clutches. Maintenance of an hydraulic clutch system involves checking of the fluid level in the master cylinder – see Chapter 4 for the front brake.*

Clutch cable freeplay should be carried out at each service. If there is insufficient freeplay in the clutch cable there is a possibility of the clutch NOT being in full engagement when the lever is released. This condition causes the clutch plates to slip; full power will not be transferred through the clutch and the plates will eventually burn out.

The two basic clutch mechanism types are described here. The first, applies to machines with an adjuster screw and locknut on the left-hand casing (most Suzuki models); the pushrod passes through the gearbox input shaft and operates the clutch which is mounted on the right-hand end of the input shaft. A small clearance is necessary in the operating mechanism and this must be set up before the cable is adjusted.

The second system is essentially a cable which connects to an operating arm on the clutch cover. The operating arm acts on a short pushrod via a rack and pinion gear arrangement.

Adjustment method for cable and pushrod system

1 Pull back the rubber cover fitted over the adjuster. Slacken the locking ring (A) and back it off so that it touches the adjuster screw (B).

Now turn the adjuster screw and locking ring in towards the clutch lever as far as it will go. Do not over-tighten it. This will create slack in the cable.

Pull the cable away from the lever and apply a smear of grease around the metal barrel end of the cable.

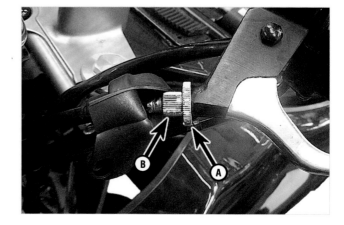

2 Trace the clutch cable down to the point it enters the engine on the left-hand side. Pull any rubber cover off the adjuster, slacken the locknut (C) and turn it so that it touches the adjuster (D). Now turn the adjuster (D) down until the locknut touches the casing.

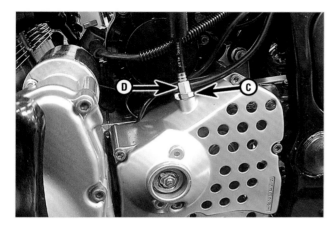

Check there is freeplay in the cable by trying to lift the cable upwards. It is not necessary for the cable to come out of the adjuster, if it does and the next step does not improve matters be prepared to renew the cable as it has probably stretched.

Whilst the cable is lifted, apply a smear of grease around the metal barrel end of the cable.

3 This engine has a rubber bung covering the clutch pushrod adjuster; yours may have something similar or even a cover plate. Whichever it is, remove it and slacken the locknut (E) by about 1 – 2 turns.

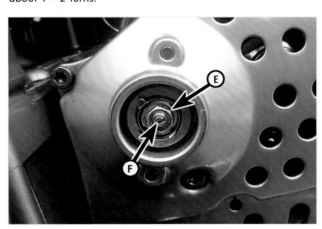

Holding the locknut, turn the adjuster screw (F) out by about 2 turns then turn the screw inwards until it just starts to seat. From this position, turn the adjuster screw back 1/4 to 1/2 a turn. Hold the adjuster screw in this position and tighten the locknut. This creates a clearance between the clutch operating mechanism and the pushrod.

4 The cable can now be adjusted. Turn the cable adjuster (D) until there is approximately 4 mm of freeplay measured at the lever stock.

Tighten the locknut (C) when this has been done. Note that some manufacturers express clutch lever freeplay at the lever end rather that at the stock, typically 20 mm freeplay.

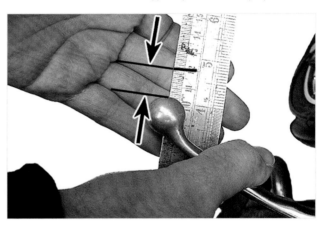

HINT

It helps to allow slightly more clearance at the lever when adjusting at the engine end. Then make any final adjustments with the adjuster at the lever.

5 Make sure that the lever locking ring is tight and any rubber cover refitted. Try to position the slot in the adjuster (B) facing towards the back of the motorcycle to help keep water out of the cable.

6 Test for correct adjustment by starting the engine engaging first gear and gently letting the clutch lever out.

Adjustment method for cable and operating arm system

1 Pull back the rubber cover fitted over the cable adjuster at the handlebar lever. Slacken the locking ring (A) and back it off so that it touches the adjuster screw (B).

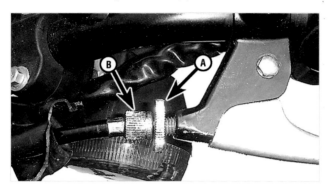

Turn the adjuster screw and locking ring in towards the clutch lever as far as it will go. Do not over-tighten it.

Pull the cable away from the lever. If it will move apply a smear of grease around the metal barrel end of the cable.

2 Trace the cable down to its lower end on the clutch cover. Slacken the locknut (C). Hold the end of the cable at the point (E) and turn the nut (D) to take most of the slack out of the cable.

Adjust the cable so that there is approximately 4 mm of freeplay at the lever stock (or 20 mm of freeplay at the lever end).

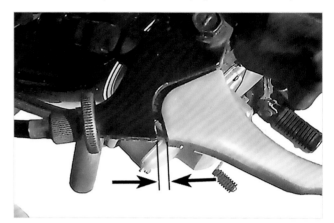

When the correct cable freeplay has been achieved, tighten the locknut (C).

HINT

It helps to allow slightly more clearance at the lever when adjusting at the engine end. Then make any final adjustments with the adjuster at the lever.

3 Moving back to the adjuster at the handlebar lever end of the cable, make sure that the lever locking ring is tight and any rubber cover refitted. Try to position the slot in the adjuster facing towards the back of the motorcycle to help keep water out of the cable.

4 Test for correct adjustment by starting the engine, engaging first gear and gently letting the clutch lever out.

8   Two-stroke engine top-end overhaul

Stripping and de-coking the top-end of a two-stroke engine is rarely necessary on a regular basis nowadays, particularly with the use of modern engine oils and if the oil pump is correctly adjusted. There are, however, a number of highly tuned, road-going motorcycles which will require this at specific mileage/time intervals.

If an engine fault is suspected, be guided by the symptoms and test each system in a logical order. The engine may be difficult to start, lack power or use a lot of fuel – all these are signs that something is not quite right. For a two-stroke engine to work it requires:

✦ Good compression pressure
✦ A spark of sufficient intensity which occurs at the correct piston position
✦ The correct air:fuel ratio

Unlike its four-stroke counterpart, a compression test of a two-stroke engine is less revealing and the results often inconclusive. In fact, many manufacturers no longer specify compression figures for two-stroke engines.

A two-stroke engine can lose compression at the cylinder head gasket joint or the crankshaft oil seals can fail. Check the obvious first – it can often be something as simple as a loose spark plug or loose cylinder head bolts/nuts; either condition may be heard as a hissing or squealing sound as the engine is turned over.

Failure of either seal on the crankshaft will produce different symptoms. The side which drives the clutch (usually right-hand side) has a double-lipped seal; its inner lip keeps the air/fuel mixture in the crankcase and its outer lip keeps the transmission oil out of the crankcase. If this seal fails transmission oil will be drawn into the crankcase and burnt with the air/fuel mixture, creating excess exhaust smoke. You may also notice a mysterious drop in the transmission oil level.

The seal on the left-hand side of the crankshaft (generator side) is usually a single-lipped type. If it fails air will enter the crankcase and cause a weak air/fuel mixture, resulting in poor running and overheating.

Other causes of low compression could be a broken piston ring, or the piston rings gummed into their grooves due to a build-up of carbon, or simply worn rings/piston or bore.

Prior to stripping down the engine first check that the fault is not due to any of the following:

+ Spark plug – clean, correctly gapped and tightened securely.
+ Cylinder head bolt/nuts – check that they are not loose.
+ Air filter – clean and not over-oiled.
+ Carburettor – fuel level/float height correct, air:fuel mixture correctly set.
+ Fuel filter – check if clean and fitted the correct way round.
+ Intake manifold – no air leaks at joint with engine and reed block/carburettor.
+ Ignition timing – incorrectly adjusted (unlikely on modern engines with electronic ignition). Excessive play in the main bearings can cause erratic igntion timing.
+ Exhaust – no air leaks at joint with cylinder barrel (usually caused by incorrect tightening sequence).
+ Exhaust system – tail pipe baffle may be blocked.

The following text in this section is divided into three main sub-sections: the top-end stripdown, the cleaning and inspection of components, and the top-end rebuild. The amount of work required to access the cylinder head/barrel will differ for every model and vary in complexity depending on whether the engine is air-cooled or liquid-cooled.

Items required

✔ Two new piston pin circlips
✔ A set of new piston rings and a new small-end needle roller bearing are advisable
✔ Oil can filled with fresh two-stroke oil
✔ Sockets, spanners, screwdrivers and a torque wrench
✔ A gasket scraper
✔ A micrometer and Vernier caliper will be necessary if parts are to be measured
✔ New top-end gasket set consisting of a cylinder head gasket, base gasket, exhaust gasket and reed valve assembly gasket. If you are using paper type gaskets, there may be a need to use proprietary gasket cement

Gaining access to the top-end

1 Remove the seat, side panels, fuel tank and any bodywork necessary to gain full access to the engine.

2 Remove the spark plug (see Section 9).

3 Remove the exhaust system.

Slacken the rearmost mounting bolt first, then work your way towards the front of the machine slackening each mounting bolt as you go. Finish with the exhaust flange nuts at the cylinder (arrowed), then remove all mounting bolts and remove the exhaust system.

4 Remove the carburettor.

Attach a hose to the drain spigot on the float bowl and place the end of the hose in a jug. Slacken the drain screw and allow the fuel from the float bowl to drain into the jug. Tighten the drain screw and disconnect the hose.

Undo the carburettor top cover and lift out the slide assembly. The machine photographed has a plunger type, cold start (choke) mechanism (A), remove it complete with its cable and place it out of the way.

Remove the oil pipe from its stub (B) on the carburettor body and place it out of the way. Some machines pump their oil directly into the inlet tract, if your machine has this type of fitting remove the pipe now. Do NOT forget to replace the pipe on rebuild or the engine will seize negating all your hard work.

You can now undo the two clips holding the carburettor to the air filter and inlet stubs and pull the carburettor away from the engine.

5 If the engine is liquid-cooled, drain the coolant and disconnect the radiator hose as follows.

Remove any cowling from the radiator. Cover the radiator cap with a heavy cloth and turn it anti-clockwise to release it.

> **Warning: Do NOT** attempt to remove the radiator cap if the engine is HOT. The cooling system is pressurised to enable the coolant temperature to exceed 100°C without boiling. If the cap is removed whilst the engine is hot, you may get coolant 'EXPLODING' at you at approximately 107°C, which can cause a very severe injury.

Locate the water pump (on this engine it is on the right-hand side) and remove the drain bolt (arrowed). Coolant will immediately flow, so ensure that you have a clean bowl under the area to catch it. Note the type of sealing washer on the drain screw. It is usually a copper or aluminium washer, which are both soft metals and can be compressed to form a watertight seal. Renew the washer if you are in any doubt about its condition, but **do not** use an ordinary steel washer.

If the pump does not have a drain screw, slacken the clamp holding the radiator lower hose (A) and pull the hose away from the water pump spigot. Place a jug under the hose to catch the coolant as it drains from the engine and radiator. The hose is likely to be stuck on the spigot so ensure that the clamp is completely free to rotate on the hose before pulling the hose off giving it a twist at the same time. **Do not** attempt to pry the hose off with a screwdriver; if you do you will most likely damage the hose or the water pump spigot or at worst, stab yourself with the screwdriver.

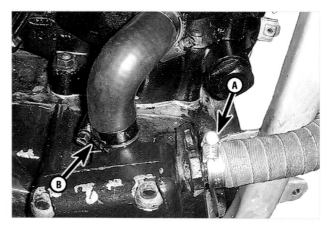

Remove the radiator top hose (arrowed), which is connected to the cooling system thermostat housing.

If the motorcycle has a coolant temperature gauge, disconnect the wire from the sender unit which is usually situated on the cylinder head. Leave the sender unit in place.

Remove the coolant drain screw from the barrel and drain the coolant into the bowl. This screw also has a soft washer sealing the drain hole. Like the water pump drain screw, this washer should also be renewed if its condition is in doubt. You can now remove the water pump to barrel hose (marked B in the photo on the previous page).

Engine top-end stripdown

1 Slacken the cylinder head bolts/nuts evenly in a **diagonal sequence** by about 1/2 a turn at a time. When **all** are slackened undo and remove each one. If the sequence is not followed, there is a possibility of distorting the cylinder head.

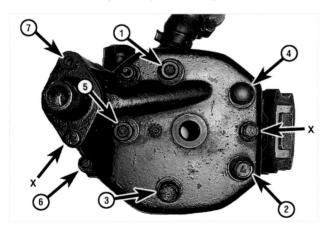

On the liquid-cooled engine photographed, the bolts marked 'X' do not need to be undone. The one on the right is a coolant bleed screw whereas the one on the left holds the thermostat cover in place. An air-cooled engine will have a much more obvious arrangement of cylinder head bolts/nuts.

2 The cylinder head can now be lifted from the engine. If it doesn't, a **gentle** tap, on the side of the head with a rubber

mallet will dislodge it. If it is still unwilling to move, check that you have not overlooked a bolt. Remove the cylinder head gasket from the top of the barrel.

3 Slacken the reed valve block bolts by about one turn before undoing and removing them all. On the reed valve block photographed, the bolt on the far right holds the oil pump cable support bracket; take note of the bracket position so that it can be refitted correctly. Similarly take note of any washers; there should be flat washers under each bolt head or flanged bolt heads (far right bolt) should be used.

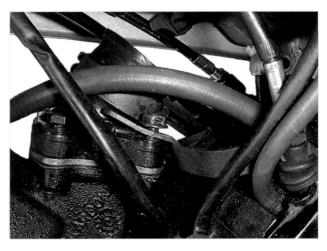

4 The fibre reed valve unit shown uses four petals; others may have only two petals and may be of fibre or steel construction. Clean any old gasket from the unit and clean the petals with a soft cloth or kitchen paper. The reeds are delicate and will be damaged if compressed air is used to clean them.

5 Remove the rotor cover and turn the rotor (in the normal direction of rotation) until the piston is at the top of its stroke and the piston crown level is level with the top of the barrel.

6 The engine photographed has four nuts holding the cylinder barrel to the crankcases, two on each side. Undo and remove all four nuts and lift the barrel by approximately one inch.

Some engines do not have separate nuts retaining the barrel; it is retained by long through-bolts which secure the cylinder head.

It is possible that the barrel will stick on its base gasket and not lift easily. Resist the temptation to insert a screwdriver between the barrel and crankcase and lever the barrel free – this will damage the barrel surface and on a liquid-cooled engine lead to coolant leaks. Gently tap the side of the barrel with a rubber hammer to break the gasket joint and give the barrel a slight 'wiggle' at the same time.

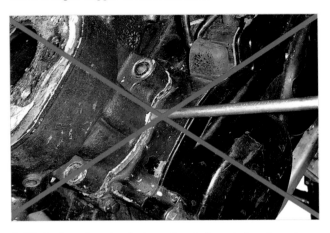

7 Lift the barrel so that it clears the studs and place two pieces of wood (approx. 10 mm x 20 mm x 200 mm) under the barrel on each side of the connecting rod. Turn the rotor so that the piston descends and sits on the wood. This will support the piston when you remove the barrel.

HINT

As you will have no idea what state the piston and rings are in, play safe and loosely pack the crankcase mouth with kitchen paper or clean cloth. If the piston rings are broken, this precaution will ensure that any loose bits of ring do not fall into the crankcases when the barrel is fully lifted, necessitating a total engine strip.

8 Hold the rotor to prevent the piston rising and lift the barrel up and off the piston. Lift the cylinder barrel gasket off the crankcase.

9 Leave the kitchen paper or cloth in place and remove both piston circlips. The type of circlip shown (arrowed) can be removed using a pair of long nose pliers.

Other types of piston circlips have no 'ears,' these can be removed using a small flat-bladed screwdriver. Place the screwdriver in the slot and GENTLY prise the circlip out of its groove. Cover the circlip with your hand because as it is released it will tend to 'ping' away.

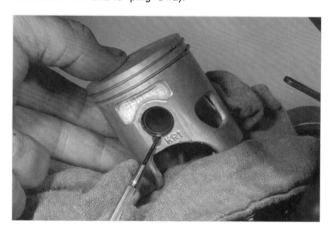

10 Check for any marking on the piston crown which would indicate its position relative to the front or back of the engine, if none is found, mark the crown with an arrow towards the front of the engine. Push the piston pin out of the piston and connecting rod and lift the piston off.

11 Slip the small-end bearing out of the connecting rod eye.

Cleaning and inspection of components

1 Before cleaning and inspecting the top-end components check the big-end bearing and main bearings for wear. If wear is apparent, the engine will either have to be fully overhauled or a new or replacement engine fitted.

The slightest up and down motion of the con-rod on its bearing is enough to condemn the big-end bearing. Check the big-end bearing as follows:

a) Hold the small-end of the con rod and rock it gently from side to side. You will feel a small amount of play in the bearing. This is normal.
b) Still holding the small-end of the con rod, use your other hand to push the big-end of the con rod to one side and hold it there.

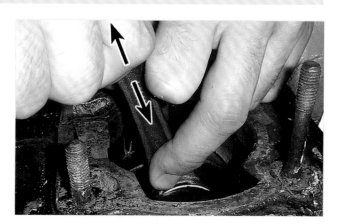

c) Try to pull and push the con rod up and down. There should be no movement at all. If you feel a small amount of movement, as in (a) the bearing is failing. Crankshaft renewal is the only option.

To check the main bearings, use both hands to grip the rotor with the thumbs and forefingers at the 12 o'clock and 6 o'clock positions as shown. Try to push the rotor up and down; there should be no discernible play. If play is present, there are two possible faults:

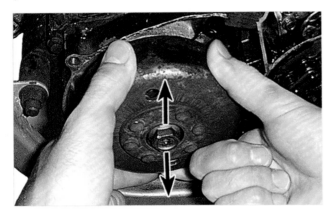

a) The rotor nut is loose. Slacken it then re-tighten it to its correct torque setting then retest.
b) If there is still a rocking motion (knocks), then the main bearings have failed and this is going to require an expensive total engine strip and rebuild.

If you remove the rotor nut for any purpose always apply one drop of locking agent to the threads and tighten it to its correct torque setting.

If the big-end and main bearings are OK, proceed to check the top-end components as follows:

2 Use a copper scraper (see Chapter 1), or carefully use a steel scraper as shown, to remove all head gasket residue from the top of the barrel. If this is not completely removed the new head gasket will not seal completely, leading to loss of compression and possibly a weak mixture due to air entering the combustion chamber. On liquid-cooled engines a poorly sealing gasket will cause leakage of coolant either externally or into the combustion chamber.

Pay special attention to the head bolt holes and clean them of any gasket material. With the top of the barrel clear of old gasket material turn the barrel upside down and repeat the process on the bottom gasket surface.

3 Turn your attention to the cylinder head and clean this of any old gasket material. Finish ALL gasket surfaces with 400 grade wet and dry paper to achieve a smooth finish.

4 Leave the kitchen paper or cloth in the crankcase mouth and remove all base gasket residue from the crankcase mating surface. Clean up the threads of the crankcase studs and the exhaust studs with a stiff wire brush. This will make reassembly much easier.

5 The final area to clean is the exhaust port. Use a copper scraper to get as much carbon off as possible, finish with 400 grade wet and dry paper. It is not necessary to achieve a mirror finish on the exhaust port but make sure the exhaust gasket face is clean. There is nothing more frustrating than to discover the exhaust 'blowing' when you first start the engine, all because the gasket face was not properly prepared.

6 Remove the rings from the piston. Line up the top ring gap with the ring groove pin. Grip the piston in both hands so that your middle fingers are opposite the ring gap and pressing the ring into its groove. This causes the ring ends to be pushed out of the groove. Use your thumbs to GENTLY spread then lift the open ends of the ring. Open the ring; just enough so that it can clear the piston. Then lift the ends so that they rest on the piston lands, just above the groove. Releasing the pressure of your middle fingers will allow the ring to be GENTLY lifted up and off the piston.

Repeat this procedure for the second ring but lift it into the first ring groove THEN lift it off the piston. Keep note of which ring fits in which groove in the piston and which way up they are fitted.

7 Clean the piston crown with 400 grade wet and dry paper until all the carbon is removed. Start at the centre of the crown and work your way to the edges. It is not necessary to produce a mirror finish.

Note the word 'IN' on the top of the piston (see photograph on page 99). This denotes that this side of the piston should face the inlet stub. Other manufacturers use an arrow and occasionally the letters 'EX' on the top of the piston denoting that this side of the piston should face the exhaust port.

Have a good look at the piston. Brown corrosion below the lower piston ring suggests that there has been a lot of 'blow-by'. This is a good indication as to the amount of ring/barrel wear. Check the piston skirt for signs of damage caused by heat seizure. Minor scuffmarks can be cleaned with 400 grade wet

and dry paper. Deep scoring or damage to the ring grooves will require the fitting of a new piston and rings.

Check to see if there is a spring steel ring in the second groove. Not all piston manufacturers use them but if yours has one, remove it now. Clean the sides of the piston and the ring grooves of any carbon. Carbon in the ring grooves can cause the rings to stick leading to a reduction in output power.

HINT

A piece of old broken piston ring with its end filed flat makes a good ring groove cleaning tool.

8 Inspect the cylinder head for warpage. A warped cylinder head will result in loss of compression and lead to a reduction in power. Place a steel rule across the cylinder head (as shown) and use a feeler gauge to measure any gap between the head surface and the rule. Note the damage to the head (arrowed) by a previous owner using a screwdriver to prise it off the barrel.

Place the rule across the head in three places when testing. If a feeler gauge greater than 0.05 mm can fit between the rule and head gasket surface then the head is warped and will need to be renewed or skimmed.

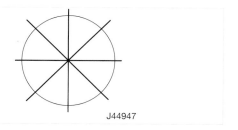

J44947

Note that skimming is a job for a specialist engineering firm. Minor irregularities can be corrected by rotating the head face-down on a sheet of 400 grade wet and dry paper stuck to a perfectly flat surface.

9 Inspect the barrel liner for scoring and deep scratches. Light scratches can be removed using 400 grade wet and dry paper. What is deep scoring? If you can feel the scoring with your fingernail it is too deep and the barrel will need to be rebored.

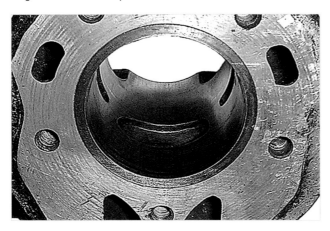

The barrel photographed has a steel liner and is thus able to be rebored and an oversize piston used. The bores on many engines are finished with an electroplated, Nickel-Silicon Carbide coating. This coating is extremely hard and is designed to last the life of the engine. In the event of catastrophic engine damage, the barrel should be renewed because reboring is not possible. If may however be worth seeking the opinion of a specialist engineering shop who may be able to replate the barrel.

10 It is necessary to 'peg' the piston rings of a two-stroke engine to prevent them moving around the piston and catching on the ports in the barrel. Check that the pegs (arrowed) in the ring grooves of the piston are in place and not loose.

11 Some manufacturers, but not all, quote a figure for the piston ring free end gap.

Lay EACH ring onto a steel rule and compare the measurement with the manufacturer's specifications. An alternative would be to measure the end gap with a Vernier caliper. If any gap is outside the tolerance, BOTH rings must be renewed. Note that the gap gets smaller as the ring wears.

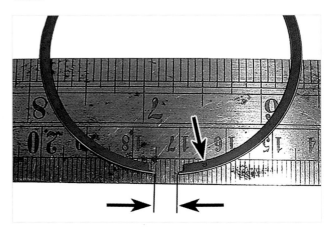

Note the 'R' marking (arrowed) or similar on one end of the ring's top surface. When refitting the rings make sure that this mark faces upwards.

12 The manufacturer usually specifies a figure for the piston ring 'installed' end gap.

Place the barrel upside down and insert one of the piston rings into the bottom of the barrel. Use the piston to ensure that the ring is 'square' in the barrel and position the ring about 20 mm below the gasket surface.

Measure the ring gap with a feeler gauge. Start with a gauge that is the same as the manufacturers standard gap size. Increase the gauge size until you find one that is a sliding fit in the ring gap; this gauge is the measurement of the ring gap. Note the size and repeat for the other piston ring. If one ring is outside the manufacturer's specification, BOTH rings must be renewed. Note that the gap increases as the ring wears.

13 If the ring end gaps are OK, refit the rings to the piston and check the ring to groove clearance. Check BOTH rings and if the clearance of any ring is outside the tolerance, it may be due to worn rings or a worn piston. To confirm, check the clearance again but this time using new rings. If the clearance is still outside the tolerance, the piston groove is worn and the piston will have to be renewed.

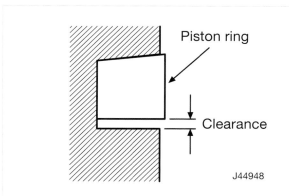

Piston ring

Clearance

J44948

14 Visually inspect the piston pin (wrist pin or gudgeon pin) for signs of heat seizure. This will usually be seen as severe damage to the hardened surface of the pin, where it is in contact with the needle roller bearing.

Use a 0 – 25 mm micrometer to measure the piston pin diameter. Measure the pin at its centre (bearing surface) and in at least two places, the second place should be 90° to the first. Compare your measurements with the manufacturer's specification.

15 To calculate the cylinder-to-piston clearance, deduct the piston measurement from the bore measurement then compare this with the manufacturer's specification.

The piston is perfectly circular at its top but not at the bottom of the skirt and its sides are not parallel. Imagine an upturned, plastic bucket with the rim slightly squashed and you have a close picture of the shape of a piston. This strange shape is to allow the piston to expand when it gets hot without causing it to seize in the bore.

You will need a large (25 to 50 mm or 50 to 75 mm) micrometer to measure the piston skirt. This measurement should be taken at right-angles to the pin holes and approximately 10 to 20 mm from the base of the piston.

To measure the cylinder bore accurately you will require an internal micrometer or telescopic gauges. These are very expensive tools and can rarely be justified by the home mechanic; they are, however, in regular use in engineering workshops. The bore should be measured approximately 20 mm from its top surface, although check your workshop manual for the exact depth specified for the engine.

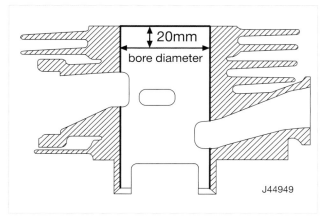

20mm

bore diameter

J44949

Once these measurements have been taken, subtract the piston diameter from the bore diameter to obtain the cylinder-to-piston clearance. Compare this with the service limit specified by the manufacturer. If the clearance is larger than the service limit, compare the piston diameter and bore diameter with the service limits specified to determine which is worn.

16 The cylinder bore can wear in different directions. It can be out of round or the bore may not be parallel (tapered). The bore should be measured in side-to-side and back-to-front directions.

Use an internal micrometer or a telescopic gauge and external micrometer and measure the bore in the three positions shown. Comparison of the three measurements will show if the bore is parallel or has become tapered.

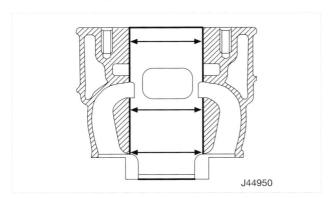

J44950

Take three more measurements at the same positions, but this time at 90° to the first set. Comparison of the top pair then the middle pair and lastly the bottom pair will show if the bore is out of round (ovalled).

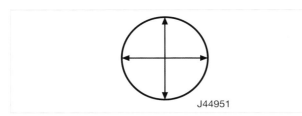

J44951

HINT

You can obtain an indication of cylinder bore wear by using one of the piston rings and feeler gauges.

Measure the piston ring gap with the ring in the bottom of the bore. Note the gap size, then move the ring to the top of the bore. Position the ring (using the piston) about 20 mm from the top of the bore and measure the gap again. Note the gap and measure again but this time with the ring at 90° to the first measurement.

If the gap has stayed the same, this is a good indication that the bore is not severely worn. If, however, the gaps differ or if any doubt exists, have the bore measured by an engineer.

If the bore is excessively tapered or ovalled, it will require a rebore and oversize piston. Note that reboring is only possible on bores with steel liners, not plated bores.

After reboring the cylinder, the engineer should chamfer the edges of the ports to prevent damage to the piston rings. If this has not been done, use a small curved file to chamfer the top, bottom and sides of each port. The figures given on the accompanying illustration apply to a Suzuki engine – refer to the workshop manual for specific figures for your machine.

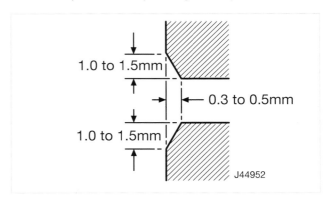

J44952

17 Fit the piston rings on the piston. The original rings can be re-used if they are not worn beyond the service limit, although it is usual practice to fit new rings due to their relative cheapness.

Piston rings are usually tapered and must be fitted the right way up. They often have a letter stamped on one end and this should face upwards when fitted.

HINT

Some ring sets have one ring with a shiny edge and another with a dull finish to its edge. When fitting this type the shiny ring is the top ring and the dull ring is the second one.

If the lower ring has an expander ring underneath it, fit this into the lower groove first. Place the piston on a flat surface and place the lower ring on top of the piston so that its gap is next to the ring peg. Place both of your forefingers at the back of the ring and gently open the ring gap with your thumbs and at the same time push the ring over the piston with your forefingers. Ease the ring into the top groove of the piston, then move the ring into the lower groove. Fit the top ring into the top groove of the piston in the same manner.

18 Check the reed valve assembly prior to rebuilding the engine.

Check that the reeds lay flat against the case and are not damaged; if they are broken, cracked or bent, they must be renewed.

If the manufacturer's figure for stopper plate height is known, you can measure the distance between the petal (A) and the stopper plate (B) and compare with this figure. If the distance is smaller than specified, the stops can be **carefully** bent to increase the gap using a pair of pliers. Note that these gaps do not change by themselves – any discrepancy is most likely due to a previous owner 'playing' with the stops or forcing the assembly into the engine on rebuild.

Do not bend the reed stopper plate so that the distance between the petal and plate exceeds the manufacturer's specifications. If the gaps are too large, there is a distinct possibility of the reeds fracturing in use leading to expensive engine damage if the broken parts are swept into the crankcase.

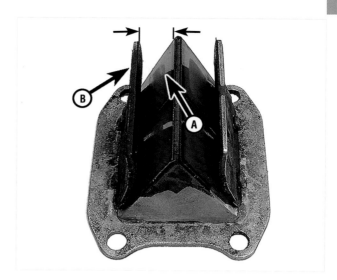

Engine top-end rebuild

1 Before rebuilding the engine, lubricate the big-end and main bearings. Use an oil can filled with fresh two-stroke oil to squirt a couple of shots of oil into the big-end bearing and down the holes (arrowed) which feed the main bearings.

2 Fit the new base gasket ensuring that it is the correct way round and matches the cut-outs in the crankcases. If it is necessary to use gasket cement, lightly coat both surfaces of

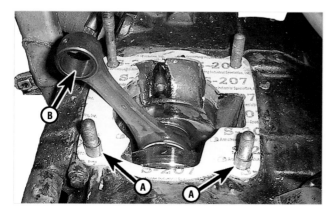

the gasket before fitting it. Make sure that the dowel pins (A) are fitted and clean. These are to ensure that the barrel lines up with the crankcases.

3 Lubricate the small-end eye (B) with fresh two-stroke oil and insert the needle-roller bearing. It is good practice to fit a **new** bearing.

4 Fit one of the **new** piston circlips to the piston so that its open end (A) is opposite the slot in the piston (B). If the piston has two slots, fit the open end of the circlip between the two slots.

Never re-use an old circlip or one which is the wrong size for the engine. Piston circlips come in differing sections, styles and diameters and it is essential that the correct type is used. If the wrong type of clip is used, there is a distinct possibility of the clip coming out of its groove and causing extensive engine damage.

5 Lubricate the piston pin with fresh two-stroke oil and assemble the piston on the con-rod, noting which way round the piston is fitted. Support the piston with the two wood blocks and stuff the crankcases with clean cloth or kitchen paper. Fit the second **new** piston circlip, using a small flat-bladed screwdriver to assist the final stage.

6 Check that the rings are correctly fitted to the piston and that the ring end gaps are positioned each side of the ring groove pegs (arrowed).

Close the rings by hand in their grooves to ensure that they close completely, if they don't then they are most likely upside down. Rings that are upside down will not fit in the barrel when it is being assembled.

7 Lubricate the bore with fresh two-stroke oil making sure that it is well covered. Although the machine will smoke for a few minutes when first fired up, the lubricant will help assembly and protect the engine on initial starting. Lubricating the sides of the piston and the piston rings will also help assembly.

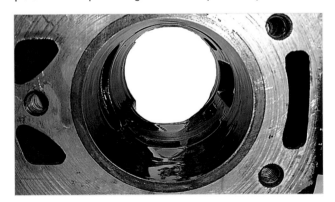

8 Turn the rotor so that the piston rests on the two wood blocks. This allows both hands to be free to fit the barrel and will prevent the piston tilting.

Squeeze the top ring so that it is completely in its groove and hold it whilst feeding the barrel slowly over the ring. Make sure the barrel is fitted with the exhaust port facing forwards. With the barrel over the first ring, squeeze the second ring, hold it and ease the barrel downwards. **Do not** use force or twist the barrel – the barrel must be dead straight when being fitted or it will jam. If the barrel will not go down, remove it and start

again. The most common cause of jamming is that the ring gaps are not exactly in line with the ring pegs.

9 Wipe any oil from the top of the piston and barrel surface, then fit the **new** head gasket, making certain that its cut-outs match those in the barrel. If gasket cement is necessary, each side of the gasket should be lightly coated.

10 Fit the four barrel nuts (two on each side (arrowed) on the engine photographed) and tighten them to the manufacturer's torque setting. Where there is no access for a socket and torque wrench, a crows foot wrench will be required (see Chapter 1).

11 Fit the cylinder head and tighten its retaining bolts/nuts in a diagonal sequence. The manufacturer will often quote two settings, initial and final torques. Tighten each bolt/nut until it is hand-tight then use a torque wrench to tighten each bolt/nut to the initial setting. When you have completed the sequence, reset the torque wrench to the final setting, and tighten the bolts/nuts.

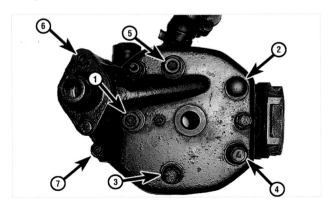

Refitting components removed for access

1 On liquid-cooled engines, fit the coolant hoses (A) onto their stubs and tighten the clamps. Don't forget to reconnect the lead to the coolant temperature gauge sender (B) otherwise the temperature gauge won't work.

Check the condition of the washers on the coolant drain plugs, then refit them to the cylinder barrel and water pump casing. Refill the cooling system as described in Section 4.

2 Fit the spark plug and tighten it to the manufacturer's torque setting. Reconnect the plug cap.

3 Place a new gasket on each side of the reed valve block and fit it into the inlet tract. Again, the use of gasket cement may be needed. Fit the inlet stub and tighten the nuts to retain the assembly to the cylinder barrel. On the engine photographed the oil pump cable bracket is secured by the reed valve block nuts.

4 Before fitting the carburettor, make sure that the two clamps are fitted to the inlet stubs. Slackening or removing the airbox mounting screws will allow the airbox to be pushed backwards; this will give you extra space when fitting the carburettor body. Secure the two clamps when the carburettor is in place.

When fitting the carburettor slide note that its cut-away (arrowed) must face the air inlet. If it is fitted the wrong way round, it will be too high in the carburettor and the machine will not start. If you try to 'bump' start the machine, and it does

fire up, the engine will rev at about 3/4 of its maximum engine speed. If this isn't frightening enough, serious engine damage may occur!

To check that the slide is fitted correctly, look into the carburettor before fitting the top cap. The slide should be sitting in the bottom of the body. If all is OK fit the top cap and, where fitted, the cable-operated cold start device (choke).

Use a syringe filled with two-stroke oil to fill the oil feed pipe which runs from the oil pump to the carburettor. Reconnect the oil feed pipe (arrowed) to the carburettor and ensure that the cable clip at each end of the pipe is in good condition. Priming the pipe with oil in this way will ensure that the engine receives lubrication immediately it is started.

5 Check the throttle cable adjustment (Section 5) and oil pump setting (Section 6).

If is was necessary to remove the oil tank to gain access to

the top of the engine, or if you have had to disconnect the oil delivery pipe (A) from the tank for any reason, the pipe will need bleeding of air before you run the engine. Refit the tank and reconnect the delivery pipe, securing it with a spring clip. Refill the oil tank. To bleed the pipe of air, undo the bleed screw (B) and allow oil to flow from this hole. After about 30 seconds to 1 minute, the flow of oil will no longer have any air bubbles in it. At this point, refit and tighten the bleed screw, having checked that its washer was in good condition.

6 When refitting the exhaust system use a **new** sealing ring (gasket) at the downpipe joint with the cylinder barrel. Loosely fit all nuts/bolts at first, then tighten the flange nuts at the cylinder and work your way to the rear of the system, tightening each mounting bolt as you go.

7 Fit the fuel tank, bodypanels and seat. Start the engine and allow it to warm up. Note that there will be excess smoke from the exhaust initially, but this should subside as the oil used during assembly is burnt off.

9 Spark plug

The spark plug is probably the most ignored component of an engine, that is until it fails. Most manufacturers recommend renewing the plug at 8000 mile intervals with a check on the gap size at 4000 mile intervals.

Spark plug check

Items required

✔ Spark plug socket
✔ Feeler gauges
✔ New spark plug(s) – if being renewed
✔ Plug gap specification

Procedure

1 Remove the HT cap from the plug by pulling it upwards. Do not pull the cap by its lead; instead grip the cap when removing it.

> **HINT**
>
> When removing the plugs from a multi-cylinder engine, check that each HT lead is labelled (arrowed) so that they can be reconnected to the correct plug. Cylinder numbering will run from the left to right side on a typical four cylinder engine.

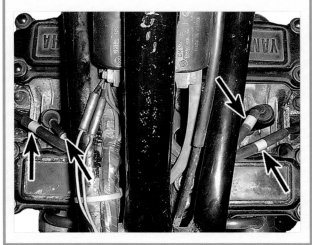

2 Before removing the spark plug, undo it by about two turns and using a soft brush, clean any dirt from around the plug hole. This will ensure that dirt does not enter the engine via the plug hole, which could cause expensive damage. Once the area is clean, continue to undo and remove the plug. This will not be possible where the plugs are deeply recessed – if available a blast of compressed air will serve to blow any debris out of the plug channel.

Always use a proper spark plug socket, of the relevant size, which will have a rubber insert to protect and grip the plug. If you use a normal, long socket, there is a distinct probability that you will break the spark plug.

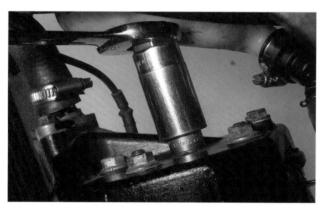

On multi-cylinder engines where the plugs are deeply recessed the plug socket will need to be thin-walled and of deep section. The tool shown below is as supplied in the machine's toolkit.

3 The condition of the old spark plug can reveal vital information about the engine's condition. It is after all, the only part of the combustion chamber that can easily be removed. Refer to the firing end guide later in this section. On a multi-cylinder engine take note of which cylinders the plugs have come from. In this way any problems can be matched to the appropriate cylinder.

In the photo below the right-hand plug has done 8000 miles, whereas the plug on the left is new. The old plug is showing signs of carbon fouling on the insulator and centre electrode and further investigation is necessary. See the information on firing tips at the end of this section. Note that as a spark plug ages there will be an increase in fuel consumption, exhaust emissions and voltage required to create the spark.

4 If fitting new plugs make sure they are of the correct type, as specified in the owner's handbook or workshop manual.

Do not assume that because the plug is new its gap will be correct. Checking the gap with a feeler gauge only takes a few seconds. The recommended gap is typically around 0.6 to 0.7 mm, but check the owner's handbook for the correct gap for your machine.

Feeler gauges are available as the blade type shown or as wire type gauges. Insert a gauge which corresponds to the plug gap specified for your machine. If the gauge is a firm sliding fit between the electrodes the gap is correct.

If the gap needs to be reset, either from new or when checking at the 4000 mile service, use a gap adjustment tool to bend the earth electrode. Do not use a feeler gauge to lever the electrode as you are likely to break the centre insulator. Likewise, damage will occur if you try to close the gap by tapping the earth electrode.

5 Install the spark plug and thread it in by hand to ensure that it does not cross-thread. The soft alloy cylinder head material can be easily damaged if care isn't taken. Thread the plug in until it seats and then use the plug socket and torque wrench to tighten it to the manufacturer's specified torque setting. As a guide the spark plug torque settings for an aluminium cylinder head are as given in the accompanying table. Alternatively the plug can be tightened through a specified angle.

Torque settings

Thread dia.	Torque setting
8 mm	8 to 10 Nm (5.8 to 7.2 lb/ft)
10 mm	10 to 12 Nm (7.2 to 8.7 lb/ft)
12 mm	15 to 20 Nm (10.8 to 14.5 lb/ft)
14 mm	25 to 30 Nm (18.0 to 21.6 lb/ft)

Tightening angles

Thread dia.	New plug	Re-used plug
8 mm	1/3 of a turn (120°)	1/12 of a turn (30°)
10 mm	1/2 to 3/4 of a turn	1/12 to 1/8 of a turn
12 mm	(180 to 270°)	(30 to 45°)
14 mm		

Where the plug hole is so deep that it is impossible to screw the plug into its thread using your fingers, use a length of tubing (8 mm bore is ideal) over the end of the plug as shown in the photo. If the plug begins to 'cross-thread' the tubing will slip on the plug. When the plug has seated, use a deep plug socket to tighten it.

6 Refit the HT cap and push it firmly onto the plug. A 'click'

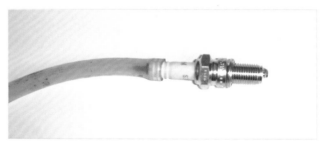

HINT

A smear of copper-based grease on the plug threads will aid installation and make subsequent removal much easier.

should be felt as the spring mechanism inside the HT cap locks over the end of the plug. The cap should resist gentle pulling, indicating that it is pushed fully home.

Note that some spark plugs come with a removable terminal cap fitted to the top. Check your HT cap to see if it can accommodate this terminal cap, if not discard it.

Used plug firing end condition guide

Normal condition

The firing end should be light brown, grey or tan coloured with a few combustion deposits. This shows that the plug is working properly and is the correct heat range for the engine.

Ash deposits

Light brown deposits can lead to misfiring and come from excessive amounts of oil in the combustion chamber or poor quality fuel.

✦ Fuel – carbon, lead and bromide
✦ Lubricating oil – calcium, sulphur, barium and zinc
✦ Other sources – aluminium, iron and silicon

Carbon fouling

Black, sooty deposits form on the firing end of the plug, causing the insulation resistance between the shell and the centre electrode to fall to zero. Misfiring occurs and in extreme cases, no spark. Caused by a rich air/fuel ratio (too much fuel – not enough air). Possible causes are:

✦ Choke/cold start device faulty or left on too long
✦ Blocked air filter
✦ Fuel level too high due to worn carburettor float needle and seat or incorrectly set float height

Wet fouling

Similar to carbon fouling but with wet, oily deposits.
Possible causes on a four-stroke engine:

✦ Worn piston rings allowing oil leakage
✦ Worn valve guides allowing oil leakage

Possible cause on a two-stroke engine:

✦ Excess lubricant caused by incorrectly adjusted oil pump
✦ Excess lubricant caused by too much oil added to the petrol (premix system)

Overheating

The insulator has a glazed white or glossy appearance and the deposits accumulated on the insulator tip have melted. This very dangerous condition must be rectified. Possible causes are:

✦ Ignition fault – over advanced ignition timing
✦ Plug heat range too hot
✦ Lean air/fuel ratio (too much air – not enough fuel) due to:
  Air leak in carburettor manifold
  Carburettor fuel level too low – incorrectly set float height
  Carburettor jet needle clip setting too low
✦ Insufficient engine cooling/lubrication
✦ Spark plug not tightened sufficiently or gasket (washer) missing

Worn plug

Corrosive gases from combustion and the high voltage spark corrode and erode the plug electrodes. The normal rate of gap growth is about 0.01 to 0.02 mm per 1000 km for four-stroke engines and twice that for two-stroke engines.

Because most motorcycle engines create a spark for every crankshaft revolution (wasted spark ignition systems) these figures can be doubled. This is why motorcycles need to have their plugs changed at half the distance for cars.

Failure to renew the plug at regular intervals can lead to poor starting in damp or cold weather, increased exhaust emission, loss of power and increased fuel consumption.

NORMAL	**ASH DEPOSITS**	**CARBON FOULING**

WET FOULING	**OVERHEATING**	**WORN PLUG**

10 Contact breaker points and ignition timing

There are still many, older motorcycles in daily use and not all of them have electronic ignition systems. This means that they will use contact breaker points to trigger the ignition and unlike electronic systems, these will need regular adjustment and replacement.

The following describes the adjustment of the contact gap and ignition timing of a twin contact set for a four cylinder, battery operated, wasted spark ignition system. The principles are the same for one set of points operating a single or twin cylinder machine with the difference being that there will be only one backplate. Several different variations are described at the end of this section.

Most manufacturers recommend checking the points gap and timing at 2000 to 3000 mile intervals.

Note: *Check the contact breaker points gap before adjusting the timing. If the points gap is correct yet there is insufficient adjustment range in the backplate to adjust the timing, the points are worn and must be replaced.*

Contact breaker points gap

Items required

✔ Feeler gauges (blade type)
✔ Variety of screwdrivers, sockets and spanners
✔ Multi-meter
✔ Size of points gap (usually 0.3 to 0.4 mm)

Procedure

1 Check that the ignition is switched OFF, then remove the points cover (usually on the right-hand side of the engine).

The four cylinder machine shown has two sets of points, one set triggers cylinders 1 and 4 (A), the other set triggers cylinder 2 and 3 (B). Those for cylinders 1 and 4 are mounted to the master backplate whereas the points for cylinders 2 and 3 are mounted to a sub-backplate, which in turn is mounted to the master backplate. The master backplate usually has stamped marks to identify the points, in this case 1.4 and 2.3.

2 Before checking the points gap, examine the point faces for signs of burning and pitting. If necessary use a thin strip of fine 'wet and dry' paper to clean the faces. If the faces are in poor condition, renew both sets of contact breaker points – see Step 7. Note that severely burnt faces indicates a failing condenser – replace the condenser if this is apparent.

3 Working on the points for cylinders 1 and 4 first, rotate the crankshaft in a forward direction (usually clockwise) until the points gap (A) is at a maximum. If you go past this point, continue to rotate the crankshaft and allow the points to close then open again. The heel of the points (B) will be resting on the peak of the operating cam when the points are fully open.

When rotating the crankshaft, always turn it in the normal direction of engine rotation (never backwards), Use a spanner on the large nut **NEVER** the smaller bolt head at its centre.

4 Use a feeler gauge to measure the gap between the point faces. If the specified gap is 0.3 to 0.4 mm this means that a 0.3 mm gauge must be able to 'slip' within the gap whereas a 0.4 mm gauge must not.

Take great care to ensure that the gauge is fitted squarely and that very little pressure is used to insert it. It is very easy to force the gauge between the points faces and overcome the pressure of the closing spring, thus producing a false reading. Note that because the point faces and heel are subject to wear it is unlikely that the points gap will be within the manufacturer's tolerance and adjustment will be required.

5 To adjust the points gap, first slacken the locking screw (arrowed) by about 1/4 turn. If the points close, tighten the screw until you feel resistance. It is important to tighten the screw just enough to hold the points open, yet still allow the gap to be altered.

Insert a flat-bladed screwdriver between the 'dimples' and slot in the points plate and gently ease the points open or closed as required. Keep checking the gap with your gauge until it is within tolerance. At this point tighten the locking screw. Always recheck the gap afterwards.

6 Rotate the crankshaft until the gap for the second set of points (cylinders 2 and 3) is at its maximum and repeat the previous steps to check and adjust this set of points.

Slacken the screw arrowed to adjust the points gap; this screw secures the points assembly to the sub-backplate. Do not disturb the two screws which retain the sub-backplate to the main backplate – these are used to adjust the ignition timing.

7 If new points are being installed, slacken the nut (arrowed) holding the feed wire to the old points then remove the screw holding the old points to the master backplate. Lift off the points, undo the nut holding the feed wire connector and remove the wire from the points.

Before you fit the new points, lightly clean their contact faces with fine 'wet and dry' paper to remove any protective coating. Connect the feed wire to the new points ensuring that the wire is positioned between the metal washer and the insulating fibre washer on the nut side, do not fully tighten the nut at this stage. If you fit the wire anywhere else, the points will be shorted out and the system will not create a spark.

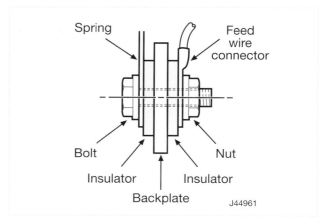

Spring · Feed wire connector · Bolt · Nut · Insulator · Insulator · Backplate · J44961

Clean the back of the points and the master backplate. This ensures that no grease or oil is present, which could act as an electrical insulator. Fit the points to the backplate so that the pivot fits into its hole in the backplate (arrowed).

Tighten the points fixing screw and feed wire nut. Ensure that the connector for the feed wire does not touch the backplate when the nut is tightened. Also check that the feed wire connector will not touch the points cover when it is replaced.

Repeat this procedure to install the other new set of points, then set the point gap on each set as described previously. Now check the ignition timing as described below.

Ignition timing check

The object of the ignition timing check is to ensure that the points begin to open at the correct piston position before TDC (top dead centre). On the engine photographed, the timing marks are marked on the ATU (automatic timing unit) and are visible through the circular cutout in the master backplate.

The following procedure describes the method of checking the timing statically (with the engine stopped) and the crankshaft turned by hand. An alternative method would be to use a stroboscopic timing lamp.

1 Check the contact breaker points gap as described previously.

2 Rotate the engine to familiarise yourself with the timing marks; on this engine the scribed line above the F 1.4 mark represents the timing mark for cylinders 1 and 4. An F 2.3 exists for cylinders 2 and 3. Ignore the TDC mark (T) and the full advance timing mark (II). Align the F 1.4 mark with the index mark in the crankcase.

3 It is not sufficient to check the points opening stage by eye. A multi-meter is used here to indicate precisely when the points open. Connect the multi-meter negative lead to a good 'earth' point (engine cases) and the positive lead to the points lead for cylinders 1 and 4. Switch the multi-meter to the ohms (Ω) x 1 range and note the reading. If the meter reads I (infinity) the

points are open, if it shows a reading (numbers) then the points are closed.

Note that a self-powered continuity tester or buzzer can be used instead of a multi-meter.

4 The ignition timing is adjusted by moving the position of the master backplate with the slots of its mounting points. Slacken the three screws (arrowed) that hold the master backplate to

the engine cases. The best method is to slacken all three screws and then **lightly** tighten them so that the backplate can just be moved using finger pressure. Note that moving the master backplate in a clockwise direction will close the points whereas an anticlockwise direction will open them. Move the backplate until the meter 'flicks' from a reading (numbers) to infinity (I), i.e. points closed to points just opened. Tighten the three master backplate screws.

5 Rotate the crankshaft almost one complete turn, then continue turning it slowly as the timing marks come into alignment. Watch the multi-meter and at the point it 'flicks' from a reading to infinity note the position of the timing marks. If the timing is correct, the 'F' mark will line up with the fixed mark at this point. If it doesn't re-adjust the backplate position until it does. **Note:** *If the backplate screws have no washers fitted, tightening them will move the backplate - ensure that the washers are in place.*

6 With the timing completed for cylinders 1 and 4, now set the timing for cylinders 2 and 3. Slacken the two screws which hold the points sub-backplate for cylinders 2 and 3 to the master backplate (arrowed). Slacken the screws sufficiently to allow adjustment of the sub-backplate position – do not unscrew them.

Connect the multi-meter positive lead to the points lead for points 2 and 3 and the negative lead to the engine cases.

Rotate the crankshaft so that the 'F' mark for cylinders 2 and 3 lines up with the fixed index mark. Using a flat-bladed screwdriver inserted between the slot and the dimples, adjust the position of the sub-backplate so that the points just open in this position. The meter readings will be as described previously.

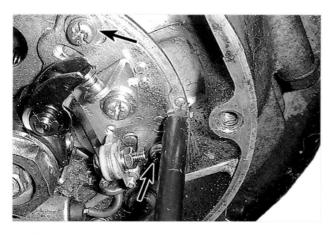

When the timing is correct, tighten the sub-backplate screws, rotate the crankshaft one turn and recheck that the points just open as the 'F' mark for cylinders 2 and 3 lines up with the fixed mark. If they don't, repeat the above.

Single cylinder four-stroke engine

On certain single cylinder four-stroke engines, the contact breaker points are housed under a cover on one end of the cylinder head, with the points being operated off a small cam on the end of the main camshaft. There will only be one set of contact breaker points and one backplate. The timing marks

will be marked on the alternator rotor edge and be visible once the crankshaft end cover has been removed.

Adjust the points gap when it is at its widest point, as previously described.

When checking the ignition timing note that because it takes two revolutions of the crankshaft to complete the four-stroke cycle, there will be two positions when the 'F' mark on the rotor lines up with the fixed mark. To ensure that you adjust the ignition timing on the correct stroke remove the cover for the inlet valve, then rotate the crankshaft whilst watching the inlet valve open (go down), then close (go up). Continue to rotate the crankshaft and the **next** time that the 'F' mark and fixed mark align the points should just open.

On other models, the points may be located behind the flywheel as described below for two-stroke models. Although it is possible to check the ignition timing via the marks on the flywheel there isn't always separate adjustment for the timing. Adjustment of the timing can only be made by varying the contact breaker gap.

Two-stroke engines

On the majority of two-stroke engines the contact breaker points (2) will be behind the flywheel rotor. They are particularly difficult to access, although checking and adjustment of their gap (1) can be done through the slots in the flywheel.

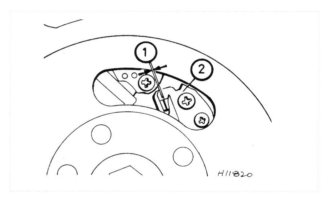

If timing marks are provided on the edge of the flywheel, the ignition timing can be checked statically (engine not running) or dynamically (engine running). The dynamic check is made using a stroboscopic timing lamp.

When checking the timing statically, note that it isn't possible to connect the multi-meter lead directly to the points as described previously. The meter should be connected to the lead from the points which exits the top of the casing - you may need to refer to the wiring diagram for the machine to identify the correct lead.

If no timing marks are provided, the ignition timing setting will be expressed in terms of the piston position before TDC (top dead centre), either in millimetres or degrees. These checks will require either a dial gauge and adaptor, or a degree disc, and some experience in their use to ensure they are properly mounted and their readings correctly interpreted. It is advised that both operations be performed by a dealer.

11 Engine compression test (4-stroke engines)

A compression test will give a good indication of the internal condition of the engine. It should be carried out AFTER each major service and a record of the results kept with your service sheets and parts bills (see Chapter 2).

Items required

✔ Compression tester
✔ 14 mm to 12 mm, or 14 mm to 10 mm adaptor to suit the spark plug hole size
✔ Oil can filled with fresh engine oil
✔ Spark plug socket, ratchet and torque wrench
✔ The manufacturer's compression figures (see Step 7)

Procedure

1 Before carrying out the compression test, the valve clearances should be checked and if necessary adjusted, and the cylinder head nuts/bolts checked for tightness.

2 Run the engine until if reaches normal operating temperature. Remove the fuel tank if necessary to gain access to the spark plug.

3 Remove the spark plug (see Section 9). Ensure that the compression tester has a good sealing ring and screw it into the spark plug hole. Press its button to zero the gauge.

If you are using an adaptor, ensure that there is a sealing washer (usually rubber) between the tester and the adaptor and another sealing washer (usually copper) between the adaptor and the cylinder head. Any leakage at these points will give false readings and could lead you to condemn a good engine.

4 If the machine has a kickstart, switch the fuel and ignition off and fully open the throttle. Operate the kickstarter until the gauge needle stops moving.

5 If the machine has electric start only, the procedure will differ depending on the nature of the ignition system.

a) Flick the engine kill switch to OFF, turn the fuel OFF and turn the ignition ON. Open the throttle fully and crank the engine via the starter motor for a few seconds until the gauge reading stabilises. Note and record the gauge reading. Turn the ignition OFF and remove the gauge.
b) On some machines, the ignition circuit will not operate with the kill switch OFF. In this case, carry out one of the following to prevent a spark being generated:

✦ Trace the wires to the ignitor unit and disconnect the unit (see photo overleaf).
✦ Trace the wires to the signal generator coils (pulse coils) and disconnect them.
✦ Trace the primary wires (thin wires) to the ignition H/T coil and disconnect them.
  With the kill switch in the RUN position and the ignition ON, open the throttle fully and crank the engine over via the starter

motor for a few seconds until the gauge reading stabilises. Note and record the gauge reading. Turn the ignition OFF and remove the gauge, then reconnect the ignition wiring.

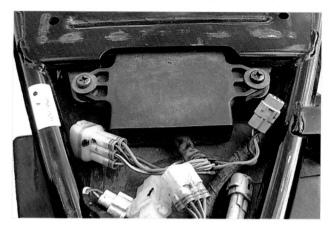

6 On multi-cylinder engines, first remove all spark plugs then repeat the test for each individual cylinder.

7 Compare the readings that you have obtained with the manufacturers figures, and be guided by your workshop manual. The manufacturer will usually quote compression pressures as follows.
✦ The compression figures (usually a minimum and a maximum standard), e.g. 142 to 213 psi (9.8 to 14.7 Bars)
✦ The service limit, e.g. 114 psi (7.9 Bars)
✦ The maximum difference allowable between cylinders of a multi-cylinder engine, e.g. 28 psi (1.9 Bars)

8 Low compression pressures can be caused by any of the following:
✦ Excessively worn cylinder bore
✦ Worn piston or piston rings
✦ Piston rings that have become jammed in their ring grooves
✦ Valves that are not seating properly due to the valve clearances being out of adjustment or burnt valve seats
✦ Failed valve stem seals
✦ A warped cylinder head
✦ A defective head gasket

9 If the figures are low, it is possible to determine where the problem lies by temporarily sealing the cylinder. Remove the gauge and use the oil can to squirt a shot or two of clean engine oil into the spark plug hole. The oil will temporarily seal the piston rings and bore. Turn the engine over for a couple of seconds. Now install the gauge and repeat the test.

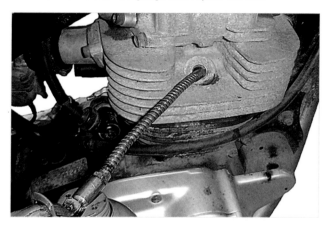

10 If the figure obtained is now significantly higher than the original figure, this suggests a problem with the piston/rings/bore. If there is little increase in gauge readings, the problem lies with the cylinder head or valves.

11 The engine should be overhauled if:
✦ One cylinder's pressure is below the service limit
✦ The difference in pressure between any two cylinders exceeds the specification
✦ The readings for ALL cylinders are below the minimum standard

12 It is particularly useful to record the compression readings and keep these with the service records for future reference. See the chart below as an example for a four cylinder engine. Don't forget to insert the date and mileage details.

	Cylinder No. 1	Cylinder No. 2	Cylinder No. 3	Cylinder No. 4
Readings obtained – Dry				
Readings obtained – Wet				

Date ....   Mileage ....

12 Exhaust system

At some time in its life the exhaust system will need to be replaced, either with an OE (original equipment) part or an aftermarket system.

On a four-stroke engine this happens because water, as a by-product of combustion, corrodes the silencer internal surfaces causing it to fall apart whereas rainwater attacks the outside. A noticeable lack of power occurs long before any rattles and increased noise level. You can waste a lot of time stripping carburettors, changing spark plugs etc. only to discover that the exhaust has disintegrated and is blocked.

Consider the age of the machine and its mileage. Are your journeys short ones (the worst thing for causing corrosion)? Has the machine been used in all weathers? Does it stay outside all day and night? Is it under a cover without air circulation and producing a lot of condensation? All these things can hasten the demise of an exhaust system. There is no hard and fast rule as to the life of an exhaust system.

HINT

Allow yourself plenty of time for this job. It should only take an hour or so but freeing the mountings of an old or corroded system may present problems. The nuts which retain the front downpipes to the cylinder head are notoriously difficult to unscrew due to corrosion and sometimes restricted access. You may discover that they have become stuck fast to the studs and any attempt to unscrew them unthreads the stud from the cylinder head, or worst still, breaks the stud off! It is recommended that a penetrating oil is applied to the nuts and studs the day beforehand.

Removal and refitting

Items required

✔ New exhaust gaskets for the engine and pipe joints.
✔ New nuts and washers (not strictly necessary but highly recommended).
✔ Appropriate spanners, sockets etc.
✔ Copper-based grease.
✔ Old ice-cream box, cardboard box or other means of supporting the collector box (see text).

Procedure

Note: *The location and type of fixings will differ for every exhaust system. A four-into-one system is used to illustrate this procedure; alternative fixings are shown on page 121.*

1 To remove the old exhaust system, first slacken all its mountings, starting at the rear of the machine and working your way to the front downpipes. Place a support under the exhaust system, then remove all the mountings nuts/bolts, again starting at the rear and finishing with the downpipe fasteners. Carefully manoeuvre the exhaust system off the engine and frame.

2 Clean up the mounting points on the machine and replace any of the rubber mountings if necessary. Fitting new mounting nuts and bolts is strongly recommended. Prise the old gasket rings out of the cylinder head exhaust ports.

3 If fitting instructions are supplied with the new system check if you need to fit sections separately rather than as a complete assembly. On the 4-into-1 system shown the downpipes for cylinders 1 and 3 are fitted separately. Note that the finned exhaust flanges from the original system have been transferred to the new downpipes.

4 Before fitting the new exhaust port gaskets, coat both sides with copper grease. This will hold them in place and create an initial seal.

5 Begin assembly by offering up the collector box and downpipes for cylinders 2 and 4. Smear copper grease on ALL of the exhaust studs. This will help to keep corrosion at bay and will aid in the removal of the nuts should this be necessary at a later date.

6 Hold the pipes with one hand and place a support under the collector box to keep them in place. Now with both hands free slide the collars fully home followed by the flanges. Fit the two half collars per pipe, noting which way they are fitted. A piece of masking tape has been applied to each side to hold the collars in place on the pipes. Slide the exhaust flanges into place.

7 You can leave the masking tape in place or pull it off as you slide the flange over the first part of the collars. You may need to give the collars and flanges a 'wiggle' to make sure that the pipes and collars are fully fitted into the exhaust ports. Before fitting the lock washers and nuts ensure that there is sufficient thread on BOTH studs for the nuts to be screwed fully home.

8 Fit the washers followed by the nuts on ONE pipe and repeat this process for the other pipe. Leave the nuts finger-tight at this stage.

9 Now fit the downpipe for cylinder number one into the collector box FIRST then repeat the above process for fitting the collars and flange. Repeat the process for cylinder number 3 downpipe.

10 Secure the downpipe clamps finger-tight.

11 Slide the silencer into place in the collector box and secure its clamp finger-tight. There should be a gasket at this joint.

12 Attach the silencer to its mounting bracket on the frame. Fit the mounting bolts, securing them finger-tight at this stage.

13 Now you can fully tighten the various nuts and bolts. Start by tightening the downpipe flange nuts to the recommended torque setting. Tighten them EVENLY, do each one up a bit at a time and work your way across the engine. Finally use a torque wrench to complete the tightening sequence.

14 Tighten the downpipe-to-collector box clamps for pipes 1 and 3.

15 The silencer-to-exhaust clamp should also be tightened to

its torque setting. Keep the open end of the clamp facing downwards out of the way of the brake lever etc.

16 Finally tighten the silencer-to-frame bolts to the specified torque setting.

17 Check over the whole system to ensure that you have not missed any bolts or nuts. It is preferable to sort them out now rather than later on the road!

18 Start the engine and check for exhaust gas leaks by running your hand NEAR the joints. Do NOT touch the exhaust as it gets HOT very quickly.

HINT

If there is a 'Blappity' sound from the front pipe that wasn't there before check the following:

✦ The front pipes may not be sealing properly. Have you followed the correct tightening sequence? Slacken ALL fastenings and retighten in the correct sequence – to tighten, start at the front downpipes and work your way towards the silencer.

✦ Are you certain that an exhaust gasket hasn't fallen out? Have a look around the floor and front of the engine. You will be amazed, how given half a chance the gaskets will make a bid for freedom.

✦ Where bolts are used to secure the downpipe flanges, do NOT use just any length bolts to hold the flanges in place. If they are too long it is almost certain that they will not tighten the flange sufficiently to prevent air leaks. Also there is a very distinct possibility that the bolt will reach the bottom of the hole and you will damage the cylinder head by trying to tighten it further. The correct size bolt or studs with nuts is essential.

Alternative exhaust fixings

Silencers

Silencers (cans) are usually retained to the exhaust system by a flange and nut fixing or a clamp arrangement. The accompanying photograph shows a typical flange arrangement, retained to the exhaust system by domed nuts and studs. When fitting the silencer, the flange joint faces must be perfectly clean and a new gasket used.

The silencer will usually be mounted to the rear footrest mounting bracket on the frame. Vibration is isolated by a rubber bush pressed into the footrest mounting bracket.

Where a clamp type joint is used between the silencer and exhaust system, always fit a new gasket ring to ensure a gas-tight joint.

Downpipe clamps

The most common downpipe-to-cylinder head fixing is the nut and flange arrangement shown on the previous page, although the collars are usually integral with the downpipes on modern designs as shown below.

On some models bolts are used to retain the flanges. The bolts thread directly into the aluminium alloy cylinder head casting, so extreme care must be taken not to cross-thread them.

Owners of vee-engined machines may encounter an unusual downpipe-to-rear cylinder exhaust fixing. On the model shown below the cupped end of the pipe is held to the exhaust stub on the cylinder head by a clamp. There is no gasket ring on this particular fixing, but it is essential to align the pipe end and stub faces exactly to prevent exhaust gas leaks.

> ### HINT
>
> If fitting an aftermarket exhaust system or silencer, note that it must comply with British Standard or European regulations (BS or E mark) to be road legal and to satisfy MOT requirements. Check with the system manufacturer whether modifications to the carburettor jetting might be necessary.

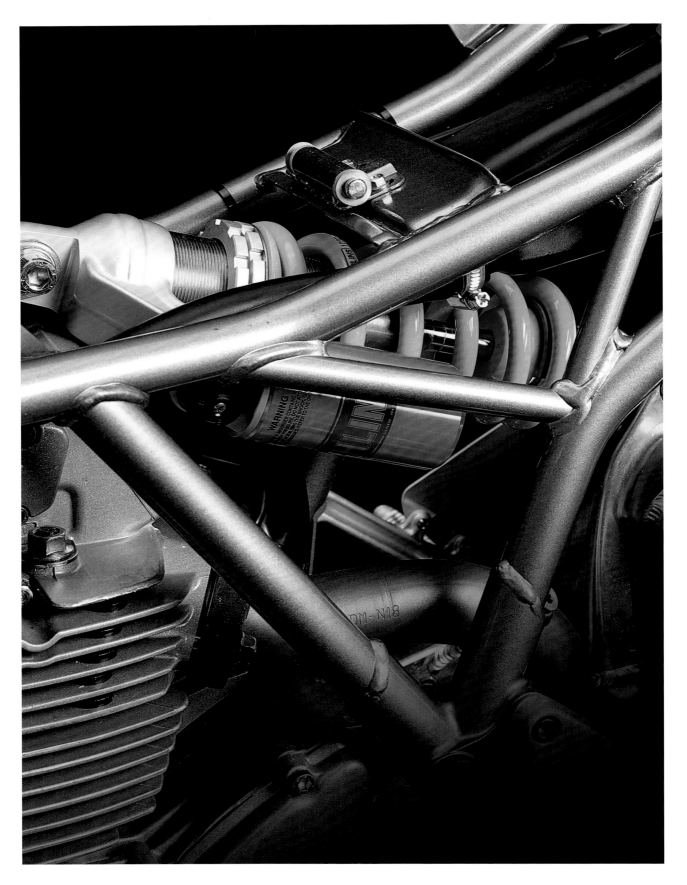

Chapter 4
Chassis

Contents

Checking chain tension

1 Check your owners manual, workshop manual or look on the swinging arm for a label like this. The information you are looking for is whether chain tension is checked with the machine on its sidestand or on its centrestand and the manufacturer's specification for freeplay.

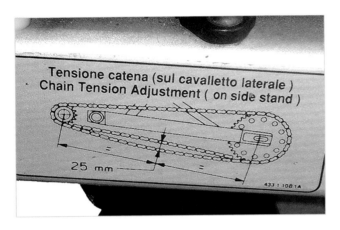

2 You will need to have the transmission in neutral and slowly rotate the rear wheel whilst testing the tension of the chain in the middle of its lower run. You will not need the rule at this stage, what you are looking for is the tightest point of the chain. If you cannot find a tight point, because the chain may be overly slack, tighten the chain (see below) and test again.

3 Once you have found the chain's tightest point, place your steel rule behind the chain (in the centre of the lower run) and push the chain downwards until it starts to resist. Do NOT force the chain any further than this point. Note the position of the lower part of the chain link against the steel rule and use a pen or pencil to mark this position on the rule.

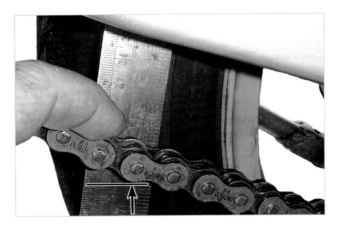

4 Hold the rule in place and push the chain upwards until it again resists, then mark the position of the lower part of the chain link against the steel rule.

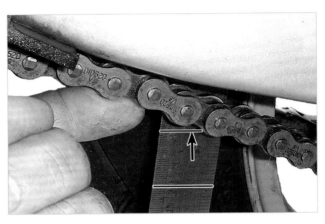

5 The distance between the two marks on the rule is the distance that the chain moves and should fall within the manufacturer's specification. If it doesn't, then the chain will have to be re-tensioned and the wheels re-aligned.

6 Some manufacturers make life easy for this regular job. This machine has an inspection window within the lower run of the chainguard.

7 To check the chain tension in this case, first place the machine on its centrestand and ensure the transmission is in neutral. Rotate the rear wheel, in the normal direction of drive, whilst looking through the window.

8 The chain tension is correct if the full end of a link can be seen within the usable range. Note that this chain is on the tight spot in this position – the lower the chain shows in the window, the greater the amount of slack.

Adjusting chain tension and aligning the wheels

Note: *Chain tension adjustment and wheel alignment check must be carried out together.*

Adjusting chain tension

Items required

✔ 12 inch steel rule
✔ Variety of spanners and sockets
✔ Torque wrench
✔ Pliers

Procedure

1 This machine has an 'R' clip to prevent the nut from coming loose. The 'R' clip can be used many times and is quick and easy to remove and refit. If you have a normal split pin, straighten its ends, remove it and throw it away. Split pins are used once only and must NEVER be used a second time because if they break and fall off the nut may become loose. Other arrangements use a self-locking spindle nut which doesn't require an R-pin or split pin.

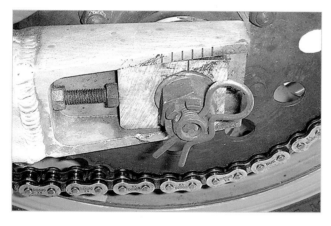

2 If your machine has a drum rear brake, refer to the procedure at the end of this Section.

3 With the 'R' clip or split pin removed, slacken the wheel spindle nut (a couple of turns is sufficient), and loosen the adjuster locknuts on BOTH sides of the swinging arm.

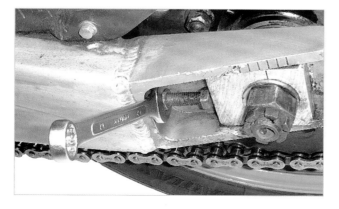

4 Turn the adjuster bolt (on the chain side only) either inwards or outwards to tighten or slacken the chain. Which way you turn the adjuster will depend on the type used (see later for other types of adjusters). Keep checking the chain tension against your rule until it is within the tolerance specified by the manufacturer.

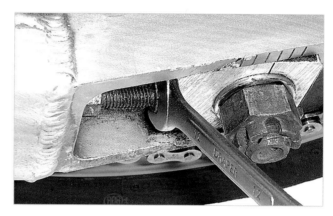

Having set the chain tension, now check the wheel alignment as described on page 130 and adjust it using the adjuster on the opposite side of the wheel to the chain.

5 Note the position of the marks on the tensioner block and swinging arm on both sides of the machine, they should be approximately the same when the wheels are aligned. Note that the marks on the tensioner block should be used as a guide only as even a 1/4 turn of the adjuster can make a large difference in alignment.

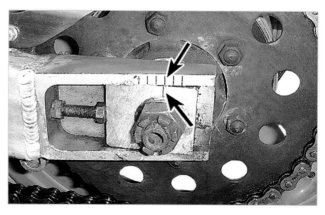

6 There are a variety of different drive chain tensioners used on motorcycles. The most common types are shown in the accompanying photos. In all cases the adjuster screws take up chain tension by pushing on the end of the swinging arm to pull the wheel spindle backwards in the swingarm slots.

This type of chain adjuster is often used on small capacity motorcycles and older motorcycles. With the wheel spindle nut slackened, undo the locknuts on both sides (A) and adjust the hexagon headed screw (B) to tension the chain. Note the notch on the upper edge of the tensioner (C) that lines up with the marks on the swinging arm.

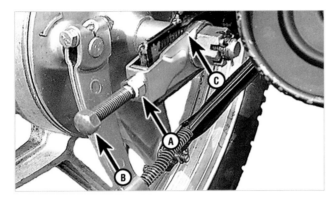

A variation on the above adjuster is shown below. The rear sprocket is bolted to a carrier, which in turn rotates on a sub axle, held in place by a nut. This quickly detachable (QD) arrangement enables the wheel to be removed without disturbing the chain and rear sprocket; it is mostly found on trail, trials and moto-cross machines. You will need to slacken the spindle nut (A) AND sub axle nut (B) to adjust the chain tension and wheel alignment.

On the arrangement below, the circlip (A) secures the nut to the adjuster and should not be disturbed. The nut rotates freely

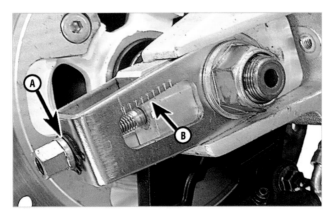

in the adjuster and moves the adjuster on the stud. With the wheel spindle loosened, turn the adjuster nuts as required to tension the chain. Note the marks on the upper portion of the tensioner (B) that line up with the end of the swinging arm.

In the example below a nut and bolt (arrow) lock the adjuster block in position; they must be removed to allow wheel removal, but not chain adjustment. Note that the ends of the swinging arm are in the shape of a sideways 'U' (not closed) and it is designed for quick and easy wheel removal. If you have one of these ensure that the nut/bolt is always tight.

7 The adjusters described in step 6 all 'pull' on the wheel spindle to tension the chain. The types shown here 'push' on the wheel spindle to tension the chain.

With the wheel spindle loosened, slacken the locknut (A) on each side and turn the adjuster screws (B) to tension the chain. Note the marks on the swinging arm behind the adjuster block; the rear edge of the adjuster block is used as the datum line.

On this arrangement (see photo at top of next page), the adjuster bolt pushes directly on the wheel spindle spacer. The spindle adjuster mark has been emphasized on the photo; it is not a bad idea to highlight your marks with a small drop of paint.

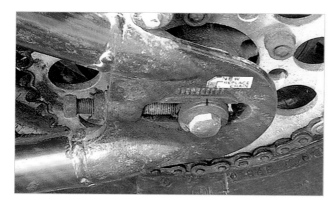

8 The marks can be seen on the adjuster block through the cut-out in the swinging arm. With the wheel spindle nut slackened, back off the adjuster locknuts (A) and turn the adjusters (B) to tension the chain. When chain tension and wheel alignment have been completed and the wheel spindle nut tightened, hold the adjuster nut with one spanner whilst securing the locknut with another. Note that the end cap (C) has been fitted upside down in this case – the two small holes at the top of the cap should be at the bottom to allow any water to drain from the swingarm.

In this example, the wheel alignment marks are stamped in the swinging arm not the adjuster block. Adjust as described above. Note that alignment is via the centre of the wheel spindle.

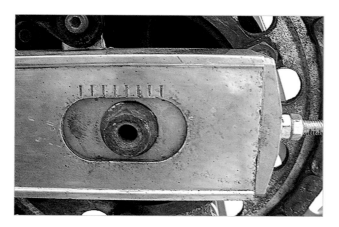

Note the sticker in the two photos on the left advising when the chain should be renewed. When the datum line on the chain adjuster or axle reaches the red zone the chain (and sprockets) should be renewed. If the adjuster bolts and locknuts are in a bad state it is advisable to renew them; smear their threads with copper grease when chain tension is completed.

The chain adjusters fitted to this Italian machine appear to be end-cap holding bolts. With the wheel spindle nut loosened, turn the bolt in each end of the swinging arm to tension the chain and align the wheels. Like all the other types, tension the chain first, then use the tensioner on the other side to align the wheels. Note that this machine should have its chain tensioned whilst it is on its sidestand. It was then placed on a paddock stand (as shown) to check the wheel alignment.

9 On machines fitted with eccentric chain adjusters it is not necessary to loosen the wheel spindle. Both locking screws (A) must be slackened before adjusting the drive chain and aligning the wheels. Adjustment is carried out by placing an Allen key in the socket (B) and turning the socket clockwise, to tighten the chain and anti-clockwise to slacken the chain. Check that the datum line (C) on the swinging arm aligns with the same position on the chain adjuster on each side, then tighten the locking screws.

10 The snail cam chain adjuster is probably the easiest adjuster to use. With the wheel spindle nut loosened, adjust the chain tension with the chain side adjuster. Align the wheels by

matching the position of the two adjusters; there are three segments between each numbered position – make sure that they are the same on both sides. Tighten the spindle nut when chain tension and wheel alignment are correct.

11 Machines with single-sided swinging arms usually have an eccentric type of adjuster incorporated into the rear wheel bearing holder. In the example shown the pinch bolt (arrow) at the end of the swinging arm is slackened and the toothed adjuster rotated by means of a large C-spanner (one is usually supplied in the machine's toolkit). Note that wheel alignment is not affected in a single-sided swinging arm arrangement.

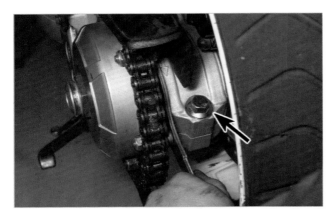

Aligning the wheels

Note: *Carry out chain tension adjustment, then align the wheels.*

Items required

✔ Steel rule
✔ Two large blocks of wood or house-bricks
✔ Two **perfectly straight** lengths of wood (rods), approximately 2 metres long with a width and depth of about 20 mm

Procedure for aligning the wheels

1 If your machine only has a sidestand, or its centrestand is in the way, then you will either need to get a friend to sit on the machine to keep it upright or purchase a paddock stand that supports the rear of the machine.

2 Place the motorcycle on its centrestand and put the two blocks (house-bricks) between the wheels as shown. You can

place the blocks either between the wheels or on the outside of the wheels. Place the two straight-edges (rods) on the blocks, each side of the machine.

3 Keeping the steering in the straight-ahead position, push both of the rods up against the rear wheel so that they touch the rear tyre at both the front and rear points of the tyre (arrowed).

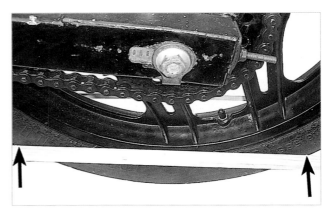

4 Keep the steering in the straight-ahead position and move to the front of the machine. In almost all cases, the front wheel is thinner than the rear wheel and the two rods represent the width of the rear wheel, therefore there should be an equal gap between the rods and the front wheel (each side of the wheel) if the wheels are in alignment.

5 This machine shown in the accompanying photo has its wheel alignment well out of true. When asked if the machine took left-hand bends better than right-hand ones the owner confirmed that this was so! This poor handling characteristic is a very good clue to the wheels being out of alignment. Correcting the wheel alignment will transform the handling of your machine.

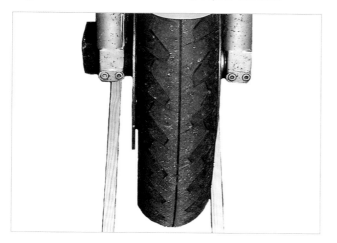

6 In the previous sub-section on chain tension adjustment, it was stated that the tensioner opposite to the chain should be slackened but not adjusted. Now use this adjuster **and this adjuster only** to bring the wheels into line.

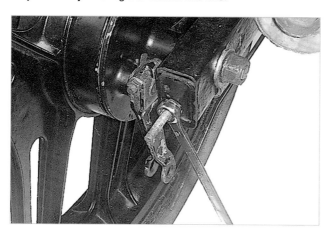

7 With the rear wheel spindle nut loosened, turn the adjuster either in or out by about 1/4 of a turn, re-position the two rods (they will have moved) and check the gap between the rod and the front wheel rim. Measure the gap at the front edge of the front wheel and the rear edge of the front wheel **on one side**, and then repeat this on the other side of the front wheel. If your wheels are in line, all gaps will be the same.

8 If the alignment has become worse then you turned the adjuster the wrong way, reverse it and carry on. If the measurements of gaps A and B are getting closer, carry on turning the adjuster (opposite the chain) by about a 1/4 turn each time until the gaps are the same.

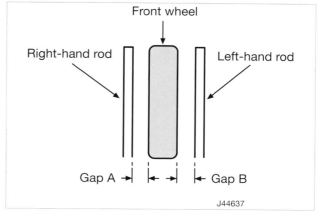

9 Repeat this process until the measurements of gaps A and B (each side of the front wheel) are the same. Do NOT be tempted to use the chain side adjuster otherwise the chain tension will become out of tolerance and you will have to re-adjust it all over again.

10 Once the wheels have been aligned, hold the tensioner bolt with one spanner whilst tightening the locking nut with another. Repeat this process for both tensioners then tighten the wheel spindle nut to its correct torque setting.

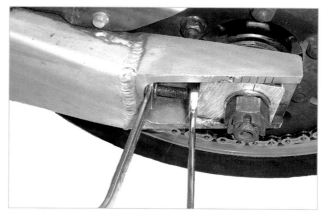

11 Before fitting the 'R' clip or new split pin, check the chain tension and wheel alignment again. One problem is that once the wheel nut is tightened to the specified torque, the slot and the split-pin hole will not line up – see Chapter 1, Section 6 for information on lining up the holes.

Drum rear brake

On machines with a drum rear brake, prior to carrying out drive chain tension adjustment, it is necessary to back off the rear brake.

1 Slacken the rear brake adjuster (A) by a couple of turns. Slacken the torque arm nut (B), where fitted. First remove and discard the split pin, then slacken the nut. Use a new split pin on rebuild.

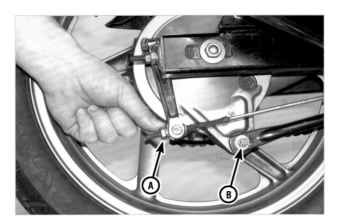

2 Slacken the rear wheel spindle nut and carry out chain tension adjustment as described previously.

3 Once the chain tension has been corrected and wheel alignment checked, it will be necessary to centralise the brake shoes **before** tightening the spindle nut. To do this, apply and hold the brake on whilst tightening the spindle nut.

Tighten the rear wheel spindle nut to the manufacturer's torque setting. Where fitted, install the 'R' clip or a NEW split pin.

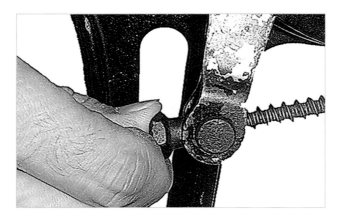

4 Turn the rear brake adjuster inwards (clockwise) to tighten the brakes and outwards to loosen them. Look in your owners or workshop manual for the specification for rear brake pedal freeplay.

5 Operate the pedal and measure the amount of lever freeplay. Do NOT force the pedal down as far as it will go, what

you are looking for is the distance the lever will travel until resistance is felt.

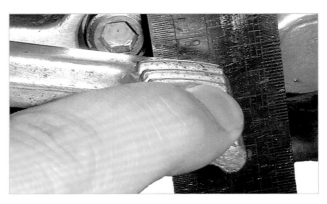

If this distance is not within the manufacturer's specification turn the adjuster (by one or two turns only) and recheck the pedal freeplay. Note that the adjuster is curved at the barrel end – this **must** align with the barrel when adjustment is complete.

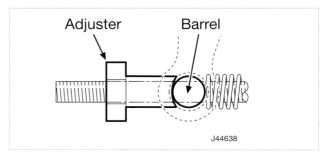

6 Don't forget to check and, if necessary, adjust the brake light switch. Tensioning the chain may necessitate re-adjustment of the rear brake light switch.

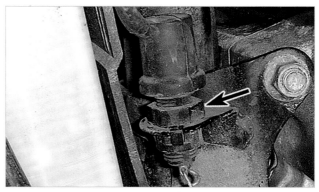

7 Press the brake pedal and check that the brake light comes on **just before resistance** is felt in the pedal, i.e. close to the end of the pedal freeplay. If necessary adjust the switch until this has been achieved.
+ Locate the switch (normally close to the rear brake pedal) and fit a spanner on the nut.
+ Holding the body with one hand turn the nut (arrowed) to raise or lower the switch.
+ Do this with the ignition switched on, make small adjustments and check between each stage.

2   Chain and sprockets replacement

The drive chain, if cleaned and serviced at regular intervals, will last many thousands of miles before it wears out. A worn chain can be felt as a 'snatching' upon acceleration, excessive chain noise and lack of adjustment range due to chain stretch. Check first, however, that the chain is not in need of adjustment and that the cush drive is not worn.

Replace the chain AND the sprockets as a set. If the chain is replaced but not the sprockets, or vice-versa, then the old items will rapidly wear out the new. This may not only lead to a dangerous situation but is also false economy. When purchasing a sprocket and chain set ensure that you purchase a chain of the correct size and with the correct number of links for your machine.

Whilst you are servicing the chain, visually inspect the condition of the chain and sprockets for any of the following possible conditions:
✦ Loose chain pins or damaged rollers
✦ Rusted, twisted or seized links
✦ Excessive wear of the chain or sprockets
✦ Lack of any further adjustment

Wear check

Sprocket check

1 See the comparison of a new and old front sprocket in the accompanying photo; the one on the right has been on the machine far too long. Notice how, on the old sprocket, the teeth are much thinner and have a 'hooked' appearance. This is a serious condition and the chain is probably so worn that it has little adjustment left and may even come off the sprockets causing a serious accident.

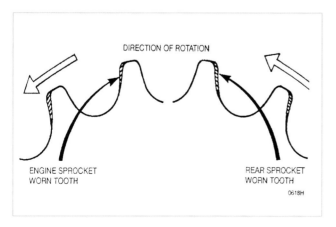

Check the sprocket teeth in the areas shown, noting that this differs for the front (drive) and rear (driven) sprockets.

DIRECTION OF ROTATION

ENGINE SPROCKET
WORN TOOTH

REAR SPROCKET
WORN TOOTH

0618H

Chain check

1 Before checking the chain for wear, clean, adjust and lubricate it as described in Section 1. Remember to adjust the chain at its tightest point on the lower run.

2 Place the thumb of your left hand over the swinging arm and your fingers under the chain and squeeze so that the chain is tightened. With the chain held tight, grip it at the three o'clock position on the rear sprocket, and try to pull the chain away from the sprocket.

3 If the chain pulls away from the sprocket then the chain is worn and must be replaced together with both sprockets. With the gap like that shown the chain is well past its 'use by date'.

Chain stretch check

1 Clean, adjust and lubricate the chain on the tight spot as before, only this time continue to tighten the chain to the point where there is NO slack on the lower chain run.

2 Using a steel rule, measure the distance between 21 pins and compare this with the maximum distance allowed by the manufacturer. Typical chain stretch limits are as follows, but check with the manufacturer for the exact limit specified for your machine. If the distance measured is at or exceeds the limit, chain and sprocket renewal is necessary.

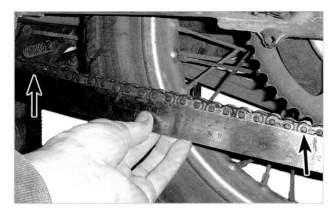

✦ Size 420 chains 259 mm (10.2 in)
✦ Size 520 chains 319.4 mm (12.57 in)
✦ Size 630 chains 383.2 mm (15.08 in)

Chain and sprocket replacement – split link chain

The following is a method of changing the chain and sprockets where a split link is used. For those of you with sports or large machines that use endless (riveted link) chains, refer to the next sub-section.

Items required

✔ New chain and sprocket kit, which should include a new split link. It may also be necessary to purchase new circlips or sprocket nut locking washers depending on the type fitted to your machine
✔ A variety of sockets, spanners and a torque wrench
✔ Ordinary pliers, and if necessary, circlips pliers
✔ Front sprocket holding tool (see Chapter 1, Section 9)
✔ General purpose grease and locking compound

Procedure

1 If the machine has a drum rear brake, it will be necessary to remove the brake adjuster, barrel and spring (A) and the split

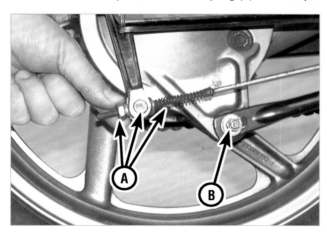

Cush drive check

1 Some machines are prone to failure of the cush drive rubbers, which are the rubber blocks that act as a shock absorber between the drive chain and rear wheel. They damp out shocks from the transmission, which would otherwise be evident on changing gear.

2 To check the condition of the drive rubbers with the components assembled, place the machine on its centrestand so that the rear wheel is off the ground. If you do not have a centrestand use a trolley-jack and stands to raise the rear wheel, alternatively use a paddock stand.

3 With the transmission in neutral, rotate the rear wheel backwards and forwards while watching the movement of the rear sprocket and rear wheel; you may need to place some load on the chain and wheel before any play is evident. If the rubbers are in good condition the rear sprocket and rear wheel will move in perfect synchronisation. If they are not synchronised, and play is evident between the rear wheel and rear sprocket, the cush drive rubbers will need replacing. Renew all rubbers as a set, never singly.

pin and nut from the torque arm (B). Clean and grease the parts on rebuild.

2 If the machine has a disc rear brake, remove the torque arm nut (A) and bolt, remembering to grease the bolt on rebuild. Slacken and remove both caliper holding bolts (B), greasing the non-threaded portion on rebuild. Once the rear wheel has been removed, place a piece of thick cardboard between the pads and hang the caliper, via a piece of string, from an upper frame member. The cardboard will keep the pads in place and supporting the caliper will prevent any stress being placed on the hose.

3 With the wheel spindle loose and the chain adjusters backed right off, it is possible (in some cases) to push the wheel forward and drop the chain off the rear sprocket. This is fine if you only want to remove the wheel but the chain split link will still have to be undone if the chain is being removed.

4 To access the front sprocket it will be necessary to remove the sprocket or generator cover. If the sprocket is retained by a nut it will usually be held in place by a lockwasher; flatten back the lockwasher tab to allow the nut to be unscrewed.

5 There are two methods of removing the front sprocket:
✦ If the chain is still in place, select first gear and use the chain to hold the front sprocket whilst you slacken the sprocket holding screws or nut. Hold the rear brake on while you do this.
✦ Alternatively, with the chain already removed, use a sprocket-holding tool as shown below.

6 Use a pair of ordinary pliers to remove the clip from the split link. Place one arm of the pliers to the left of the pin and the other arm against the open end of the clip. Close the pliers and the clip will 'spring off' the right-hand pin. Turn the clip so that it is at 90° to the back plate and push it upwards off the left-hand pin. It's fiddly because you do not have a lot of metal to grip – the trick is to ensure that the pliers are perfectly square to the clip and the open end is central to the pliers' arm. Remove the front plate followed by the back plate then remove the old chain.

7 The component parts of the split link are shown in the accompanying photo (A – back plate and pins, B – front plate and C – spring clip). The split link is a 'use once only' item and MUST be renewed if it is disturbed. If the spring clip breaks or comes off, the chain will come apart with disastrous results.

8 Remove the rear wheel, noting the position and direction of any spacers and washers used.

9 Lay the wheel on a flat surface, taking care not to damage the brake disc (where applicable) and grip the sprocket at the 3 o'clock and 9 o'clock positions. Try to twist the sprocket in a rotary motion. This will test the condition of the cush-drive rubbers; there should be no discernable play. If play exists then the cush-drive rubbers have failed (indicated by transmission snatch) and will need replacing.

10 Use a socket and short extension bar to remove the rear sprocket securing nuts. If you use a spanner, and it slips, you may lose a lot of skin from your knuckles!

11 On the machine shown, the nuts are of the self-locking type (Nyloc nuts) and the sprocket is held to the carrier by a large circlip (arrow). Use external circlips pliers to remove the circlip and replace it with a new one on rebuild.

12 On the machine shown, the rear sprocket is bolted directly to its carrier and the nuts are held in place by locking washers. The locking washers have their tabs turned up against the side of the nut to prevent it coming loose and use two washers that lock one nut to its neighbour. Use a cold chisel to flatten the tabs and discard the washers once the nuts have been removed. Fit new washers on rebuild, and use an adjustable pipe wrench or a hammer and punch to fold their tabs against the flat of each nut once the nuts have been tightened to the correct torque setting.

13 Remove the old sprocket, clean the carrier/wheel hub face and any circlip groove.

14 Fit the new rear sprocket, noting that it is usually fitted with its markings (number of teeth, e.g. 43T) facing outwards. Apply one drop of locking agent to the thread of each stud before fitting and tightening the nuts to their specified torque setting.

15 Where a circlip is fitted, install the large washer and new circlip. Note that the circlip must be fitted with its square edge in the direction of thrust. Circlips are stamped from sheet steel and careful inspection will show a rounded edge to one face. The action of the sprocket will cause it to try to come off the carrier, therefore the rounded edge must be fitted against the sprocket.

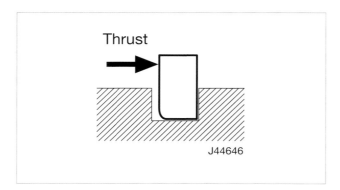

Thrust

J44646

16 If failure of the cush drive rubbers was noted previously (see **Wear check** at the beginning of this section), prise the old rubbers from the rear wheel and fit new ones.

17 Fit the new front sprocket with its markings (usually the number of teeth, e.g. 14T) facing outwards. Where a locking plate is fitted (as shown in the photo) slide it over the shaft splines then rotate it in the shaft groove to align the bolt holes. Other machines may use a locking tab washer which fits between the sprocket and nut – it is advisable to renew the tab washer every time it is disturbed.

18 Apply one drop of locking agent to the threads of each securing nut/bolt. Hold the sprocket with the special tool whilst tightening the nut/bolts to the correct torque setting. If a locking tab washer is used, bend a portion of the washer up against one flat of the nut. Note that it may be easier to tighten the sprocket nut/bolts when the chain is installed and can be used to hold the sprocket.

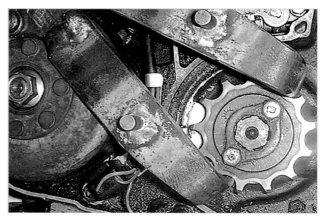

19 Refit the rear wheel but leave all nuts etc. loose at this stage, then fit the chain over the rear sprocket. Make sure that the wheel is as far forward as it will go and if necessary back off both chain adjusters to achieve this. Feed the chain through the chainguard, over the swinging arm, and onto the front sprocket. Pull the chain round the front sprocket and position its two ends so that they are in the centre of the lower run. In some instances, it may be easier to remove the chainguard to facilitate fitting of the chain.

20 Fit the NEW split link back plate and pins through the chain ends then fit the front plate. Rotate the wheel so that the split link is on the sprocket in the 3 o'clock position and position the new spring clip as shown. It is imperative that the **closed end** of the clip is fitted in the normal direction of chain travel. If fitted the other way round there is a danger that the clip may come off with disastrous results.

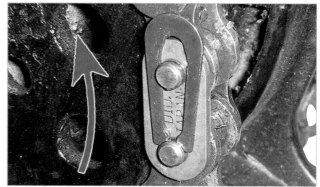

A small squirt of chain lubricant on the pins, front plate and spring clip will help to ease the clip into the pin grooves.

21 Use an ordinary pair of pliers to fit the spring clip. Place the lower jaw so that it is under the pin and the upper jaw above the spring clip's closed end. Closing the pliers will force the spring clip to seat in the grooves of both pins. This can be a fiddly job, so take your time and keep the spring link flat against the front plate.

22 Now rotate the rear wheel so that the split link is on the lower run of the chain. Place a pair of long nose pliers between the back plate and the front plate and open the pliers as much as you can. This pushes the front plate tight against the spring clip and helps to hold it in place.

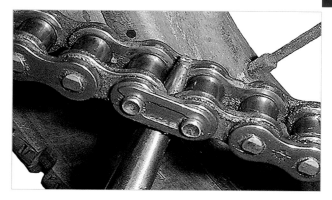

23 With the chain and sprockets fitted carry out the following tasks:
+ Fit all removed parts such as brake caliper, torque arm etc.
+ Adjust the chain tension and align the wheels (see Section 1).
+ Recheck chain tension and alignment then tighten all nuts and bolts. Don't forget to fit new split pins where necessary. Lubricate the chain.
+ If a drum rear brake is fitted, apply and hold the rear brake on whilst tightening the wheel spindle (see Chapter 1, Section 6, for a method of lining up the nut castellation and spindle hole). This will centralise the brake shoes giving the best braking action possible. Adjust the rear brake (see Section 1).
+ If a disc rear brake is fitted, check that the brake pads are seated properly over the disc and that the brake operates correctly.
+ Adjust the brake light switch.
+ Road test the machine.

Chain and sprocket replacement – riveted link chain

Drive chains for all but small bikes are continuous and do not have a split-type link. The chain must be broken using a chain breaker tool and the new chain securely riveted together using a new soft rivet-type link. Various chain breaking and riveting tools are available, either as separate tools or combined as illustrated in the accompanying photographs – read the instructions supplied with the tool carefully.

Refer to the previous section for details of sprocket replacement.

 Never use a clip-type connecting link instead of a rivet-type link.

The need to rivet the new link pins correctly cannot be overstressed – loss of control of the motorcycle is very likely to result if the chain breaks in use.

1 Rotate the chain and look for the riveted soft link. The soft link pins look like they have been deeply centre-punched

instead of peened over like all the other pins and its sideplate may be a different colour (see Step 8). Position the soft link midway between the sprockets and assemble the chain breaker tool over one of the soft link pins.

2 Operate the tool to push the pin out through the chain. On an 'O' ring chain, remove the 'O' rings and carry out the same procedure on the other soft link pin. Note that certain soft link pins (particularly on the larger chains) may require their ends being filed or ground off before they can be pressed out using the tool.

Chain sizing

◆ Chains are sized using a three digit number, followed by a suffix to denote the chain type. Chain type is either standard or heavy duty (thicker sideplates), and also unsealed or 'O' ring/'X' ring type.
◆ The first digit of the number relates to the pitch of the chain, i.e. the distance from the centre of one pin to the centre of the next pin. Pitch is expressed in eighths of an inch, thus:

Chain size	Pitch
415, 420, 428	1/2 inch (12.7 mm)
520, 525, 50 (530), 532	5/8 inch (15.9 mm)
630, 632	3/4 inch (19.1 mm)

◆ The second and third digits of the chain size relate to the width of the rollers.

Chain size	Roller width
415	0.187 in (4.76 mm)
420, 520	0.250 in (6.35 mm)
428	0.313 in (7.94 mm)
525	0.312 in (7.93 mm)
50 (530), 532, 630, 632	0.375 in (9.53 mm)

3 Check that you have the correct size and strength (standard or heavy duty) new soft link – do not reuse the old link. Look for the size marking on the chain sideplates.

4 Position the chain ends so that they are engaged over the rear sprocket. On an 'O' ring chain, install a new 'O' ring over each pin of the link and insert the link through the two chain ends.

5 Install a new 'O' ring over the end of each pin, followed by the sideplate (with the chain manufacturer's marking facing outwards).

On an unsealed chain, insert the link through the two chain ends, then install the sideplate with the chain manufacturer's marking facing outwards.

6 Note that it may not be possible to install the sideplate using finger pressure alone. If using a joining tool, assemble it so that the plates of the tool clamp the link and press the sideplate over the pins.

Otherwise, use two small sockets placed over the rivet ends and two pieces of wood between a G-clamp. Operate the clamp to press the sideplate over the pins.

7 Assemble the joining tool over one pin (following the maker's instructions) and tighten the tool down to spread the pin end securely. Do the same on the other pin.

8 Check that the pin ends are secure and that there is no danger of the sideplate coming loose. If the pin ends are cracked the soft link must be renewed. The pin end (A) is correctly riveted and the pin end (B) has yet to be riveted.

---

3 Steering head, wheel and swinging arm bearing checks

Steering head bearings check

Check every 6000 km (4000 miles) or every 12 months.

The motorcycle steering pivots on a shaft (stem) that runs through the headstock of the frame. The forks are held in two yokes, one above and one below the headstock. The yokes are connected to the pivot shaft (steering stem) via bearings that sit in the headstock and occasionally require adjustment to compensate for wear.

If the bearings are over tight the balls/rollers will skid rather than roll, causing flats to be worn in them as well as on the track surfaces. The steering will not be smooth and the machine will weave from side to side – it may become so bad that notches appear in the bearing surfaces. This will cause the steering to self-centre and ruin the bearings at the same time. If the bearings are too loose they will rapidly be destroyed. Both extremes cause stability problems at all speeds, in a straight line and when cornering. If too slack, a 'knocking' may be heard or felt through the handlebars when braking. Check the bearings as follows:

There should be no slack in the bearings but the handlebars should move freely from lock to lock.

Checking for loose bearings

1 Place the motorcycle on its centrestand or support it so that the front wheel is off the ground.

2 With the wheel in the straight-ahead position, grasp the bottom of both fork legs and push then pull the forks.

3 If there is any play in the bearings, this will show up as a knocking at the headstock. If you are unsure as to whether there is any play, get a friend to hold the headstock at the place shown.

With you pushing and pulling the forks as shown any play will be easily felt at this point. Any play will need to be taken up by adjusting the bearings.

If pushing and pulling at this point causes a knocking, this may be:

+ Loose steering head bearings – adjust as described below.
+ Loose fork yoke clamp bolts – slacken then tighten them to their specified torque settings. Re-check bearing play afterwards.
+ Worn front fork bushes – if the head bearings are correctly adjusted and fork yoke clamp bolts are tight, the fork bushes may have worn.
+ Motorcycle rocking on its centrestand.

Checking for tight bearings

1 Place the motorcycle on its centrestand or support it so that the front wheel is off the ground and the steering is in the straight-ahead position.

2 Use a piece of string and a small fishing scale (as shown) and gently pull on the scale. Note the reading on the scale when the bars first start to move and compare this figure with the specifications in your workshop manual. Do this on both sides of the bars. As a 'rule of thumb', the figure is normally between 200 to 500 grams.

Steering head bearings adjustment

1 If the bearings need adjustment, first remove any items necessary to gain access to the top yoke, e.g. headlamp, fairing, instruments. On certain machines it may also be necessary to remove the handlebars to gain access to the steering stem nut. See Section 6 on handlebars for information on the rebuild. If you are careful, removal of the fuel tank isn't necessary but highly recommended, to prevent damage to its finish should a tool slip.

2 Note that it helps to remove the front wheel as this takes a lot of weight off the steering head, although this is not essential.

3 Slacken the two top yoke fork clamp bolts (A) then slacken and remove the steering stem nut (B) and its washer. Ease the top yoke up and off the steering head.

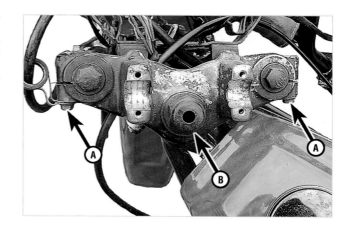

Note that it isn't always necessary to completely remove the top yoke, the bearing adjuster is often easily accessible or can be accessed by lifting the top yoke slightly.

4 Support the lower yoke with one hand and slacken the adjuster nut slightly, then retighten it until resistance is just felt. Turn the bottom yoke from left to right as you tighten the adjuster nut to ensure that the bearings seat properly. By supporting, and turning the lower yoke, you can feel the effect a quarter turn of the adjuster nut makes. Refit the top yoke and nip up the top nut and top yoke bolts.

5 Note that some machines use a locking nut and washer above the adjuster nut. The locking nut must be slackened off before the adjuster nut can be turned. Once the adjuster nut setting is correct, the adjuster nut must be held in position with a C-spanner whilst the locking nut is tightened against it.

6 Where a tab type lockwasher is fitted between the adjuster nut and locking nut, the top yoke will require removal to enable the lockwasher tabs to be straightened and the nuts slackened. It is recommended that a NEW lockwasher is fitted every time.

7 This fitment shows a lockwasher design where the long tabs of the washer locate in the slots of the two nuts. When the

adjuster nut setting is correct, it is held in position with a C-spanner whilst the locking nut is tightened so that its slots align exactly which those of the adjuster nut.

8 If the steering head bearings haven't been adjusted for some time, the adjuster nut can be extremely difficult to undo by hand and a C-spanner may be necessary.

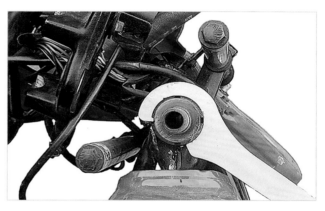

9 Re-check the head bearings as described previously. If the adjustment setting is correct, slacken the steering stem nut and top yoke bolts. Re-tighten the steering stem nut **then** the top yoke bolts and to their correct torque settings. Check the headraces again after tightening the bolts/nut, as it has been known for the races to become too tight after tightening the steering stem nut. If they have tightened up, remove the top yoke and re-adjust.

10 If it proves impossible to adjust the bearings successfully, or the steering action feels notchy, the bearings are most likely worn and should be renewed. Refer to your workshop manual for details of bearing replacement.

⚠ **Caution: Take care not to apply too much loading on the bearings because this will cause premature failure. The object is to remove all freeplay, yet allow free movement of the steering.**

Wheel bearings check

1 Place the machine on its centrestand or support it upright so that the wheel to be tested is off the ground.

2 Make sure that the wheel spindle is tight.

3 Grip the wheel with both hands as close to the top and bottom of the wheel as possible.

4 Push with one hand and pull with the other. Try to 'rock' the wheel about its spindle. If any play is felt then the bearings will have to be renewed.

HINT

To feel what is meant by 'play', slightly loosen the wheel spindle (1/2 to 1 turn) and repeat the above. Tighten the wheel spindle when done.

Swinging arm bearings check

1 Place the machine on its centrestand or support it upright so that the rear wheel is off the ground.

2 Grasp the rear tyre at the 3 o'clock position and place your other hand on the swinging arm pivot.

3 Push and pull the tyre with one hand (side-to-side) whilst feeling for any 'knock' with the other.

4 If any 'knock', can be felt and the swinging arm pivot is tight, then the swinging arm bearings will need renewing. Refer to your workshop manual for details of bearing renewal.

5 It can be difficult to assess bearing wear with the rear wheel and suspension unit(s) in place. To confirm your findings, remove the rear wheel, detach the shock absorber(s) from the lower mounting and recheck for play in the swinging arm pivot by holding the ends of the swinging arm and repeating the test above.

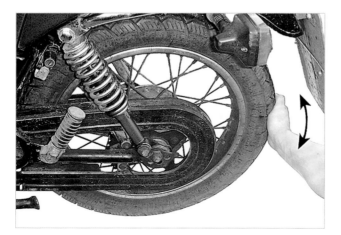

4   Wheel bearing replacement

Check the wheel bearings as described in Section 3. Wheel bearing renewal is a straightforward process. **Note:** *The use of high pressure water or steam washers tends to drive the grease out of wheel bearings, causing their life to be much reduced.*

Items required

✔ Hammer and appropriate drifts (steel rods). The copper/rawhide hammer is good for many jobs but for this task, a hammer with some weight is required
✔ Two new wheel bearings. Leave them in their wrappings until you are ready to do this job
✔ New wheel bearing seal(s)
✔ Two blocks of wood to support the wheel
✔ Large socket or length of tubing that is the same diameter as the outside of the bearing
✔ Grease and clean cloths
✔ A hot air gun or some method of heating the hub may be required

Bearing removal

1 Remove the wheel and lift out the wheel spacers from each side of the hub (take note of their positions). If working on the front wheel remove the speedometer drive unit (where fitted) from the hub. If working on the rear wheel, lift out the sprocket coupling and its spacer.

2 Most wheels will have rubber seals fitted to prevent dirt and dust entering the wheel bearing. This seal must be taken out before the bearings can be removed. The use of a small, bicycle tyre lever or large flat-bladed screwdriver makes an ideal tool for this job. Don't re-use the seals, obtain new ones for the rebuild.

> **HINT**
>
> Don't try to remove the seal in one go. Work the seal out of the hub by easing it up at one place, then moving the lever to a new position that is 90° to the first position and gently lift again. If the seal hasn't come out by this time, move the lever round the seal by a further 90° and repeat the process until it comes out.

3 With the seals removed, access can now be gained to the bearings. If you are working on the front wheel, you may need to remove the speedometer drive plate from one side of the hub – this is often retained by a circlip.

Bearings are usually destroyed during the removal process, so make a double check now of their condition by rotating the inner race with your finger. A bearing in good condition should turn smoothly, without rough spots or noise.

Prior to removing the bearings, check for any circlips retaining the bearing in the hub – remove them if found.

4 Place the wheel on the blocks of wood so that the wheel hub is supported by the wood. Check that the wood supports the hub and **not** the brake disc otherwise the disc could be distorted. Also, do not support the wheel by the rim because you are likely to damage the spokes.

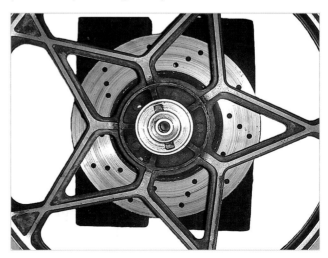

5 Between the wheel bearings will be a spacer (tube). This spacer must be moved aside slightly to enable a drift to be used to knock out the first bearing.

6 Place the drift about halfway into the centre of the wheel and lever the spacer to one side. This will leave part of the lip of the spacer showing and allow you to tap the lower bearing out with the drift.

7 The bearings are an interference fit in the wheel hub. This means that the bearing has a very slightly bigger outside diameter than the inside diameter of the wheel hub. This way the hub grips the bearing outer race allowing the wheel to rotate on the ball rollers.

Although not essential, applying heat to the aluminium bearing housing will cause it to expand and ease removal of the bearing.

The safest method of applying heat is with a hot air gun, such as a domestic paint stripper. In the example shown it took about ten minutes to get the hub to a temperature where it was hot to the touch but did not burn the skin. Work the tool in a circular motion around the hub and close to the bearing. With the hub hot enough, flip the wheel over and make sure the hub is supported by the wood blocks. The use of a gas type blow torch is not advised because the heat is too localised and there is a high risk of damage to the hub.

HINT

If the bearings fall out when cold, or need virtually no persuasion to leave the wheel hub, it is likely that the hub is badly worn, especially if there are signs that the bearing has been spinning in the hub. Your dealer may recommend a bearing locking compound.

8 Place the drift through the first bearing and position the edge of the drift onto the edge of the lower bearing.

Pull the top of the drift towards you so that the bottom of the drift is away from you and give the drift a sharp, firm tap with the hammer. Reverse the position of the drift (top away from you, bottom towards you) and tap the drift again.

Now move the drift to the right and tap, then to the left and tap. Work your way around the bearing (12 o'clock, 6 o'clock, 3 o'clock then 9 o'clock) until the bearing, then spacer fall out.

9 With the first bearing out of the hub, turn the wheel over and drive the second bearing out. It isn't usually necessary to heat this side of the hub as you have a lot more bearing to work on.

Bearing and hub check

10 With the bearings out, clean the hub bearing surfaces then inspect them for damage. If the bearings have been replaced before, and they haven't been fitted squarely, there may be witness marks on the hub surfaces.

Minor scratches can often be removed with very fine 'wet and dry' paper. Deep grooves will require expert inspection.

11 Always renew both bearings in the hub at the same time, never singly, and ensure that the new bearings are of the same type as the originals. This can be ensured by purchasing them from a motorcycle dealer.

Bearing markings

Ball bearings come in many sizes and are used inside the engine as well as in the wheels. They can be:

✦ Without any seals. These are often found inside the engine and have the basic bearing number, e.g. 6301.
✦ Single seals (usually rubber) would have the bearing number followed by the letters RS, e.g. 6301-RS.
✦ Two seals would have the bearing number followed by the designation 2RS, e.g. 6301-2RS.

The bearings used on motorcycles are 'C' grade (automotive quality) bearings.

12 It is a common misconception that bearing manufacturers do not put enough grease in the bearing and that they have to be packed solid with grease before fitting them. In fact, if a bearing is over packed, there is a strong possibility that the bearing will overheat and suffer damage. The colour of the grease in the bearing on the right shows distinct signs of overheating.

13 Non-sealed bearings can be cleaned by immersing them in a clean solvent such as white spirit or paraffin and then dried in a clean jet of dry compressed air. Place the bearing on a clean surface and direct the air at the bearing. NEVER hold the

bearing whilst drying it with compressed air. Bearings should NOT be spun by the air. The balls will skid, damaging the races and rolling elements. With the bearing clean and dry, lightly oil the rolling elements.

14 To check the bearings for wear, hold the bearing inner race between thumb and finger, whilst slowly rotating the outer race with the other hand. Check for abnormal noise (when worn they grate) and any notchiness as it rotates. There should also be little play when 'rocking' the inner race against the outer race.

Bearing installation

Note: *Although the original bearings can be cleaned and checked as described above, it is recommended that new bearings are always used.*

15 Apply a smear of grease around the outer race of the new bearing and a smear of grease in the hub. This aids the initial fitting of the bearing.

16 Place the bearing squarely onto its housing with its identification numbers uppermost. If the new bearing is sealed on one side only, it must be fitted with the sealed side facing outwards.

17 Place a large socket or metal tube over the bearing so that it contacts the bearing's **outer race** only. Hitting the inner race or balls will damage the new bearing.

18 Hold the bearing and socket with one hand, and give a firm, sharp tap to the end of the socket with a large hammer. Continue to tap the socket ensuring that you hit it in the centre and that the bearing enters the hub squarely. Take your time and check that the bearing is still square to the housing, between hammer blows. When the bearing is fully home there will be a distinctive 'thunk' as the bearing contacts its seat in the hub.

19 Flip the wheel over and insert the spacer that will have dropped out when the first bearing was removed. It isn't necessary to coat the spacer with grease but a light coating won't hurt.

20 Fit the second bearing by repeating Step 18. Clean off any excess grease and fit new seals. The seals must be fitted with their lips facing inwards and size markings outwards.

5   Gear lever, brake pedal and footrests

Gear lever pivot lubrication

This is a fairly simple task that along with lubricating the brake pedal pivot point should take no more than a couple of hours. Lubricate the lever pivot every year to reduce wear on the pivot and keep the lever action sweet.

Items required

✔ Variety of spanners and Allen key sockets
✔ Torque wrench
✔ Wire brush, clean cloth and 'wet and dry'
✔ Copper grease or multi-purpose grease
✔ Locking agent, new split pins or 'R' clips
✔ Parts tray to put the bolts etc. in

Procedure

1 Check the lever clamp to see if it has a master spline or some other means by which it can easily be returned to its original position on the shaft.

Some manufacturers provide a punch mark on the shaft that lines up with a corresponding punch mark or the slit in the clamp. Others use a master spline that means it is physically impossible to get the relationship between the shaft and clamp wrong. Slacken and remove the clamp screw (arrow).

2 Slacken and remove the assembly mounting plate screws (arrows). Remove the clamp and assembly mounting plate as one piece.

3 On the arrangement shown, the gear lever pivots on a shaft that is part of the footrest assembly. The footrest assembly is screwed to the mounting plate. With the mounting plate removed, turn it over and locate the screw that holds the footrest in place and remove it.

4 With the parts removed and disassembled:

✦ Clean and grease the pivot bearing in the lever (A).
✦ Clean and grease the bearing surface on the footrest assembly (B).
✦ Although the bearing surface on the footrest is round, there will often be a slot machined at the end that locates in a similar slot in the mounting plate (C). This is to ensure that the relationship of the footrest and mounting plate is always correct. Clean the slots in both the mounting plate and the footrest.
✦ Clean any old locking agent from the footrest mounting screw (D) then put one drop of fresh locking agent onto the threaded portion and allow it to flow down and around the threads.

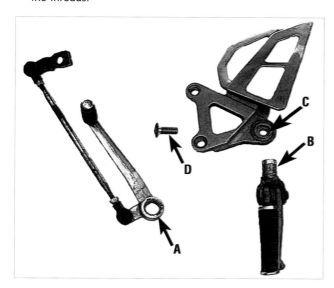

5 Mount the gear lever on the bearing surface of the footrest. Locate the footrest/gear lever into the mounting plate. Fit and tighten the footrest mounting screw to its torque setting. Check your workshop manual for this figure. Clean any excess grease from the assembly.

6 Clean any old locking agent from the threads of the mounting plate screws, then place one drop of fresh locking agent onto the threads of the two screws.

7 Fit the clamp to the gear lever shaft, lining up the original marks, then fit and tighten the locking bolt.

8 Offer up the mounting plate to the machine and fit the lower mounting plate screw but do NOT tighten it more than 2 or 3 turns at this time. Fit the upper screw and tighten it by 2 or 3 turns. The screws on this machine have shoulders built into them (see brake pedal section) that locate in the mounting plate.

9 Tighten each screw until it is finger-tight, ensuring that its shoulder fits squarely into the socket in the mounting plate. This gives a flush fitting to the screw heads.

10 Finally, tighten each screw to its recommended torque setting.

Brake pedal pivot lubrication

This is another of those jobs that should be done once a year. This helps to reduce the wear on the pivot shaft and pedal bush, and keeps the lever action smooth.

Items required are the same as for gear lever pivot lubrication described previously.

The following procedure describes brake pedal removal on an hydraulically operated system. A similar method of attachment is used on a drum braked system.

1 Slacken, but do NOT remove both of the rear brake master cylinder mounting screws (A). Slacken both mounting plate screws (B) then remove each in turn.

2 With the mounting plate detached from the frame, turn it around and locate and remove the split pin that secures the master cylinder (via a clevis pin) to the end of the brake pedal. Throw away the old split pin and have a new one ready for the rebuild.

> **HINT**
>
> Dispose of the old split pin in the dustbin. Do NOT be tempted to leave it lying on the floor, it is almost guaranteed that the split pin will be picked up by your tyres and cause a puncture.

3 Remove the clevis pin and examine it for signs of wear. If it is showing signs of wear (grooves in its bearing surface) replace it. Note which way round the clevis pin is fitted.

4 With the clevis pin removed, undo the two brake master cylinder mounting screws and place the master cylinder in a safe position.

5 With the master cylinder removed from the mounting plate, remove the brake light switch spring from the brake lever by expanding the spring and unhooking it from the brake lever peg. Remove the brake light switch mounting plate and place this item out of harm's way. Similarly, remove the lever return spring by unhooking one end from the brake lever peg.

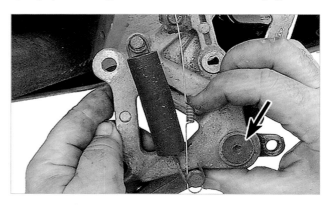

This is a good time to check the condition of the springs, clean, lubricate them with light oil, and lubricate the switch rod.

6 With the mounting plate removed from the machine, the screw (arrowed in the above photograph) can now be undone

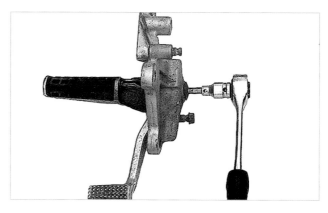

which will release the footrest and brake pedal pivot mount. It will probably be very tight, so use an Allen key socket and long bar to break the seal.

7 With the components stripped from the mounting plate:

✦ Clean and grease the brake pedal pivot bush (A) and the return spring locating peg (B).
✦ Clean and grease the footrest mount bearing surface (C).
✦ Clean and grease the clevis pin (D).
✦ Clean any old locking agent from the threads of the footrest mounting screw (E). Place one drop of new locking agent onto the threaded portion and allow it to run down and around the threads.
✦ There will be a 'flat' machined into the footrest mounting and a corresponding 'flat' cast into the mounting plate. This is to ensure that the footrest/plate relationship is correct. Clean any dirt or corrosion from the plate (F).

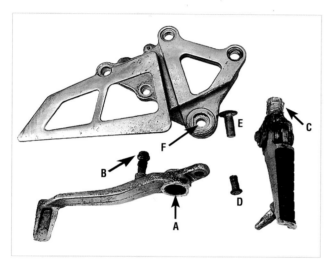

8 Reassemble the brake pedal and footrest, fit the locking screw and tighten it to its recommended torque setting. Clean any excess grease from the assembly when done. **Note:** *Make sure that the 'flat' in the peg mount (C) locates with the 'flat' in the mounting plate (F) BEFORE tightening the screw (E).*

9 Use one drop of locking agent on the brake light switch securing screw and refit the brake light switch assembly.

10 Clean and grease the brake pedal return spring pivot, on the mounting plate, and refit the pedal return spring. Refit the brake light switch spring and check the action of both items.

11 Clean the threaded portion of the master cylinder mounting screws and put one drop of locking agent on each screw. Allow the locking agent to flow down and around the threads.

12 Install the master cylinder on the mounting plate and fit the lower mounting screw. Tighten it by 2 or 3 turns only then fit the upper screw. Tighten both screws finger-tight only at this stage. **Note:** *Make sure that the shouldered portion of the screws fit within the recesses in the mounting plate.*

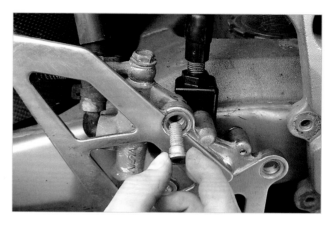

13 Locate the master cylinder rod assembly to the end of the brake lever and fit the greased clevis pin through the holes in both. Note which way round the clevis pin is fitted. Fit a NEW split pin, cut it to length and bend the ends open to prevent it coming out (arrow).

14 Clean the mounting screw threads and apply one drop of locking agent to each thread. Allow the agent to flow down and around the threads.

15 Place the mounting plate against the frame and fit the lower mounting screw. Tighten it by 2 or 3 turns only at this stage. Fit the upper mounting screw and tighten it finger-tight ensuring that the screw shoulder fits snugly into its recess in the mounting plate.

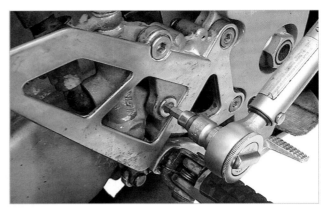

16 Tighten the lower mounting screw until it is finger-tight with the shoulder fitting snugly into its recess, then tighten both screws to the recommended torque setting.

17 Return to the master cylinder mounting screws and tighten both to their recommended torque setting.

18 Operate the brake pedal and check for:

✦ Correct operation of the brakes
✦ Correct operation of the brake light switch
✦ Correct brake pedal height

Footrest pivot lubrication

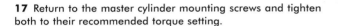

Items required

✔ Grease (copper-based)
✔ Screwdriver and pliers
✔ New 'E' clip or split pin where appropriate
✔ Old toothbrush, cloth and cleaning spray

1 This footrest pin is held in place by an 'E' clip. With a flat-bladed screwdriver, use a twisting motion to GENTLY prise the clip out of its groove. Take great care because this is a spring clip and if you are heavy handed it is going to ping away.

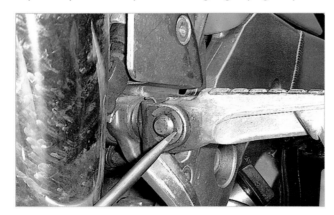

2 If the footrest is held in place by a split pin, straighten the pin, then remove it. Remove the washer behind the split pin.

3 Whether an 'E' clip or split pin is fitted, always use a new one when you assembly the component. Split pins, 'E' clips and circlips are 'use once only' items because opening them weakens their construction. Should the clip fall off or a split pin break, there is nothing securing your footrest to the machine.

4 Before you pull the footrest pin out, note the position and direction of the return spring. Nothing is more frustrating than to rebuild the unit and find that the spring is on the wrong way round.

5 Use your cleaning spray, cloth and old toothbrush to remove the grit and dirt from all of the parts. If necessary, clean any rust off the pin with 'wet and dry' paper or a wire brush.

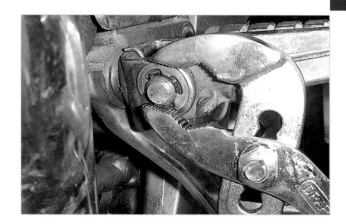

6 Pull the rag through the footrest pin holes to make sure these are clean. Dirt and corrosion here will cause the footrest to seize. Where the pin is secured by an 'E' clip, make sure that the groove in the pin is clean and free from rust; use a small, flat-bladed screwdriver or wire brush to clean it.

7 Grease the pin and pin hole and re-assemble the parts, ensuring that the pin is fitted with its flange uppermost.

8 Where an 'E' clip arrangement is used, position the NEW 'E' clip and lock it into its groove with pliers.

9 Where a split arrangement is used, install the washer then insert a NEW split pin through the hole in the footrest pin and bend its ends securely around the pin.

Brake pedal height check and adjustment

This is a simple task that once set should not go out of adjustment and can make the ride more comfortable and safer.

1 Use a straight-edge (piece of wood) parallel to the ground and resting on the footrest and a rule to measure the brake pedal height. The measurement is taken with the pedal 'at rest' and is usually expressed as the distance of the pedal tip below the upper surface of the footrest.

2 On this disc-braked model, if adjustment is required slacken the locknut (A) and rotate the master cylinder pushrod via (B) until the specified brake pedal height is achieved. Hold the nut (B) tighten the locknut (A).

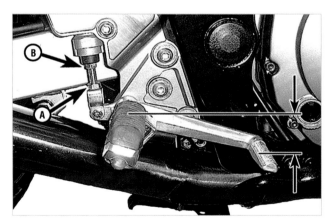

3 Check the operation of the brake light switch and adjust if necessary. The brake light should illuminate at the end of the pedal freeplay just as resistance is felt in the pedal.

4 On this drum-braked model, first back off the brake adjuster at the rear wheel (see Section 1). Slacken the locknut (A) and turn the adjuster screw (B) until the required brake pedal height

has been achieved. Tighten the locknut, then adjust the rear brake and brake light switch.

5 Another type of drum-braked pedal height adjuster is shown. Having slackened the brake adjuster at the brake drum, slacken the locknut (A) and turn the adjuster screw (B) until the required brake pedal height has been achieved. Tighten the locknut, then adjust the rear brake and brake light switch.

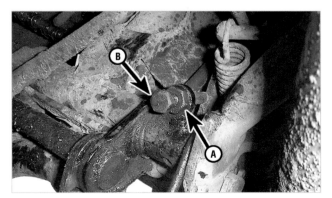

6	Handlebars, levers and cable lubrication

Handlebar removal and installation

If the handlebars have been fitted incorrectly or if you have to remove them for steering head bearing adjustment or fork removal, the following procedure should be noted.

Items required

✔ Various sockets and extension bar
✔ Torque wrench
✔ Copper grease and locking agent

Procedure

1 One-piece handlebars have two clamps holding the bars in place. Check if there are any markings on the clamps to indicate which way round they should be fitted.

On the clamp shown, a small punch mark (arrow) indicates the forward facing end of the clamp. It is often hidden under the flange of the bolt.

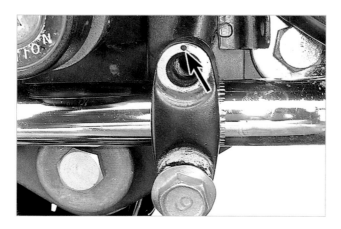

If there are no markings, inspect the clamp to see if one side is wider than the other (asymmetrical). In the accompanying photo, the front end is thicker than the rear end. The clamp should be fitted with the clearance facing the rear of the machine.

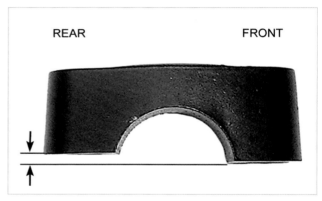

REAR   FRONT

If the clamp is symmetrical (both ends equal width), it must be fitted with equal gaps. See Step 6 for this type.

2 Fit the handlebars so that any serrations are central to the two lower clamp pieces. It is not always possible to fit the serrations perfectly within the lower clamps. What is important is that the bars are central to the two lower clamps. Do not worry if your bars do not have the serrations, not all manufacturers use them.

3 Have a look at the bars to see if there is a punch mark or a longer serration. This (if it is there) will indicate the manufacturer's recommended bar position and any mark should line up with the mating surface of the lower clamp.

4 Before fitting the upper clamps and bolts, smear copper grease on the non-threaded portion of each bolt. This will help to keep corrosion at bay. Put ONE DROP of locking agent on the threaded portion and allow it to run down the threads. This will help to lock the bolt in place. Any more than one drop and you will have an immense amount of trouble removing the bolt later.

5 If asymmetrical clamps are fitted, fit the clamps so that their wider ends (forward part) seat on the lower clamp surface. Fit the four bolts and tighten them by approximately two or three turns, then tighten the two FRONT bolts until they are finger-tight.

Tighten the two REAR bolts until there is approximately 2 to 3 mm of clearance between the bolt flange and the clamp.

Now use a torque wrench to tighten the TWO FRONT BOLTS to the setting recommended by the manufacturer. Use of a long socket or socket and short bar will keep the torque wrench away from your fuel tank, so that you don't scratch it.

With BOTH front bolts tightened to their torque setting, check that the position of the bars hasn't changed then tighten the two rear bolts to their torque setting. This will leave the gap for BOTH clamps at the rear of the bars as shown.

6 If symmetrical clamps are fitted, i.e. both ends of the clamp are the same height, they must be fitted so that there is an EQUAL GAP at the front and rear of the bars.

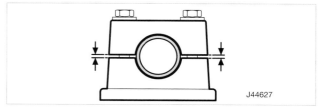

J44627

Grease the unthreaded portion of the bolts, use one drop of locking agent on each bolt and install all four bolts.

Tighten each bolt by approximately 2 to 3 turns then tighten the two FRONT bolts until the gap at the front of the clamp is approximately the same as the gap at the rear.

Check the position of the handlebars then tighten the two REAR bolts to the torque setting recommended by the manufacturer. Recheck the torque setting for the two front bolts.

7 On machines with individual handlebars which clamp around the front forks, either above or below the top yoke, there will be a means of locating the handlebar in position and clamping it to the fork.

In the example shown, an Allen headed screw (A) mounted in the handlebar unit locates in the top yoke clamp to position the handlebar at the correct angle, and another Allen screw (B) clamps the handlebar to the front fork.

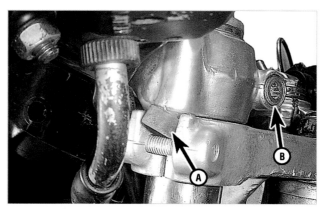

Control cable lubrication and handlebar lever replacement

The control cables should be lubricated periodically to ensure their smooth operation. This section describes the procedure for lubricating the clutch cable and, on a drum front brake system, the front brake cable. Although lubricant can be applied to the exposed parts of the cable without disconnecting it from the lever, the most effective way of lubricating the entire cable is to disconnect it from the lever and use a cable luber tool and aerosol cable lubricant.

This section also describes how to remove the levers, either to lubricate their pivots or to replace a broken lever damaged as the result of dropping the machine.

1 Slacken and turn out the adjuster lock ring (A) so that it is close to the adjuster (B). Turn the adjuster (B) and lock ring (A) as far into the lever as possible whilst ensuring that the slots in the lever and adjusters line up. Lining up the slots will allow the cable inner to be removed from the lever assembly.

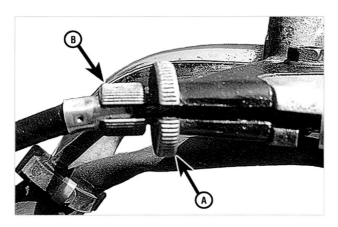

2 Whilst holding the cable close to the adjuster with one hand, operate the lever with the other hand. Slowly release the lever, whilst at the same time, pulling on the cable. This pulls the outer cable end cap out of the adjuster. With the end cap clear of the adjuster, pull the inner cable out of the adjuster via the slots. Once it is out, the barrel (at the end of the inner cable) can be removed from the underside of the lever.

3 The lever's pivot pin is usually screwed into the lower part of the lever holder and is secured with a nut (arrow). If your machine has an ordinary nut fitted then a locking washer should be used. Other makes of machine may use a self-locking nut and no washer may be present.

Undo and remove the locking nut, then undo and remove the pivot pin and remove the lever.

4 With the lever's pivot pin removed, check the condition of the threads, clean any corrosion from the pin and lightly grease the pivot area. If the threads are damaged, usually caused by over-tightening of the pivot pin, a new pin will be required.

Whether you are replacing a broken lever or cleaning the old one, clean the inside of the lever assembly then lightly grease the pivot end of the lever. With both items clean, place the lever into its holder.

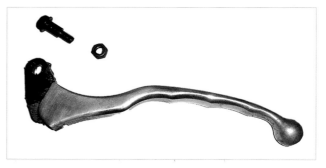

Screw the pivot pin back into the assembly and tighten it to its torque setting. This will be quite low as most of these pins have 6 mm threads. With the pin in place, hold the pin with one spanner or socket and tighten the nut on the underside of the lever holder.

5 Proper lubrication of the cables once a year, will ensure smooth operation. Damage to the outer covering of cables may allow the inner cable to rust, which will interfere with the smooth operation of the cable. Replace the cable if it is damaged and lubrication does not improve the situation.

Before lubing the cable, inspect the inner cable for signs of damage. Kinked or broken strands (even one strand) will mean that the cable MUST be replaced. The cable may snap at an inappropriate time or even become jammed. A broken front brake cable or a sticking throttle cable can lead to a very dangerous situation.

If your cable has a nylon liner, use graphite based grease.

HINT

If you need to replace the cable, do NOT remove the old cable without taking note of its routing. It is advised that you route the new cable alongside the old one or tie the upper end of the new cable to the lower end of the old cable to allow the new cable to be drawn into place as the old one is pulled free.

6 Fit the cable luber tool so that the outer cable is as far into the rubber sleeve as possible. Note that the rubber has two sizes of inner sleeve, one for clutch and brake cables and the other for throttle cables.

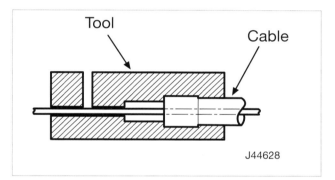

Fully tighten the screw, insert the spray pipe, fit the pipe to the spray can and operate the spray nozzle until lubricant can be seen coming from the other end of the cable. Stop and wipe off any excess lubricant.

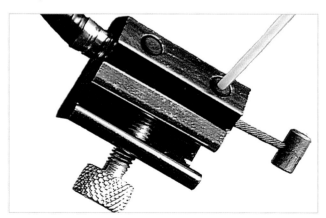

If the cable has not been lubricated for some time, it is very likely that the spray will not penetrate to the end of the cable. This is because dirt and corrosion has entered the cable, and this can normally be felt as a stiff lever action.

7 If the cable is still sticking, it will be necessary to detach the cable from its lower end (from the clutch or front brake, as applicable) and work the inner cable back and forth whilst holding the outer cable.

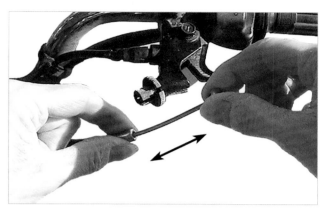

Reconnect the lower end of the cable to the clutch or front brake, as applicable.

8 Pull the inner cable out of the outer cable as far as it will go and grease the exposed inner cable and barrel end.

9 Ensure that the adjuster and lock ring have their slots lined up with the slot in the lever assembly. Fit the barrel into the lever ensuring that the cable is fitted into the slots and that the end of the outer cable is fitted close to the lock ring (as shown).

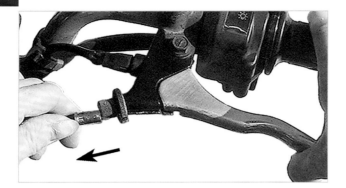

Holding the outer cable with one hand, gently operate the handlebar lever with the other hand. Once the lever has reached the handlebar, slowly release the lever and pull the outer cable away from the adjuster. As the cable is pulled away from the adjuster, slide the end cap into the adjuster.

10 With the cable fitted, adjust the cable freeplay as described in Chapter 3, Section 7 for the clutch cable, or Section 13 of this Chapter for the front brake cable.

Brake lever freeplay

In an hydraulic brake system, it is essential that there is freeplay between the front brake lever and the master cylinder piston. If there is no play between the lever and piston, the brake could seize on, locking the front wheel.

On the majority of machines, this setting is not adjustable, the necessary degree of freeplay having been built into the lever. If your machine has a screw and locknut it can be adjusted as follows:

1 Slacken the locknut (A).

2 Turn the screw (B) in to reduce freeplay or out to increase it. Refer to your workshop manual for the specified amount of freeplay.

3 Hold the screw (B) and tighten the locknut (A).

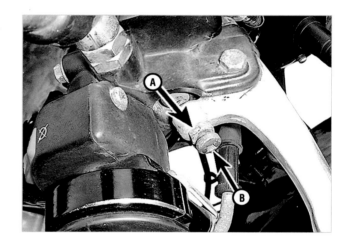

Lever span adjusters

To compensate for different size hands, some machines come with a means of positioning the lever closer to, or further from, the handlebar. There are many different types of adjuster. On the type shown the procedure is as follows:

1 Push the lever forwards, away from you and hold it in this position. This will allow the rod (A) to come out of its groove in the lever assembly.

2 The wheel has four separate positions with four different depths of groove. Turn the wheel to select a different groove, aligning the number on the wheel with the arrow (B).

3 Release the lever and 'wiggle' the wheel to ensure that the rod locates in its groove.

4 Check that the distance between the bar grips and levers allow a firm, un-stretched grasp of the lever.

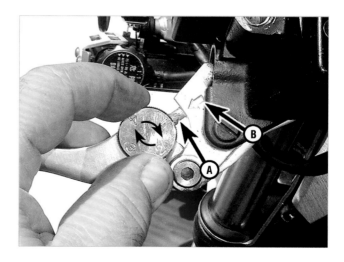

7   Front suspension maintenance

Technical – front forks

The basic telescopic front fork is a very simple device, consisting of a tube moving within a tube with a coil spring to absorb the bumps and ripples of the road. Oil damping of the spring's energy is used to prevent the spring oscillating causing the wheel to bounce along the road. This would lead to a very unpleasant ride and loss of traction.

All but basic front forks have a form of adjustment, but it is important to note that adjustment should only be made once everything has been checked and set to the manufacturer's original settings – what you decide works for you is a very personal decision. It is very easy to spend hours fiddling with the suspension settings only to make the ride and handling even worse. Remember that suspension settings which apply on a smooth race track will rarely give a good ride on a normal road. Carry out adjustment in a logical order as follows:

+ Set the suspension to the standard settings recommended by the manufacturer (see the owners manual).
+ Change the front fork oil.
+ Make minor suspension changes – do one thing at a time, see what the results are and act accordingly.
+ Have patience – this is a long, drawn out process that cannot be achieved overnight (unless you are extremely lucky)

One area that is often ignored is the quality and quantity of front fork oil used. As the miles 'clock up' the quality of the damping oil slowly deteriorates and the performance of the suspension suffers. This is such a slow process that it is only noticed when the oil is changed and full performance is restored.

Fork seal check

Periodically inspect the area around the front fork dust seal for signs of oil. If you find any then a fork seal has failed and will have to be replaced. Gently lever the dust seal off the fork slider to inspect the area directly above the oil seal.

layer of the steel tube (whether chrome or titanium), leading to corrosion then pitting and flaking of the surface. The resultant sharp edges tear the seal lips as the fork works over bumps and ripples, leading to oil loss.

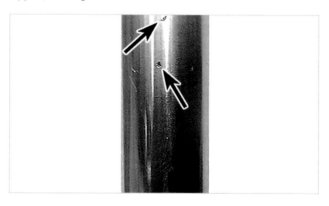

Fork oil seeping from the seal (due to the pumping action of the forks) will reduce the amount of oil in the fork, adversely affecting the damping characteristics.

Depending on the complexity of the fork, seal replacement can be straightford or require special tools. Refer to your workshop manual for the procedure or leave the job to a dealer.

Fork seals are sold in pairs and it is a false economy to replace one seal without replacing both of them. When replacing a seal the fork oil will be replaced as well. Both forks should have the seals and oil changed at the same time.

One cause of failed fork seals is pitting of the fork stanchions. Stones which fly up off the road surface damage the protective

Inspect the few inches of fork stanchion directly above the dust seal. This is the working area of the fork and must be perfectly smooth.

Note that replacing the fork seals without doing something about the pitted fork stanchions will be a waste of money, as the seals will soon fail a second time. To remedy this problem have the stanchion replaced or re-chromed; both are very expensive. A cheaper option is to degrease the pits and fill them with Araldite smoothed off with the old fork seal.

> **HINT**
>
> Fitting fork gaiters to the stanchions will prevent damage from stone chips. See Chapter 6 for details.

Fork oil change (with fork removed)

Note: *This procedure applies to forks which are non-adjustable or to forks which have pre-load adjustment only. Forks with rebound damping adjustment have a complex method of securing the fork top cap to the damping adjustment rod inside the fork and usually require a special tool to compress the fork spring whilst the two components are separated; reference should be made to the appropriate workshop manual for specific information.*

Items required

- ✔ Sufficient fork oil of the correct grade. 5W, 10W, 15W etc. Be guided by your workshop manual or dealer recommendations.
- ✔ Jug and funnel
- ✔ Variety of sockets, spanners and torque wrench
- ✔ Steel rule
- ✔ Fork oil level gauge (see Chapter 1, Section 8)
- ✔ A box to hold small, removed parts

HINT

Some machines, particularly older models, have an oil drain screw at the bottom of the fork leg to enable the oil to be drained without removing the forks. Note, however, that the screw is often difficult to remove and if the oil has not been changed for some time, it may have formed a sludge which is impossible to drain fully. It is preferable that the forks are removed from the machine and the oil changed as described below. However, a procedure is given at the end of this section for draining the oil via the drain screw.

Procedure

1 If the forks have preload adjusters, set the preload adjuster (arrow) on both forks to the SOFTEST setting. Refer to the owner's manual for details, but this usually involves rotating the preload adjuster fully anti-clockwise.

2 Note the position of the forks relative to the top yoke BEFORE you dismantle anything. The fork shown in the bottom left photo is almost flush with the top yoke, but on other models the top surface of the fork may be raised above the top yoke.

3 Remove the front brake caliper(s), front wheel and mudguard to enable the forks to be removed. Note which side the wheel spindle is fitted through. If a split pin is used to secure the spindle nut, replace it with a NEW split pin on rebuild.

With the brake caliper(s) removed, place a piece of cardboard between the brake pads to prevent them falling out and to ensure that they do not completely close if the brake lever is inadvertently operated. Tie a piece of electrical wire or string to the caliper(s) and hang it from the bottom yoke. This prevents any strain on the brake hose that the weight of the caliper will impart.

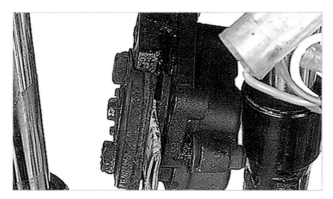

If a drum front brake is fitted, it will be necessary to fully unscrew the front brake cable adjuster (A). With the adjuster removed, pull the cable from its stop on the brake backplate (B) and reassemble the spring and cover, trunnion (small round item usually left in the brake arm) and adjuster onto the cable.

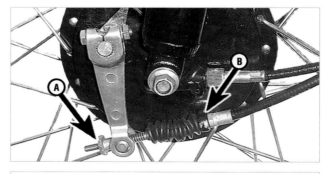

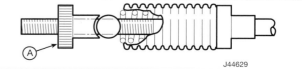

It is recommended that the fuel tank is removed to prevent expensive damage should a tool slip. If the machine has a fairing, you may want to consider removing it to improve access to the fork clamps in the yokes.

4 Always work on ONE FORK AT A TIME to avoid parts getting mixed up. Once you have completed the work on one fork, replace it BEFORE starting work on the other.

5 Slacken BOTH of the fork top caps whilst they are held in the fork yokes. DO NOT completely unscrew these caps at this stage, just slacken them. If you remove a top cap the spring tension will be released when you are not expecting it. Where the fork top caps are obscured by the handlebars, first remove the handlebars as described in the previous section.

If the forks are fitted flush to the top yoke it may be necessary to slacken the top yoke clamp bolts before slackening the fork caps. Keeping the lower yoke clamp bolt tight will hold the fork stanchion (the fork component that is clamped to the yokes) tight and prevent the stanchion revolving when you slacken the fork top cap.

Once the fork top cap has been slackened, the lower yoke clamp bolt can be slackened; only slacken the bolt for the fork you are working on at this time. Note that some machines have decorative covers fitted over the lower yoke, which will have to be removed first.

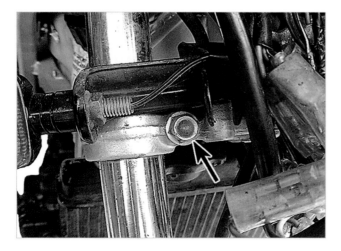

Now slacken the top yoke clamp bolt, again only on the side you are working on.

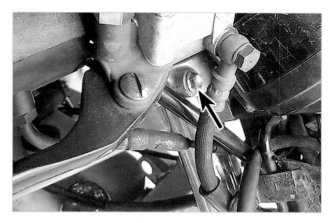

6 Having slackened the top and lower yoke clamp bolts, the fork can be slid downwards out of the yokes. The fork is usually a tight fit in the yokes and twisting it whilst pulling downwards will usually get it to move. If it doesn't want to move check that you have slackened the clamp bolts sufficiently.

✦ DO NOT hit the top of the fork leg as this will only damage the very fine thread of the fork cap – check that all components have been removed.
✦ DO NOT pry the yoke clamps further apart with a screwdriver or any other device, you will only damage an expensive component and you may injure yourself in the process.

Where separate handlebar assemblies are fitted, the handlebar assembly must be removed (if above the top yoke) or its clamp slackened (if mounted below the fork yoke). In the example shown, the handlebar clamp bolt has been slackened and the fork slid slightly upwards through the top yoke to allow removal of handlebar retaining circlip. The circlip was removed using a small flat-bladed screwdriver and a lot of care to prise it out of the groove.

On many small machines, the forks are held in the top yoke by the fork top caps rather than by clamp bolts. On this type of top yoke undo the top cap and remove it and its washer for

BOTH forks BEFORE slackening the lower yoke clamp bolt for ONE leg.

On this particular machine there is a thick rubber 'O' ring in the top of the fork leg. This may stick to the underside of the top yoke as you slide the leg down. Remove the ring, put it in your parts box and remember to refit it on the rebuild.

7 With the fork leg removed from the machine, you can now unscrew the fork cap. If you previously set any spring pre-load to the softest setting, the spring will not put too much force on the cap as you undo it. Take care as you undo the last turn or two, as the spring will still 'pop up' slightly when the cap is removed.

8 Remove any spacer, washer and the spring and note the way they are fitted, particularly the spring. If necessary make notes as an aid to reassembly.

9 Invert the fork over a jug and drain the oil into it. Pumping the fork will help to expel the oil quickly. Empty the jug then leave the fork upside down in the jug to drain fully.

10 While you are waiting for the fork to drain, clean the spacer (where fitted), washer and spring.

Measure the spring length and note it down so that you can compare it with the spring in the other fork leg. If you have a workshop manual you can also compare the length of both springs with the service limit specified by the manufacturer. If one spring is outside the tolerance, the springs must be

replaced as a pair. Fork springs will sag over a period of time and reduce in length from their nominal lengths when new.

Note the closer wound coils at one end of the spring photographed. This is a dual-rate spring and the close wound coils will close up first when you ride over a bumpy surface. When installing this type of spring, the open wound coils should usually be fitted first leaving the close wound end towards the top of the fork. Some manufacturers, however, fit the springs the other way round so it is important to check your workshop manual for the correct fitting. Whichever way they are fitted, it must be the **same** for both forks.

11 Refer to your workshop manual for the fork oil type, quantity and level. A typical recommendation might be 10W fork oil, 382 ml per leg, 99 mm from the top of the stanchion with the fork fully compressed. This information will differ for every model, so it is essential to establish the correct data for your machine.

It is almost impossible to measure the amount of oil accurately using home workshop equipment. What is more important, however, is that the oil in each leg is at the same level.

12 Using the fork oil level gauge described in Chapter 1 is the best method of ensuring the forks are filled to the correct level. If the tool is available, measure into a jug slightly more oil than is recommended by the manufacturer. In the above example measure out 390 to 400 ml and fill the leg.

Push the stanchion FULLY DOWN into the slider. With the tool adjusted to the correct figure (99 mm in the above example), insert the tool and draw out the excess oil.

13 If a fork oil tool isn't available, measure out the fork oil quantity as accurately as possible and pour the oil into the fork.

Use a steel rule or length of welding rod inserted into the top of the stanchion to measure the oil level. Add or subtract oil until the level is correct.

14 With the fork oil at the correct level, pull the stanchion as far out of the slider as it will go. Fit the spring into the fork with the close wound coils uppermost (or as found on dismantling – see earlier note). Fit the top-hat washer and any spacer. This will leave the spacer/spring slightly proud of the top of the stanchion.

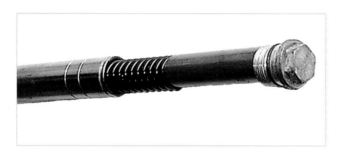

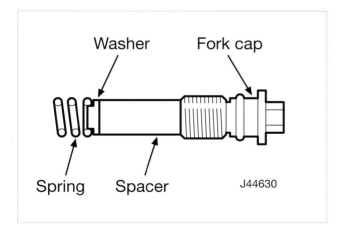

Washer   Fork cap

Spring   Spacer   J44630

15 The fork top cap is made from an aluminium alloy and has a very fine thread. Before fitting it:

✦ Use a light oil spray such as WD40 and an old clean toothbrush to clean the threads of old oil or dirt. Even the small amount shown (arrow) will cause problems.

✦ Check the condition of the rubber 'O' ring and replace it if it is damaged.

✦ Lubricate the 'O' ring with fresh fork oil to prevent it catching and tearing when the cap is screwed home.

The thread on the fork top cap is very fine and it is very easy to cross-thread it when you are fitting it. Provided you have thoroughly cleaned the thread it should not be a problem to fit.

Lubricate the threads with clean fork oil and holding the stanchion firmly fit a socket and ratchet on the fork top cap head. Push downwards to compress the spring and keep the fork top cap square to the stanchion whilst carefully screwing the cap into the stanchion.

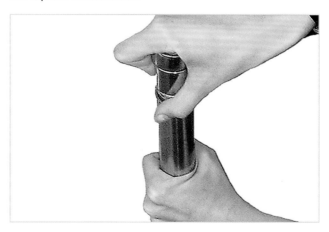

The top cap will be relatively easy to screw into the stanchion, but if it starts to bind STOP, undo the cap and start again. If you damage the thread, you will need a new top cap.

16 Before refitting the fork leg in the yokes, pump the leg 5 or 6 times to distribute its damping oil.

17 Clean the inside of the top and bottom yoke clamps and slide the fork back into the yokes. If the insides of the clamps are heavily corroded, use 400 to 600 'Wet and Dry' paper to clean them.

18 Line up the fork in the yokes. On the motorcycle photographed, which has separate handlebar assemblies positioned above the top yoke, a groove in the stanchion must be flush with the top of the top yoke. On other machines, where the handlebar is mounted via clamps, the top of the stanchion is usually fitted flush with the top yoke – see your workshop manual for details.

19 Tighten the top yoke clamp bolt to the recommended torque setting, followed by the lower clamp bolt and finally the fork top cap.

Where separate left and right handlebar assemblies are fitted (such as on the machine photographed), it is now necessary to fit the handlebar to the fork. Secure the handlebar by fitting the clip and tightening the Allen headed clamp bolt to the recommended torque setting. Whether the handlebar is mounted above or under the top yoke, there will be some method of keying it in place to ensure that it is fitted at the correct angle.

20 Re-check that you have not left anything loose, strip out the other fork and repeat the process of oil change, rebuild and re-assembly.

21 Refit the mudguard, wheel and brake caliper or cable (as applicable), noting the following points:

22 Fit the speedometer drive into the wheel BEFORE fitting the wheel into the forks. Make sure that the lugs in the wheel (arrows) fit in the spaces on the drive unit. If you don't do this, it is likely that both sets of lugs will lie on top of each other causing damage.

To prevent the speedometer drive from spinning round the wheel, when the brake is applied, some form of stop is provided. This speedometer drive mechanism has a slot built into it which locates in a small abutment cast into the fork leg. Whatever system is used on your machine, ensure that the assembly is correctly fitted BEFORE you tighten the wheel spindle.

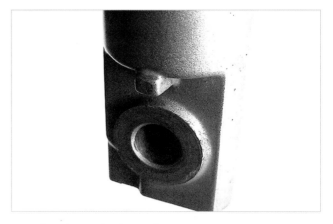

23 When fitting the front wheel, note that not all machines have a front wheel spindle which passes through holes in the forks. Some have the spindle clamped to the forks via lower clamp pieces (just like handlebars) which located over studs in the ends of the forks; nuts with plain and spring washers secure the clamps. Where clamps are used, note the following before fitting them:

✦ The asymmetrical type clamp (see photo) is fitted with its wider end facing forwards. Fit the clamp so that the gap is at the rear of the clamp and tighten the front nut until it is finger-tight. Tighten the rear nut but leave it slightly loose. Switch to the other fork and repeat this process. Now tighten both FRONT nuts to their correct torque settings followed by the two REAR nuts. This will leave the gaps at the rear as shown.

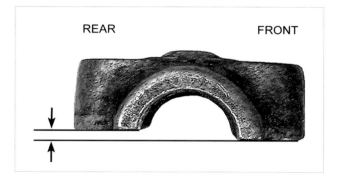

REAR   FRONT

✦ The symmetrical type clamp (both ends of equal thickness) is fitted so that there is an EQUAL gap at the front and rear of the fork leg.

Clean the wheel spindle, removing any corrosion with fine

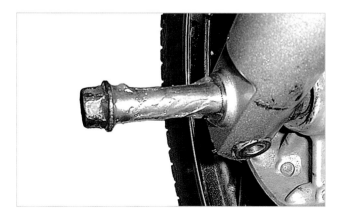

grade 'Wet and Dry' paper, and give the spindle a coating of general-purpose grease before fitting it. Clean off any excess grease when the spindle has been tightened.

Many machines have a spindle without a locking nut. Instead the spindle screws into the opposite fork leg.

Once the spindle has been tightened to its correct torque setting, a clamp bolt is used to lock the spindle and prevent it coming loose. A small amount of general purpose or copper grease, on the non-threaded portion of the bolt will reduce corrosion. This will make later removal of the bolt that much easier.

24 After fitting the front wheel assembly and before tightening the wheel spindle, nut or clamps:

✦ Slacken the bottom yoke screws/bolts and the steering stem nut.
✦ Remove any cardboard placed between the brake pads and slide the caliper(s) back over the brake disc(s). Refit the caliper bolts.
✦ Apply and hold the front brake, compress then release the front suspension (bounce the forks) about six times. This will align the forks and yokes.
✦ Tighten the steering stem nut and then the bottom yoke bolts, finishing with the wheel spindle.

25 Some machines have a specific sequence for tightening the front wheel spindle. This ensures that the brake calipers do not foul the brake discs. Check with your owners or workshop manual to see if your machine has this requirement.

26 Use a NEW split pin (where fitted) for the wheel spindle nut and check that nuts/bolts are tightened correctly.

27 Check that the speedometer is working by spinning the wheel BEFORE you take to the road.

28 Where a drum front brake is fitted, adjust the brake then apply and hold the brake on while you tighten the wheel spindle nut. This action will centralise the brake shoes giving you the best action that can be obtained from this type of brake.

Fork oil change (via drain screw)

Where drain screws are fitted in the base of the fork sliders, the fork oil can be changed without removing the forks from the machine. Note that this is not always desirable – see Note at the beginning of the main *Fork oil change* procedure.

1 Position the machine on its centrestand, or on a paddock

stand if only a sidestand is fitted. Place a support under the crankcase so that all weight is off the front wheel.

2 Working on one fork leg at a time, unscrew the fork top bolt. Take GREAT CARE as the top bolt is unscrewed because it will be under tension from the fork spring and may be forcibly released once the last threads are unscrewed.

3 Place a jug or other type of container under the fork leg and have a piece of card ready to act as a chute to direct the oil into the container. Remove the drain screw and washer from one fork leg and allow the oil to drain into the container.

4 Hold the front brake on and GENTLY compress the forks to expel the last drops of oil. Avoid rapid compression of the forks because this will cause the oil to spurt out.

5 Leave to drain for a few minutes. When fully drained, refit the drain screw and washer, then fill the fork with the correct type and quantity of oil.

6 Refit the fork cap and tighten it to the specified torque setting.

7 Repeat the process on the other fork leg.

Link type front suspension

This type of front fork is mainly found on the 'step-thru' type of machine and certain scooters. Carry out this task at major service intervals (4000 miles) or every six months, whichever comes first.

Items required

✔ Variety of sockets, spanners, screwdrivers and a torque wrench.
✔ Multi purpose grease, cleaning cloths and 'wet & dry' abrasive paper.

Procedure

1 Remove any covers to gain access to the wheel spindle (A) and

link pins (B). First, remove the speedometer drive (C) and the brake adjuster (D) and cable before removing the wheel spindle and wheel. Note that this is an ideal time to clean and lubricate the speedometer drive cable and service the front brake.

2 To test the link pins (bearings), grasp the end of the link (at the wheel spindle end) and try to move it from side to side. There should be virtually no sideways play, but the link must be free to move up and down.

If there is excessive play the bearings/bushes will need to be replaced. This will necessitate a visit to your local dealer.

3 Undo the nuts holding the pivot bolts and remove any bushes (A). Note the way that the bolts have been fitted. In most cases, they are fitted with the head of the bolt facing in towards the wheel.

The rubber bush (B) should only be removed if it is to be replaced. This will require special tools and techniques to remove and replace it.

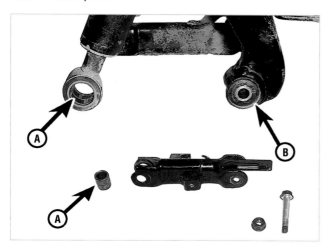

4 Clean all the components and grease the pivot bolt(s) and bushes. Reassemble the link arm and components, clean off any excess grease and repeat the process for the other arm.

5 When both arms have been serviced, hold the pivot bolt head

with a suitable spanner and tighten the nut to its torque setting. Repeat this for the other arm.

6 Fit the brake backplate into the wheel, position the wheel between the link arms and locate the lug on one of the link arms in the slot in the brake backplate, then fit the wheel spindle and nut. Do not tighten the spindle nut yet; two or three turns will be sufficient for the moment.

7 Before fitting the speedometer cable, gently spin the wheel and make sure that the speedometer drive is fully engaged (see section 11 – the speedometer cable). Fit the speedometer cable (C) then fit and adjust the brake cable (D).

8 Hold the front brake on whilst tightening the wheel spindle to its correct torque setting.

---

8   Suspension checks and adjustment

Suspension checks

Motorcycle suspension systems consist of springs to absorb the bumps in the road and hydraulic (oil) damping to control the spring oscillations. Simple machines have damping that is the same for both the compression and rebound strokes whereas sports and larger machines have separate damping for both compression and rebound strokes.

The bump stroke (compression stroke) is when you hit a bump or ripple in the road surface and the suspension is compressed.

The rebound stroke (extension stroke) is when the wheel has travelled over the bump and the suspension extends to its normal position.

Front suspension check

1 Take the machine off its stand.

2 Grip the handlebars and push downwards to compress the

suspension. Still holding the bars, allow the suspension to return to its normal position.

3 If the suspension is working correctly, the machine will return to the normal position reasonably quickly, give one small bounce then settle into its normal position. If the suspension continues to bounce then the damping has failed. Change the oil in the forks or in the case of link type front suspension **both** suspension units.

4 On telescopic forks look for signs of oil seeping past the seals, which indicates that the fork seals have failed. The machine photographed, with upside down (USD) forks, has a ring of oil around the stanchion, indicating that the seal on this leg has failed. The fork seals in both forks should be replaced; refer to your workshop manual for details. Do not leave it for too long or the handling will rapidly deteriorate.

Rear suspension check

1 With the machine off its stand, have a friend support the machine by holding the front handlebars.

2 Place both hands on the seat (over the rear wheel) and firmly press down on the rear of the machine. Push the rear of the machine as far down as you can, then let go off the seat.

3 If the suspension is working correctly, the machine will return to the normal position reasonably quickly, give one small bounce then settle into its normal position. If the suspension continues to bounce, the damping has failed. The shock (or both shocks on a twin shock system) must be replaced.

4 Check the shock for signs of oil leakage where the damper rod enters the main body of the damper. Also check for bending of or corrosion on the damper rod, which would cause the damper seals to wear and lead to oil loss. Check for damage to the damper body.

Front suspension adjustment

Front forks will either have no adjustment whatsoever, pre-load adjustment, or on the most sophisticated models, pre-load, rebound damping and compression damping adjustment. It is essential that the adjustment settings are the **same on both** forks.

Spring pre-load

Pre-load adjustment controls how much the springs compress (sag) under the machine's weight. Use an open-ended spanner or a socket (where possible) to adjust the pre-load. Measure the height of the adjuster or use the grooves on its body as a guide. Always set both pre-load adjusters to the same height.

The standard setting for the ZXR400 photographed is 16 mm (6.5 grooves).

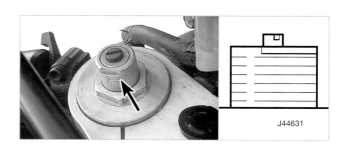

J44631

Pos.	Spring	Setting	Load	Road	Speed
20 mm	Weak	Soft	Light	Good	Low
↕	↕	↕	↕	↕	↕
5 mm	Stronger	Hard	Heavy	Poor	High

Rebound damping

Rebound damping adjustment controls the rate at which the forks extend after they have been compressed.

This machine has different characteristics for rebound damping which can be varied by turning the screw set in the centre of the pre-load adjuster (arrowed). Adjustment is made by turning the screw fully clockwise then back to the required position via a series of 'clicks' or a specific number of turns.

Pos.	Damping	Setting	Load	Road	Speed
12 ↑	Weak ↑	Soft ↑	Light ↑	Good ↑	Low ↑
↓ 0	↓ Stronger	↓ Hard	↓ Heavy	↓ Poor	↓ High

Compression damping

Compression damping adjustment controls the rate at which the spring compresses when a bump in the road is struck or the brakes are applied. Adjustment is made by turning the screw at the bottom of the fork (arrowed) and can be via a series of 'clicks' or by turning the screw by a number of degrees. Turn the screw in until it seats, then out to the specified position.

Pos.	Damping	Setting	Load	Road	Speed
7 – 9 ↑	Weak ↑	Soft ↑	Light ↑	Good ↑	Low ↑
↓ 1	↓ Stronger	↓ Heavy	↓ Heavy	↓ Poor	↓ High

Rear suspension adjustment

Twin shock suspension

This type of spring pre-load adjuster is very common on machines that use twin rear shocks. The pre-load can be changed by turning the adjuster with a 'C' spanner so that a different slot sits on the peg.

The owner's manual will give a standard setting for pre-load, although experimentation will allow you to find a setting that is suitable for you. As a 'rule of thumb', the least amount of pre-load is for solo riding whereas the maximum pre-load is for riding with a passenger/luggage.

To ensure good handling and stability, it is essential that both suspension units are set to the same pre-load setting.

HINT

Note that changing the spring pre-load will not change the spring rate. Spring rate is measured by the amount of force required to move (close) the spring by a set amount. For example, a spring rated as 90 lbs/inch would require a force of 90 lbs to close it by 1 inch, 180 lbs to close it 2 inches.

Monoshock rear suspension

A monoshock usually has pre-load and rebound damping adjustment, with the more sophisticated units also having compression damping adjustment.

Spring preload on most models is adjusted by a stepped collar which is turned using a 'C' spanner. A suitable 'C' spanner is usually provided in the machine's toolkit.

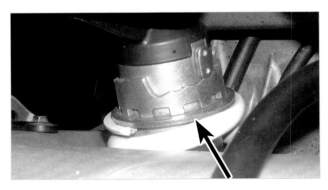

An alternative pre-load adjuster consists of two threaded rings on the shock body. To make adjustment, slacken the top (locking ring) and then adjust the spring pre-load with the second (adjuster) ring. Use a large 'C' spanner to make the adjustment.

Manufacturers usually specify pre-load settings as a dimension, which is a measurement of the length of the compressed spring measured from spring collar to spring collar. Don't forget to tighten the locking ring against the adjuster ring after making adjustment.

Rebound and compression damping adjusters usually take the form of slotted head screw adjusters. Their settings are usually expressed in the 'number of turns out' or 'number of clicks' from the fully turned in position. Most units have a label or inscription alongside to indicate which way to turn the adjuster (S and H are commonly used to indicate Soft and Hard).

Refer to the owners manual for standard settings recommended by the manufacturer. These settings will usually be shown as a table. Where the front and rear suspension is adjustable, the table will give recommendations for compatible front/rear settings to suit solo and pillion riding.

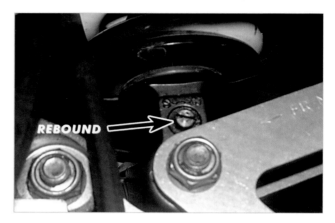

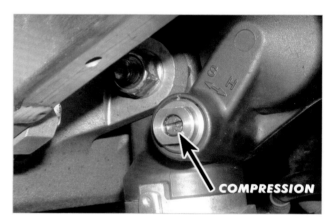

9 Rear suspension maintenance

Twin shock rear suspension units

Each unit should be removed (in turn) and the pivot points greased once a year.

1 Undo the nuts/bolts that secure one suspension unit then remove it.

2 Clean and grease the pivot points and inspect the rubber bush in the eyelet(s). Some machines have bushes in both the top and bottom eyelets, other types have a bush in the top eyelet only. If

the bushes have deteriorated then it is probable that the suspension unit will also have failed, although new rubber bushes can usually be purchased separately. Note that suspension units must always be replaced as a pair, never singly.

3 If all is ok, refit the unit, tighten the nuts/bolts and then repeat for the other unit.

4 Single-sided units, fitted to scooters, can be difficult to remove and fit as the engine unit weighs on the suspension. Use a couple of pieces of wood inserted between the rear wheel and ground as shown, to take the weight of the engine unit when removing/fitting the suspension unit.

Monoshock rear suspension systems

Checking for pivot bearing wear

1 Place the machine on its centrestand or support it (via the engine) so that the rear wheel is off the ground and the swinging arm is free to move.

2 Grasp each leg of the swinging arm, as close to the rear wheel spindle as is possible and lift up, then push down on the swinging arm.

3 There should be no movement of the swinging arm without a corresponding movement of the suspension unit.

If a 'clicking' can be heard or felt the bushes/bearings are probably worn.

Re-greasing the rear suspension

This should be done every two years to keep the system in good working order. This can be quite a long job so allow at least half a day to complete this task.

The machine shown in the accompanying photographs has the top bush of its suspension unit connected to the frame with the lower bush connected to a rocker arm. There are many variations but most machines have a similar set up.

1 Remove the rear wheel (see Section 2 of this Chapter).

2 Undo the bolt securing the top of the suspension unit to the frame.

HINT

There will be a number of different sized bolts used. Remove each bolt and replace it in the frame/rocker arm so that you won't lose it or fit it in the wrong place on the rebuild.

3 Moving to the underside of the machine it will be necessary to slacken each of the following (see photo overleaf):

✔ Suspension unit to rocker arm mounting (A).
✔ Suspension arms to frame mounting (B).
✔ Suspension arms to rocker mounting (C).
✔ Rocker arm to swinging arm mounting (D).

Now remove the bolts holding the suspension arms to the frame (B) and the rocker arm to the swinging arm (D) and lower the assembly out of the machine.

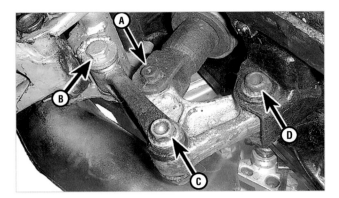

4 Strip the nuts/bolts from the component parts and lay them out for cleaning and greasing. Note the positioning of the suspension unit on the rocker arm before separating them.

Clean any corrosion from the pivot bolt shafts and, if necessary, use a thread file (see Chapter 1) to repair any thread damage. Replace any bolts which are in a poor condition.

Push out each bearing inner sleeve in turn and wipe off the old grease. Use kitchen paper or a clean cloth to 'pull through'

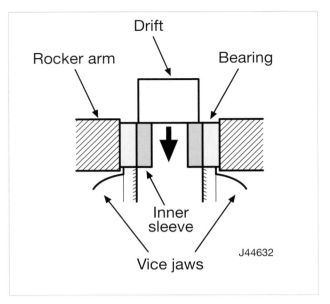

J44632

each bearing. If this task has not been done for some time, it may be necessary to GENTLY drive each inner sleeve out of the bearing.

Check the fit of each inner sleeve in its bearing. If there is significant movement between the two components, the bearing should be replaced. The bearings are a tight fit and will require pressing out using a drawbolt tool.

5 Apply fresh grease to the bearings and insert their inner sleeves.

6 Clean the bearing end caps and check the condition of the rubber seals. If they appear to be damaged, replace them with new ones. These are important items as they help to keep grease in and dirt out. Refit each end cap to its respective bearing end to ensure that they are a good fit. Different sized end caps may be fitted, so do not get them mixed up.

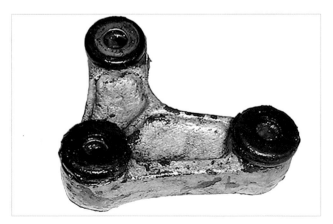

7 As an alternative to end caps with rubber seals, some machines use narrow oil seals which are a press fit in the rocker arm casting, and locate each side of the bearing. They can be carefully prised out with a large flat-bladed screwdriver.

8 Grease the shanks of ALL pivot bolts before fitting them, and put one drop of locking agent on each thread before fitting the nuts.

9 Offer up the suspension arms (with the end caps fitted) to the frame mount. Fit the bolt and nut and tighten it finger-tight only at this time. Check that the arms swing freely. If it is too tight, remove and disassemble it and try again.

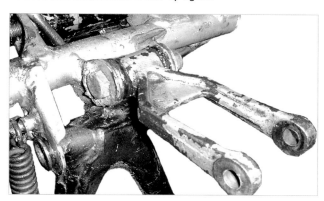

10 Connect the suspension unit to the rocker arm and fit its bolt and nut finger-tight only. Check that the unit can swing freely on the rocker arm and that it is positioned the right way round.

11 Push the suspension unit up through the frame and offer up

the rocker arm to the swinging arm mount. Fit the rocker arm to swinging arm mount bolt and nut and tighten this finger-tight as well. Check that the rocker arm can swing freely in the swinging arm mount.

12 Finally fit the last two end caps and connect the suspension arms to the centre bolt hole on the rocker arm. Fit its bolt and nut finger-tight only.

13 Move to the top of the suspension unit and fit the pre-greased top bolt. It may be necessary to 'wiggle' the swinging arm to ensure that the top of the suspension unit lines up with its mounting point.

14 The manufacturer may specify a sequence for tightening the bolts/nuts to their correct torque setting. See your workshop manual for details. On the machine photographed, the pivot bolt nuts are tightened in the sequence 1 to 4.

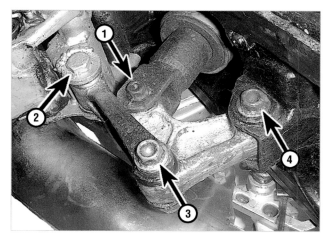

15 Check the action of the suspension system, then refit the rear wheel, check and adjust the chain tension, wheel alignment and brakes.

10 Tyres and tyre changing

Tyres – technical

Over the years, tyre technology has advanced with machine improvements with tyres being an integral part of the handling and suspension of a modern motorcycle.

Tyres are designated by their size description (A) which represents the nominal tyre width, the aspect ratio, the identification letter for the type of tyre and the rim diameter, and by their service description (B), which is the load index and speed symbol.

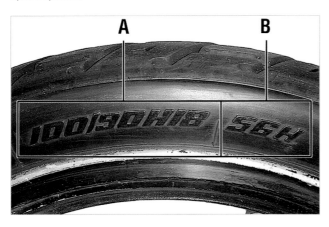

+ The first figure (100) refers to the nominal tyre width in millimetres. Some tyres are still quoted in inches e.g. 3.25 – H18.
+ The second figure (90) is the aspect ratio. This is the tyre's section height as a percentage of its width, e.g. tyre height = 90% of tyre width.
+ The third figure is the speed index; the 'H' denotes that this tyre is rated for speeds up to 130 mph. See later section for speed and load ratings.
+ The 18 refers to the wheel rim diameter in inches.
+ The fifth figure (56) is the load index (LI), which corresponds to the maximum load for the tyre at its maximum speed. If the tyre has MC in small letters between the wheel diameter and load index figure, this merely relates to it being for motorcycle rather than car use.

Tyre construction and design can be categorised as follows:

+ Diagonal design, formally known as 'conventional' tyres (cross-ply tyres) – these have a hyphen (-) in the size designation e.g. 3.50-18 or a single speed rating.
+ Diagonal-belted design, also known as bias-belted tyres – these have the letter B in their size description e.g. 150/80B16.

+ Radial design. This is the modern tyre fitted to many sports machines and has the letter R in its tyre description e.g. 150/70ZR17.

Speed index (SI) table

Z/ZR	speeds over 150 mph (240 km/h)
Y	speeds up to 187 mph (300 km/h)
W	speeds up to 168 mph (270 km/h)
V/VB	speeds up to 149 mph (240 km/h)
H	speeds up to 130 mph (210 km/h)
U	speeds up to 124 mph (200 km/h)
T	speeds up to 118 mph (190 km/h)
S	speeds up to 112 mph (180 km/h)
R	speeds up to 106 mph (170 km/h)
Q	speeds up to 100 mph (160 km/h)
P	speeds up to 93 mph (150 km/h)
N	speeds up to 87 mph (140 km/h)
M	speeds up to 81 mph (130 km/h)
L	speeds up to 74 mph (120 km/h)
K	speeds up to 68 mph (110 km/h)
J	speeds up to 62 mph (100 km/h)
G	speeds up to 56 mph (90 km/h)
F	speeds up to 50 mph (80 km/h)
E	speeds up to 44 mph (70 km/h)
D	speeds up to 40 mph (65 km/h)
C	speeds up to 37 mph (60 km/h)
B	speeds up to 31 mph (50 km/h)

 Warning: Do NOT fit a radial tyre to the front wheel with a cross-ply or bias-belted tyre on the rear wheel, not only is it dangerous, but in the UK it is illegal. It is also illegal to fit a bias-belted tyre to the front wheel with a cross-ply tyre on the rear wheel.

Important safety observations

When replacing a worn tyre match the replacement with the tyre still on the machine; this keeps the tyres as a matched pair. The rear tyre will usually last half the life of the front tyre, so ensure that when purchasing a new rear tyre it is compatible with the existing front tyre. If you want to change to a different

Load index (LI) table

Load index (LI) = maximum load and maximum speed. Kg = kilograms

LI	Kg	LI	Kg	LI	Kg	LI	Kg	LI	Kg	LI	Kg
0	45	21	82.5	42	150	63	272	84	500		
1	46.2	22	85	43	155	64	280	85	515		
2	47.5	23	87.5	44	160	65	290	86	530		
3	48.7	24	90	45	165	66	300	87	545		
4	50	25	92.5	46	170	67	307	88	560		
5	51.5	26	95	47	175	68	315	89	580		
6	53	27	97.5	48	180	69	325	90	600		
7	54.5	28	100	49	185	70	335	91	615		
8	56	29	103	50	190	71	345	92	630		
9	58	30	106	51	195	72	355	93	650		
10	60	31	109	52	200	73	365	94	670		
11	61.5	32	112	53	206	74	375	95	690		
12	63	33	115	54	212	75	387	96	710		
13	65	34	118	55	218	76	400	97	730		
14	67	35	121	56	224	77	412	98	750		
15	69	36	125	57	230	78	425	99	775		
16	71	37	128	58	236	79	437				
17	73	38	132	59	243	80	450				
18	75	39	136	60	250	81	462				
19	77.5	40	140	61	257	82	475				
20	80	41	145	62	265	83	487				

type of tyre, do this at the time both tyres are due for replacement.

When choosing what tyres to fit be guided by the motorcycle manufacture, tyre manufacturer or more importantly the tyre fitting company. All have a vast amount of knowledge relating to your machine and what tyres are suitable for it.

If your machine has Z/ZR tyres as standard, do NOT believe that just because you will never exceed the legal speed limits you can fit cheaper V or H rated tyres. Top speed is not the only factor influencing the choice of tyre, braking and acceleration forces play a big part in what construction your tyres have, and it is extremely dangerous to try to save a small amount of money on cheaper but unsuitable tyres. The tyres fitted must be capable of matching the speed of the machine.

Do NOT let the tread depth become so low that the tyre has virtually no tread pattern left. The tread pattern is necessary to remove water from under the tyre when it is raining and without it, there will be virtually no grip in the wet.

Tyre markings and construction

Some tyres have a weight mark painted on the tyre which can be a white or yellow dot, or a white or yellow ring. When the tyre is manufactured, it is made with an area that is slightly lighter than the rest of the tyre. This is to allow for the weight of the valve in the rim. When fitting the tyre, the mark should be placed next to the valve.

This gives some degree of wheel balance but you should get your wheels balanced professionally as soon as possible.

When tyres are manufactured, the base tread area is made in one piece, wrapped around the carcass, joined and cured. The tyre is then placed in a mould and the tread pattern injection moulded. There are two basic methods of joining the ends of the tread: the butt joint and the tapered joint.

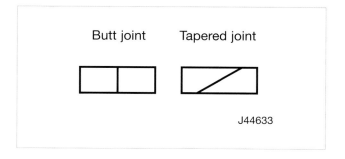

Butt joint   Tapered joint

J44633

The tapered joint has a longer area of contact and is stronger than the butt joint. There is one major disadvantage in that if the tyre is fitted in the wrong direction the tread may break at the joint under braking for the front wheel or acceleration of the rear wheel.

To overcome this the tyre manufacturers mould a directional arrow into the tyre wall. When fitting a tyre with this marking check the forward direction of the wheel and fit the tyre so that the arrow matches the wheel. The photograph shows a rear rotational arrow; there may be a front rotational arrow on the other side of the tyre where the tyre is of the 'dual fitment' type. Note that most tyres are either for front use only or rear use only.

Tyre changing (tubed tyre)

Changing a tyre requires technique, not great strength, and for scooters and small motorcycles this task can be easily undertaken by the owner. For larger motorcycles, where the aspect ratio is low (wide tyre, narrow walls) this task should be entrusted to the professionals. They have the specialist equipment needed to replace and balance these tyres.

The following procedure relates to the removal and fitting of a **tubed type tyre** and replacement of a punctured inner tube. **Do not** be tempted to remove a tubeless type tyre, not only does this require specialised equipment, but there is a risk of rim damage.

Items required

- ✔ Pair of tyre levers
- ✔ Wire brush, piece of chalk and NEW inner tube
- ✔ Valve core removing tool. These can be bought where one end is the tool and the other end is a valve cap
- ✔ Rim protectors or thick cardboard (especially if working on an alloy wheel)
- ✔ Tyre soap or weak solution of washing up liquid
- ✔ A couple of blocks of wood to support the wheel hub

Procedure

1 Place the wheel on the wood blocks so that the wheel hub is supported. Only one block was needed for this small scooter wheel.

2 Remove the valve cap and loosen the valve stem securing nut. Depress the centre of the valve core to release as much of the air pressure as possible. Undo and remove the valve core to deflate the tyre completely. Releasing the air pressure BEFORE removing the valve core prevents it 'flying' out and being lost, or even ending up in your eye!

3 If the tyre has been punctured, mark the tyre with chalk at the position next to the valve (this reference can be used later to identify the position of the puncture).

4 With the tyre deflated, push down on the tyre to force the tyre away from the bead seat area. Work your way around one side of the tyre then turn the tyre over and repeat for the other side.

5 Lubricate the bead area on both sides of the tyre with a tyre soap solution.

6 If working on a rear wheel, place the sprocket side downwards to prevent 'skinning' your knuckles.

7 Starting at the valve, place one lever under the tyre bead approximately one inch to the left of the valve. Place the second lever approximately one inch to the right of the valve. Make certain that the curved end of each lever is under the bead area. Note the use of the cardboard as rim protectors – dedicated plastic versions are available.

8 Pull back on the first lever to lift the tyre over the rim. Whilst holding it down, pull back on the second lever to lift more of the tyre over the rim. Holding the second lever down, remove the first lever by sliding it through 90° (whilst keeping it flat) until it comes out from under the tyre bead.

9 Now place this lever approximately three fingers width to the right of the existing lever and insert it under the tyre bead. Pull down on the lever to lift a bit more tyre over the rim. Continue this process until the tyre is off the rim on this side.

HINT

The trick is to take small 'bites' and not to try and remove too much tyre in one go.

10 With the tyre off the rim on one side, remove the valve securing nut and push the valve into the tyre. Pull the inner tube out of the tyre.

11 Place a tyre lever between the first rim and the second bead and push the tyre off and away from the wheel.

12 Use a stiff wire brush to clean any corrosion from the inside of the wheel. Pay special attention to the bead seat area, any rust or old rubber in this area will cause the tyre bead to be incorrectly seated. On wire spoked wheels it is important that the rim tape is in place over the spoke ends which protrude through the centre of the rim.

13 Inflate the inner tube and locate the puncture. A hissing can often be heard, and felt where the tyre is punctured. Failing that, laying the inflated tube in water will show the puncture point via a stream of bubbles.

14 Mark the puncture point on the tube by circling it with chalk. Now lay the tube on the tyre and line up the valve with the chalk mark on the tyre. Mark the tyre, with chalk, opposite the puncture point. Turn the tube over and mark the tyre again.

This will give two points on the tyre where whatever penetrated can be located. Inspect the inside and outside of the tyre at these two points by spreading the tyre walls and remove any nails, sharp pieces of steel etc.

15 On the grounds of safety, it is recommended that a punctured inner tube is replaced, rather than repaired. Equally, it is recommended that a new inner tube is fitted every time the tyre is renewed, even if the original tube is not punctured. Modern inner tubes are made from synthetic rubber and the old one would have taken the shape of the old tyre.

16 Slightly inflate the new inner tube and push it into the tyre, then remove the valve core.

17 Some tyres have a mark on the tyre wall that is used as a balance point. If the tyre has one of these, position this point next to the valve. Lubricate the bead areas on both sides of the tyre and push one side of the tyre over the rim lining up the balance point with the valve hole in the rim.

18 Feed the valve through the rim and secure it with either its cap or nut. If using the valve nut, turn it by only one or two turns. Do NOT tighten the nut fully yet.

19 Starting opposite the valve, push the second bead onto the rim.

20 Work as much of the tyre onto the rim by hand. Pushing the tyre into the rim well helps to get more of the tyre onto the rim. Use tyre levers to work the rest of the tyre over the rim.

21 When working the final area of tyre over the rim, push and hold the valve into the tyre slightly as you lever over the last piece of tyre. This will prevent trapping and 'nipping' of the tube, which is the major cause of punctures when fitting tyres.

22 Fit the valve core. Inflate the tyre ensuring that the beads 'pop' out onto their seating area. Do NOT over inflate the tyre. If you have cleaned the rim properly, the tyre should have seated before the correct tyre pressure is reached.

23 Clean the rim and bead area and check that the tyre is seated correctly. Most tyres have a line on the sidewall (arrowed) that should be the same distance from the rim all around the tyre. Check on both sides of the wheel.

24 If the distance between the rim and line is not identical, deflate the tyre, lubricate the bead area that has not moved onto its seat, then re-inflate the tyre and check again.

25 Adjust the tyre pressure, tighten the valve nut and fit the valve cap. Always have the wheel balanced after a new tyre has been fitted.

 When a new tyre has been fitted, full power should **NOT** be applied until the tyre has been 'scrubbed in'. This usually takes about 100 miles (160 km) of riding.

Tyre pressure check

Incorrectly inflated tyres can lead to uneven tread wear, poor handling and can in extreme cases cause an accident. It takes a few minutes to check the tyre pressures and this should be done before each ride. Tyre pressure should always be checked with the tyres COLD.

Pressure check

There are a variety of different tyre pressure gauges available, from the simple pencil type to electronic gauges with digital readouts. The dial type gauge shown in the photographs holds the reading even after you remove the gauge. Pressing the red button on its housing resets the gauge to zero.

1 Unscrew the valve cap. Zero the gauge then press it onto the valve ensuring that it fits squarely.

2 Remove the gauge and read the scale. The red scale reads in Kg/cm^2 (bar) whereas the black scale reads in lb/sq. in. (psi). Refit the valve cap and check the pressure in the other tyre.

Tyre inflation

Air pressure is measured in barometric pressure (bar), kilopascals (kPa), kilograms per centimetre squared (kg/cm^2), or pounds per square inch (psi). The latter is probably the measurement you will be most familiar with.

A typical gauge of a common tyre inflator as found on many garage forecourts is shown in the accompanying photograph. The thin red line across the gauge is the datum line and the red scale (on the left) is measured in bar with the black scale (on the right) in psi. Each red division equates to 0.2 bar with each black division equating to 2 psi. Note that a footpump and separate pressure gauge can be used as an alternative to the garage forecourt tyre inflator.

Neither over inflate nor under inflate your tyres. Apart from poor handling, over inflation will rapidly wear the centre portion of the tyre whereas under inflation rapidly wears out the edges of the tyre. Keeping your tyres at the recommended tyre pressures will give a comfortable ride, good handling and maximise tyre life.

1 Unscrew the valve cap. Before fitting the inflator depress its pressure lever for a few seconds to release a very short burst of air through the nozzle. This clears any dirt or grime that may be on the nozzle prior to inflating the tyre – point the nozzle away from you whist you do this.

2 Press the nozzle firmly onto the valve. If it is on squarely, no air will come out of the tyre. Hold the nozzle firmly onto the valve and fully depress the pressure lever to allow air to enter the tyre. Release the lever when the correct pressure is shown on its gauge.

3 Over-inflate the tyre, but only by a small amount. An example would be to inflate the tyre to 34 psi when a reading of 30 psi is required. These gauges appear to be more accurate when the pressure is being released rather than when being applied. Bring the tyre pressure DOWN to the correct reading by pressing the gauge lever HALFWAY down. At the halfway stage, the gauge releases air from the tyre instead of pumping it in.

Operating the lever (halfway down) in a series of short bursts will give better control and allow the correct reading to be easily obtained. When the correct reading has been obtained release the lever and remove the nozzle.

Note that tyre inflaters on garage forecourts have been known to be inaccurate. Where possible verify the tyre pressure with your own gauge.

4 Refit the valve cap. A valve cap should be fitted to both tyre valves at all times – it keeps dirt out of the valve and forms a secondary seal should the valve fail. Do NOT run your machine without the valve caps fitted because if the valve core fails, the cap could be the only thing saving you from a rapidly deflating tyre.

Tyre tread depth check

Local law will state a minimum tread depth that the tyre must have to be legal for the road. This is usually a lower figure than the tyre and motorcycle manufacturer will recommend. Most manufacturers recommend a minimum tread depth of 1.6 mm for the front tyre and 2 mm for the rear tyre, beyond which the handling may suffer.

Note that the tyre manufacturer usually provides wear indicator blocks in the tyre tread. When the surrounding area of tread wears down to the level of the block the tyre should be renewed. A symbol or TWI (tyre wear indicator) mark on the sidewall indicates where to look on the tread.

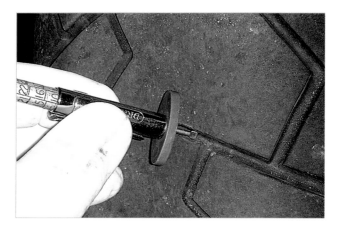

1 Place the tread depth gauge into the tyre groove at the point of greatest wear (usually the centre of the tread). Do not force the tool into the tyre; just let its flat end rest lightly in the bottom of the tyre groove.

2 Turn the tool so that it is at 90° to the tyre and press the tool flange (green part) against the tyre. Turn the scale until the end of the outer sleeve lines up with one of the marks on the scale and read off the depth of the tyre groove.

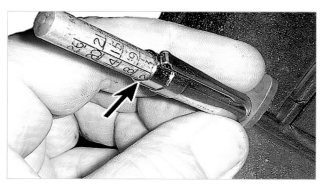

3 Repeat this process two or three times across the tyre and in approximately four places around the tyre. The smallest reading is the one to note.

4 Whilst checking the tread depth, inspect the tyre for any signs of damage and especially for any cuts in the tyre sidewall. If you find any cuts you are unsure about, take the bike to a tyre fitting shop or dealer where they will advise you.

---

11   Speedometer cable and drive

This section applies to cable-driven speedometers.

Speedometer cable

Lubricating the speedometer cable is a simple task that is often ignored, resulting in the cable breaking and the speedometer not working. Removing the cable inner, cleaning and coating it with light motor oil at major service intervals (or every 12 months) will keep it working for many years.

1 Disconnect the lower end of the speedometer cable, where it enters the drive unit on the front wheel. If a knurled ring retainer is fitted, slacken the ring (A) using pliers or a pipe wrench and pull the cable free. Watch out for a sealing 'O' ring (B) between the outer cable and drive unit (C).

Where a screw type fitting is used, remove the screw and pull the cable free of the drive unit. Note that this screw can prove very difficult to remove, especially if the wrong size screwdriver has been used previously and the screw head is damaged.

2 Draw the inner cable completely out of the outer cable. Pull the cable through a rag to wipe off all old oil and check for any damage or kinks in the cable.

3 Use a light mineral oil or WD40 to clean and lubricate the inner cable. A light coating is all that is required.

4 Before refitting the inner cable, inspect the cable plastic outer for damage, if necessary disconnecting it from the speedometer to allow full inspection. Slight damage can be repaired using heat shrink sleeve (see Chapter 1). If water gets into the cable, rust will cause the inner to corrode, become jammed and break.

5 Slide the inner cable into the outer and push it as far as it will go, giving the inner cable a twist to ensure that it locates into the speedometer head.

6 Locate the lower end of the cable in the drive unit, ensuring that its squared or forked end (as fitted) meshes corrected with the drive mechanism. Slowly rotate the front wheel to help them to engage.

7 Apply a smear of copper-based grease to the threads of the retaining ring or to the screw (as applicable) to ensure that it can be easily removed next time.

Speedometer drive

1 To inspect the speedometer drive unit, remove the front wheel and lift the drive out of the wheel hub (see Section 7).

2 Make sure that the speedometer drive is free to rotate by holding the body and turning the two lugs (A). While you are rotating the lugs, have a close look at the cable drive spigot (B) and ensure that this is also turning smoothly.

3 Clean any old, dirty grease from the unit using rag or a small, clean paintbrush and lightly repack the unit with fresh general-purpose grease.

4 When fitting the front wheel it is necessary to ensure that the speedometer drive 'ears' are correctly fitted into their slots. If this is not done the 'ears' will be damaged and there will be no drive between the wheel and drive unit.

5 Note the importance of aligning the speedometer stop when refitting the front wheel (see Section 7).

12   Disc (hydraulic) brakes

Fluid level check

The brake fluid level should be checked before each journey and also at each service. The fluid should be completely replaced every two years.

The brake fluid level will drop gradually as the pads wear and the caliper pistons move out to take up the space between the pads and disc. Fluid from the reservoir takes the place of the displaced pistons. If the fluid level drops rapidly, however, it is likely that a leak has occurred and this should be investigated immediately.

1 Keeping the bike upright, turn the handlebars so that the front brake master cylinder reservoir is parallel to the ground and check the fluid level through the sightglass in the side of the reservoir.

2 The brake fluid should be above the LOWER mark on the side

Brake fluid types and warning

Brake fluid is rated as DOT 3 and DOT 4 (mineral based) and DOT 5 (silicone based). DOT 4 is the usual recommendation for motorcycle use, but check the marking on the master cylinder cover and the owners manual for your machine.

DOT 3 and DOT 4 fluids are hygroscopic, meaning that they absorb water from the air, which lowers the boiling point. For this reason, new fluid added to the system should always come from a freshly opened container. The fluid will also damage paintwork so care should be taken to avoid fluid spills.

DOT 5 does not absorb water from the air, but care must still be taken to avoid water getting into the system.

NEVER mix brake fluid types – they are not compatible and can corrode the brake system. Always use the brake fluid type specified by the motorcycle manufacturer.

of the reservoir. Some machines have a plastic bodied reservoir which has UPPER and LOWER level lines – the brake fluid level should be between the two lines.

3 If the reservoir needs topping up, wrap a cloth around the master cylinder to prevent fluid getting on any paintwork, which would ruin it. Place a thick cloth over the fuel tank.

4 Undo the two screws holding the cover in place. Plastic-bodied reservoirs usually have a screw type cap, occasionally with a tamper-proof clamp to lock it in place.

5 Remove the cover and rubber diaphragm and add the specified type of brake fluid until it is level with the upper mark cast inside the reservoir, or on plastic-bodied reservoirs until it lies between the two level lines. Do not overfill.

6 Check the condition of the rubber diaphragm. It should have no tears or breaks, if it is damaged replace it.

7 The level of fluid in the rear master cylinder should be checked and topped up as described above for the front master cylinder.

Pad condition check

1 Some calipers have a cover that must be removed to allow inspection of the pad thickness. Lever the cover off to gain access. Note that the outside of the cover has writing on it; make sure that this is facing outside when the cover is replaced.

2 The amount of pad wear can be checked by inspecting the pad thickness.

Some manufacturers have a wear line or cut-out (arrowed) built into the pad friction material; others quote a minimum pad thickness. The wear line is usually 1 mm thick and 1 mm from the metal backplate, giving a minimum thickness of 2 mm. If the pads are worn to this line, replacement is required.

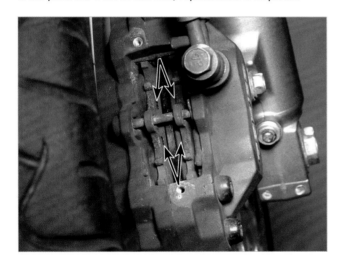

 Do NOT allow the pads to wear down below the minimum limit. Not only does this present a dangerous safety situation but the metal backing plates will score the disc. Check the amount of pad wear regularly.

3 Note the comparison of the new set of pads (left) with those on the right which have been allowed to wear down to the metal backing plates.

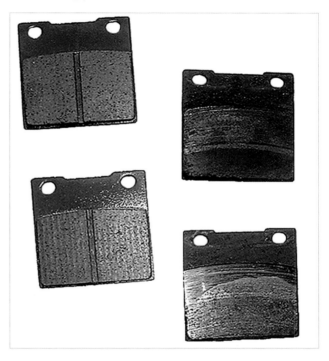

Hose condition check

The flexible brake hoses should be replaced every four years and the fluid changed every two years. This is because as the hoses age they tend to expand (when the brakes are applied) thus needing more pull on the lever to get the same result.

Regularly examine the hoses for splits, bulges and cracking, especially near the end connectors. Replace any hoses which are in poor condition.

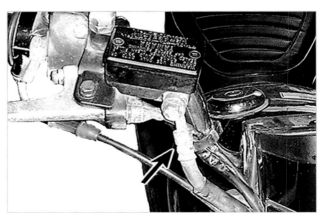

Pad replacement

Brake pads need to be removed from the caliper for replacement, or for cleaning of the existing pads and caliper area. The pads and caliper pistons are in an exposed location and corrosion from road dirt and salt will result in a build up of corrosion occurring if cleaning is neglected. An annual clean is advised, especially if the machine is used all year round.

Items required

✔ Various sockets, spanners, Allen keys and a torque wrench
✔ Brake cleaner, clean cloth and an old toothbrush
✔ Caliper piston retracting tool (see Chapter 1, Section 9)
✔ Brake grease or copper grease and silicon grease
✔ Small syringe
✔ New brake pads
✔ Hammer and thin drift

If you have a twin disc front brake then replace both sets of pads at the same time.

When working on the brakes it is necessary to have everything spotlessly clean, before rebuilding the unit.

The following procedure and photographs illustrate a twin piston sliding caliper. When the brake lever is operated, the pistons move out towards the disc and push on the brake pad. When the pad touches the disc, further pressure causes the caliper to slide on its pins so that pressure is applied to the other pad, and the disc is squeezed between both pads. If the caliper pins seize then only one pad pushes against the disc which will drastically reduce braking efficiency and over a period of time can cause the disc to become warped.

An opposed piston caliper design is shown in Step 16.

Procedure

1 To gain access to the pads, undo the lower slider pin (A) and remove it. This will allow the lower end of the caliper to be pivoted upwards (at point B) where it can then be removed from the carrier slider pin. Do not disconnect the hydraulic hose from the caliper or operate the brake lever/pedal whilst the caliper is off the disc.

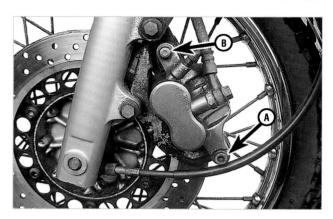

2 The pads for this machine are mounted to the carrier. Remove the old pads and use brake cleaner solution to clean the carrier and its end plates.

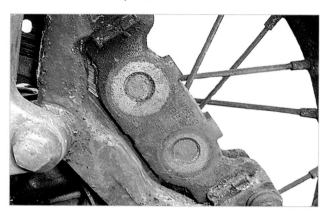

3 If the pads are to be refitted it is necessary to clean them and de-glaze their braking surface. Use sandpaper and not emery cloth or 'wet and dry' paper to clean the brake surface. If emery cloth is used, there is a possibility that very hard pieces from the emery cloth will embed in the pad material, which will damage the disc surface.

4 Measure the thickness of the remaining pad material. If worn down to or below the manufacturer's minimum thickness, or down to the wear limit indicators, the pads should be replaced. See the comparison between a new and worn pad below.

5 The end plates on each end of the carrier are fitted to protect the carrier ends and to prevent the pads rattling. Remove the end plates, clean the carrier and the plates and refit them. Smear silicon grease on the end plates.

6 Check the condition of the rubber gaiters at each end of the carrier where the slider pins fit. If they are damaged, dirt and road salt will get in causing the caliper to seize on the pins. The piston side pad will be the only one working and this will not only reduce the efficiency of the brake, but can distort the disc by pressing on one side of it only.

7 Fit the cleaned, or new, pads on the carrier and ensure that they are correctly positioned with their friction surfaces facing the disc. Smear brake grease or copper grease on the back of the pad that the pistons bear on. This helps stop the pads squealing when the brakes are applied. Do NOT put too much grease on the backplate or it may melt and contaminate the pad material.

8 Attention can now be turned to the caliper body. This is the sort of corrosion that can occur with only 12 months of riding. The machine is used every day and road salt and grit (from winter

---

HINT

If you are a little heavy handed or are worried that you may push the pistons out too far, place a wooden block between the pistons and the caliper. This will prevent the pistons from moving too far.

---

use) can make a real mess of the caliper. The pistons can seize in the caliper or the pads can seize in the carrier. Both conditions will reduce the braking efficiency to below acceptable limits.

9 Operate the brake lever gently so that the pistons move out by no more than a millimetre. The photograph clearly shows a small amount of clean piston. This will provide room to clean the pistons and thus allow them free movement in the caliper.

10 Remove the pad spring plate for cleaning later. Clean the pistons and the inside of the caliper using brake cleaner fluid, clean cloth or kitchen paper. A clean, old toothbrush can be used to clean the area between the pistons and other awkward to get at places. Do NOT be tempted to use carburettor cleaner to clean the brake caliper – the fluid will take the paint off the caliper.

When the brake is applied, fluid pressure acts on the back of the pistons and this in turn is transmitted to the pads. The pistons move through seals (within the caliper), which distort and then pull the pistons back to their original position when the lever is released. As the pads wear, the distance the pistons move is increased so that the seals cannot distort anymore. At this point, the piston slips through the seals and when it is returned it assumes a new, slightly further forward position.

As the brake pads wear, the pistons automatically move outwards to take up the space, thus there is no requirement for regular adjustment as there is with a drum brake system. The distance moved each time is minute.

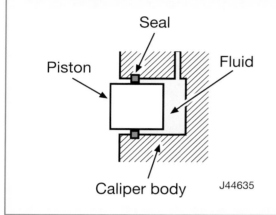

J44635

11 With the caliper and pistons cleaned, it will be necessary to push the pistons back into the caliper to allow sufficient clearance for the new pads to be installed. This can often be done with firm hand pressure.

Screwdrivers and metal rods can be a bit savage and can easily damage the pistons or caliper body. This tool, taken from the car world, has two thick plates connected via a course threaded screw. Turn the screw so that the plates are together, fit the plates between the pistons and the caliper body and turn the screw to open the plates. As you turn the screw, the pistons will be forced back into the caliper.

Before you use the above tool, it will be necessary to check the fluid level in the master cylinder. Use a small syringe to draw fluid out of the reservoir to allow for the fluid to be

displaced back into the reservoir when the pistons are pushed back. Do NOT draw out so much that the feed and return holes (in the bottom of the reservoir) become exposed to air. If you do, the system will need to be bled.

12 With the pistons pushed back into the caliper, refit the cleaned pad spring plate and smear silicon or brake grease around the piston heads.

13 Lubricate the gaiters and the fixed slider pin with silicon grease and refit the caliper. Clean and lubricate this removable slider pin with silicon grease, line up the caliper and pin hole and screw the pin into its hole. Tighten the pin to its specified torque setting.

Check that the ends of the pads are correctly positioned in the carrier. Refitting the caliper can knock one end of a pad out of its mounting. If this happens and you ride the machine, the pad may jam or fall out. Both are likely to cause an accident.

14 If it was necessary to remove the pad carrier from the fork leg, for example to be cleaned, observe the following points when refitting it:

Clean the threads of the fixing bolts and place one drop of locking agent on the threaded area of each bolt. Place a smear of copper grease on the non-threaded portion of each bolt. Fit and hand tighten both bolts before tightening them to their specific torque setting.

Note that caliper or pad carrier mounting bolts are special high tensile bolts. Do not replace them with ordinary engineering quality bolts even if they are the same size.

15 After reassembling the caliper, check the fluid level in the master cylinder and top up if necessary. Apply the brake lever (front) or pedal (rear) to bring the pads back in contact with the disc, then recheck the fluid level and top up again if necessary.

16 This front caliper, with its cover removed, has opposed pistons (two per side) and has no sliding elements. The caliper will have to be removed from the fork leg (front brake) or carrier (rear brake) to enable the pads to be removed.

These pads have a single pin that is held in place by an 'R'

clip (arrowed). Use pliers to pull the 'R' pin out, then withdraw the pad retaining pin. The pads can now be withdrawn from the caliper. Clean the pad retaining pin and apply a smear of brake grease or copper-based grease to it on installation.

This caliper has heat insulators fitted to each piston to prevent the heat generated in the pads from reaching the pistons (arrowed). Note the damage which can be done to the piston heads and caliper body when screwdrivers etc. are used to push the pistons back into the caliper.

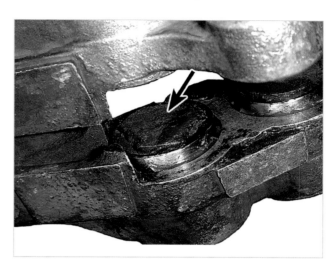

17 Early machines used neoprene or nylon rings (washers) between the back of the brake pad and the piston. This device prevents heat being transferred from the brake pad to the caliper piston. If the pistons were subjected to the full heat generated under heavy braking, this heat would be transferred to the fluid in the caliper. This would heat up the fluid causing it to boil and dramatically reducing the braking efficiency, leading to brake fade. If your system has this type of ring, don't forget to fit it on the rebuild.

Brake disc check

Check the disc visually for cracks or damage especially where the disc is mounted to its carrier. Unless the disc is of the floating type, there should be no movement between the disc and its carrier.

Visually inspect the disc surface; it should be perfectly flat, without any ridges. If the surface has pronounced ridges or bumps the disc should be replaced.

Measure the disc thickness. Use a micrometer and measure in the centre of the pad contact area. If the thickness is at or below the maker's minimum thickness, the disc should be replaced. Note that the disc's minimum thickness is often stamped into its inner rim.

Disc run-out can accurately be checked only with the use of a dial test indicator and stand, which is the not the sort of equipment found in an owners toolkit.

There is a way of telling if the disc is badly warped.

+ Ride the machine and listen for an intermittent 'knock' from the front wheel area that changes as speed changes. This could be the disc tapping on the brake pads.
+ A pulsing in the lever when the brakes are applied or a need to pump the lever to regain pressure is another sign of a warped disc.

Clean the edge of the disc with fine wet and dry paper and its braking surface with brake cleaner and a cloth.

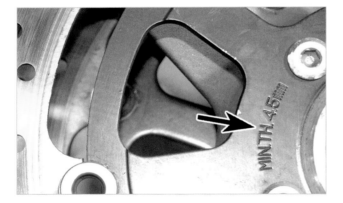

Modern materials technology has allowed discs to be made thinner and therefore lighter but the brakes have a harder job stopping the very powerful machines that are produced today. Discs may not be cheap but your life is priceless, if the disc is warped, damaged or below the maker's specification, renew it.

> ⚠ If replacing a front disc on a twin disc set-up, always replace both discs. Always fit new brake pads if a disc is replaced.

Brake fluid change and system bleeding

Brake fluid will degrade over time and manufacturers recommend that it be changed every two years.

Items required

✔ Brake bleeding kit. This kit has a 'one-way' valve allowing it to be easily used by one person

✔ A glass jar or plastic jug to collect the old fluid
✔ A small syringe
✔ A NEW bottle of brake fluid of the type specified by the motorcycle manufacturer, or as marked on the reservoir cap (see beginning of this section).

Procedure

1 Place clean cloths or clean rags around the brake master cylinder and also remove or cover the fuel tank. Most brake fluids can 'eat' paint. If you do get brake fluid on your paintwork, wash it off immediately, however prevention is better than cure.

2 Remove the master cylinder reservoir cap, plate and rubber diaphragm and place them out of the way for later inspection. Use a small syringe to draw most of the fluid from the reservoir and place it in the jar. Do not allow the two holes in the bottom of the reservoir to be exposed to the air.

3 Fill the reservoir to the upper level with fresh brake fluid.

4 Remove the bleed nipple cover and fit the ring end of a spanner to the bleed nipple. Fit the bleed kit to the nipple and place the other end in your jar. Note the positioning of the white plastic plate; one end supports the bleed pipe whilst the other is pushed over the bleed nipple. This secures the pipe and keeps it from falling off the nipple.

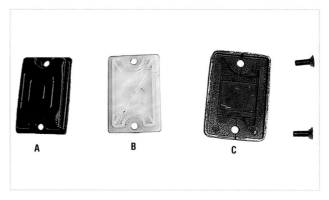

5 Loosen the bleed nipple by turning it about 1/3rd of a turn and operate the brake lever/pedal. Release the lever/pedal and repeat this action to pump brake fluid and air into the jar via the bleed kit. Because of the one-way valve, fluid will not return when the lever is released. If you find that fluid returns up the pipe, place some old fluid into the jar so that the ball end is below the surface.

6 Keep the reservoir topped up so that the holes in the bottom of the reservoir are never exposed. If they are exposed, air will enter the system and this MUST be bled out, which can take a lot of time.

7 Continue to operate the lever/pedal, and top up the reservoir until fresh fluid appears in the bleed kit pipe. Keep the lever/pedal squeezed and tighten the bleed nipple. Operate the lever/pedal until its action becomes firm. Remove the pipe, top up the master cylinder reservoir and refit the rubber diaphragm (A), plate (B) and cap (C).

A   B   C

8 The procedure in Steps 5 to 7 applies when using a 'one-man' brake bleeding kit. If a kit isn't available, connect a length of clear tubing to the bleed nipple and submerge its end in a jar containing brake fluid.

9 Pump the lever/pedal three or four times and hold it in (front) or down (rear) while opening the bleed nipple. Brake fluid will flow out of the caliper into the tubing and the lever will move towards the handlebar (front), or the pedal will move down (rear). Keep the lever/pedal squeezed and tighten the bleed nipple. Repeat this procedure until no air bubbles can be seen in the tubing.

Back bleeding

When fitting new hoses one way to speed up the bleeding process is to 'back bleed' the system.

a) Use a NEW oil can and fill it ¾ full with brake fluid.
b) Fit a piece of plastic tubing to the metal spout of the can.
c) Pump the oil can lever a few times to prime it.
d) Fit the tubing to the bleed nipple, open it and pump the oil can lever to force fluid into the system.
e) Pump the lever until the reservoir level starts to rise.

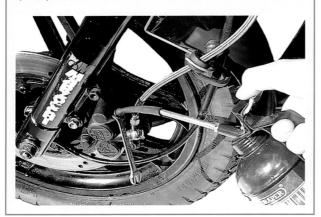

Vacuum type brake bleeder

A vacuum brake bleeding kit will draw the fluid out of the system, via the bleed nipple, when the vacuum pump is operated. It is not necessary to pump the brake lever/pedal, only to keep the master cylinder topped up. This system is often more successful than the conventional means of brake bleeding, especially where the machine's hydraulic system contains small-bore metal pipes such as on linked brake or ABS systems. It is, however, essential to obtain an air-tight seal between the bleed nipple and brake bleeder hose.

Brake hose replacement

The brake hoses should be replaced every four years because the hoses get 'tired' over a period of time. When the brake is applied the hoses tend to expand, this reduces the braking pressure at the caliper meaning more lever action is required to compensate. Replacing your existing rubber hoses with braided hoses will transform the system.

Items required

✔ New armoured hose, banjo bolts and copper washers. Do not be tempted to use the old ones otherwise they may not seal properly
✔ Fresh brake fluid. Once the seal under the cap has been broken, use the fluid and dispose of any left over. Never use old brake fluid as it absorbs moisture from the atmosphere. If this water is subjected to the high temperatures of the braking system it will 'boil', leading to vapour locks and a loss of brakes
✔ Brake bleeding kit and jar or jug
✔ Brake hose clamp

The round connectors on the ends of the hose are called 'banjos' and the connecting bolts are banjo bolts. It is advisable, but not necessary, to replace the bolts with new ones when replacing the hose(s). Always use new copper sealing washers.

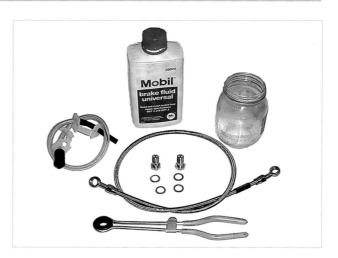

Before you start this task, it will be necessary to determine the thread size of your system. Referring to the photograph on the following page, the bolt on the left is a new one that has a thread pitch of 1.25 mm, whereas the one on the right is an original with a pitch of 1 mm. If you try to fit either into the wrong hole, you will irreparably damage both the bolt and the master cylinder. If you are unsure as to which thread pitch is required, consult your dealer or the company supplying the new hose.

Procedure

1 Remove the master cylinder cover, plate and diaphragm and using a small syringe, draw out the brake fluid from the master cylinder reservoir. Removing the fuel tank to protect it from contact with the brake fluid and wrap the master cylinder with a clean cloth to catch any spillage.

2 Fit the bleed kit and place the tube end into a jar or jug. Slacken the bleed nipple, operate the lever, and pump the fluid into the jar. When you have pumped out as much as possible close the bleed nipple.

HINT

Note the position of the spanner in the bottom left photo.
✦ The ring end is being used as this gives a better grip on the bleed nipple.
✦ The ring end is invariably angled at 15° to the shank, allowing the spanner to be positioned so that you can get the maximum swing on it when in confined spaces. In some situations, there is insufficient room to use the spanner both ways. Before you try to undo the bleed nipple, check which way up will give the most swing.

3 As an alternative to draining the fluid, a hose clamp can be used as shown to squeeze the old hose closed. Wrap a cloth round the caliper and remove the lower banjo bolt. Place the hose end into the jar, then open and remove the clamp allowing the fluid to drain into the jar.

4 Before removing the old hose, note its routing. The new hose must follow the route of the old one to prevent the hose being stretched when the handlebars are turned (front). In the case of a new rear brake hose, take note of how the old hose is routed and clipped to the swinging arm.

5 Place a cloth under the master cylinder banjo bolt, and slacken and remove it. Fit the new hose to the master cylinder ensuring that two new washers are used (one each side of the banjo union) and that the fitting follows the path of the old one.

6 Remove the old hose from the caliper and fit the end of the new hose in its place using new washers. Not all hoses have straight fittings. The hose in the second photograph has a straight fitting at the master cylinder end and a slightly angled fitting at the caliper. If your hose has different end fittings, check which way they are fitted.

7 With the new hose in place and the banjo bolts tightened to

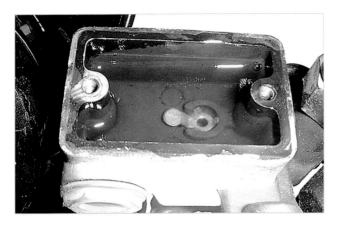

their correct torque setting, fill the master cylinder reservoir to its upper mark with fresh brake fluid. Fit the rubber diaphragm to prevent brake fluid spraying out when the lever/pedal is operated. Note the hole in the bottom of the reservoir, this is the feedhole and under the cover to the left is the return hole. The cover prevents fluid spraying upwards when the lever/pedal is released.

8 Ensure the brake bleeding kit is still correctly connected, then slacken the bleed nipple by about 1/3rd of a turn and bleed the brake following the procedure in the previous sub-section on 'Brake fluid change and system bleeding'.

9 Whilst you are refilling and bleeding the system, keep an eye on the fluid level in the master cylinder. Never let the feed and return holes become exposed or air will enter.

10 When the bleeding operation is complete, top up the master cylinder to the correct level and refit its cover.

11 Check that there is no sign of brake fluid leakage from the new hose or banjo union connectors. Check that the brake works correctly before riding the machine.

Brake light switch adjustment

Refer to the end of Section 13 for details.

---

13   Drum brakes

Brake overhaul and shoe replacement

Regular adjustment of the drum brake is necessary to compensate for shoe wear, whereas brake shoe replacement should be undertaken only when the shoes have reached their service limit. It is impossible to give time/distance intervals when replacement will be needed as the amount of shoe wear will depend on how you ride.

The following procedure describes the service and replacement of rear drum brake shoes; front drum brakes are virtually identical.

Items required
✔ Tray into which to put your removed parts
✔ Glass paper (sandpaper)
✔ Steel rule and stiff wire brush
✔ Appropriate size sockets, spanners or Allen keys
✔ Hammer and metal drifts (steel or aluminium rods)
✔ Multi-purpose grease and brake cleaner
✔ New brake shoes
✔ Clean cloth and a paintbrush (1/2 inch is ideal)

Wear assessment

Most drum brake systems have some external means of indicating when the shoes are worn and need replacement. The machine photographed has a washer (with a pointer) attached to the brake spindle and a fixed mark on the brake backplate.

If the arrows line up when the brake is applied, or if they are close to each other, then it is time to replace the shoes.

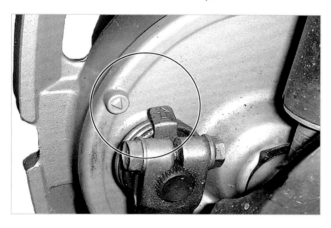

Failure to replace the shoes will result in extremely poor braking, possible breaking up of the shoe material causing the brakes to lock on and result in an accident, or damage to the brake drum which will require an expensive wheel rebuild.

You should service the brakes long before the shoes are worn out (at major service intervals). Brake servicing doesn't just involve the shoes, but also the operating spindle and shoe return springs. If the brake spindle seizes, the brakes will lock on, with a noticeable drop off in power and the wheel becoming progressively more difficult to rotate.

If left too long without attention, the sort of damage that will be done can be seen in the accompanying photo. A cast iron brake drum is incorporated in the wheel hub and the two light brown lines (arrowed) are deep grooves. This wheel hub is not only useless but also dangerous and a new wheel or new hub and wheel rebuild is necessary. Don't be tempted to just replace the brake shoes in this situation.

Procedure

1 Undo and remove the brake adjuster nut then operate the brake pedal to draw the brake rod from the trunnion block and brake arm. Either place the adjuster nut, trunnion and spring in your parts tray or reconnect them to the brake rod for safekeeping.

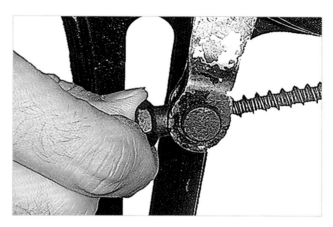

HINT

The brake rod hangs down and often gets in the way. If you move the machine for any reason, it is guaranteed that the rod will be seriously bent. Tying the rod to the swinging arm with string will keep it out of harm's way.

2 The torque arm (where fitted) prevents the drum backplate rotating with the wheel when the brake is applied. It consists of a metal bar connected to the backplate at one end, and to the swinging arm or frame at the other. The bolts used to attach it have an 'R' clip or split pin to prevent the nut coming off.

Remove the clip, nut and bolt at the backplate and move the torque arm up and down. If it is stiff in its action, remove the nut/bolt at the other end and service it.

Clean any corrosion from the shoulder of the bolt, which is the area that the torque arm pivots on. Then grease the bolt shoulder. Clean any corrosion from the end of the torque arm and grease the end and pivot hole. Reconnect the torque arm to the frame or swinging arm, tighten the nut to its correct torque setting. Refit the 'R' clip or use a NEW split pin to secure the nut. Check that the arm moves freely.

3 Slacken off the chain adjusters (see Section 1 of this Chapter). Undo the wheel spindle nut and remove its washer.

4 Remove the wheel spindle noting the position and lengths of spacers and lower the wheel to the ground. Disengage the chain from the sprocket and withdraw the wheel from the swingarm.

5 Remove the backplate from the wheel and check the operation of the brake cam. This spindle has jammed in the backplate and will have to be driven out (see Step 7).

6 Some brakes have marks for aligning the brake arm with the spindle. If yours has, highlight the marks before removing the backplate. If there are no marks, make your own with a permanent marker. This will help to set the correct relationship between the arm and spindle on rebuild. Other brakes have a master spline. Remove the brake arm pinch bolt and nut and pull the arm off the spindle splines.

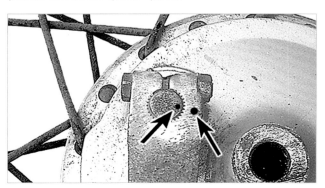

7 Remove the brake shoe assembly by lifting one shoe (at the centre of the shoe) until it is 90° to the other shoe, then lift off both shoes; do not worry if the springs come out of their holes in the shoes, as you need to inspect them anyway. Note the way in which the springs are fitted, both springs fit over the shoes. Other makes have the springs over one shoe but under the other. This all depends on the type of springs that have been used.

If the spindle has jammed in the backplate, check that the brake arm pinch bolt and nut have been removed, and that the brake shoes have been removed. Support the backplate in a vice. Do not tighten the vice, instead close its jaws so that the spindle will come out but the jaws support the backplate.

Use a steel drift (round bar) and hammer and GENTLY tap the drift to remove the spindle.

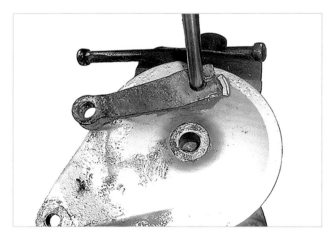

8 Clean all corrosion off the brake spindle. Clean the brake cam spindle hole with 'wet and dry' or sandpaper and pull through with a cloth dampened with brake cleaner. Heavy corrosion, as shown in the photo below, will require the use of a stiff wire brush to remove.

9 Clean the backplate using brake cleaner, a clean cloth and paint brush. Pay special attention to the brake shoe pivot stem (arrowed in the photo overleaf) and check the backplate for cracks or other signs of damage.

10 Clean the brake spindle splines with a wire brush.

The wide master spline locates with either a projection on the brake wear indicator (arrowed), or an equivalent slot on the brake arm. If there is no equivalent slot on the brake arm the master spline lines up with the open end of the arm.

Grease the brake spindle and fit it in its hole.

Fit any brake wear indicator washer and the brake arm. Note that some manufacturers fit a rubber 'O' ring or felt washer on the outside of the backplate around the brake spindle and under the arm. If this is the case, put a smear of grease on the rubber 'O' ring or two drops of clean oil onto the felt washer.

11 Before fitting and tightening the arm locking nut and bolt, check that the lever arm is free to operate, and that you have fitted it the right way round. If this is not the case, just remove the arm, turn the spindle through 180° and refit the arm.

12 Smear a **small** amount of grease on the pivot and cam faces and lay the backplate to one side until later.

13 Measure the thickness of the shoe friction material at its thinnest point, which is usually just off the centre of the shoe, towards its leading edge. Repeat this for the other shoe and compare the smallest reading with the maker's service limit. As a 'rule of thumb', the usual thickness of new shoe material is 4 mm with a service limit of 2 mm.

If the thickness of the friction material of one shoe is at or close to the minimum specified, replace BOTH shoes.

Do not be tempted to turn the shoes around or replace only one shoe.

If the shoe material is within specification:

✦ Check the condition of the shoe springs. The springs used are often extension springs, i.e. they are close wound. If there are any gaps when the spring is not operated then they are tired and should be replaced. Check also for damage or fatigue of the spring hooks.

✦ Check for damage to the brake shoes. Look for any cracks or breaks, especially where the springs locate.

✦ Clean the glaze from the shoe material using glass paper. Do not use emery cloth or 'wet and dry' as this will embed particles into the shoe material and likely cause damage to the shoe and/or drum.

14 Fit both springs to the shoes and place the first shoe against the pivot point and cam face. Place the second shoe at 90° to the first one.

Hold the first shoe against its pivot and cam face and push the other shoe over its pivot and cam face. Take your time, the shoe will drop into place. If it wedges against the pivot or cam face, carefully operating the lever will often cause the shoe to settle into its proper position.

When the shoes are in place, operate the arm to ensure that the shoes move and then 'snap' back into place when the arm is released.

15 Spray brake cleaner inside the wheel hub and clean the drum with a clean cloth or kitchen paper. Dispose of the cloth or paper in a sealed plastic bag when you have completed the task.

With most of the brake dust out, all that remains is to clean the brake drum with emery cloth or 'wet and dry'. Give the drum a final wipe with a kitchen paper.

16 Place the backplate into the wheel.

17 Refit the wheel and loop the chain over the sprocket. Ensure that the spacers have been returned to their original positions, then slide the wheel spindle through the wheel making sure that it passes through the chain adjusters and spacers. Install the washer and nut on the end of the spindle, but don't tighten the nut at this stage.

18 Clean the trunnion, spring, adjuster nut and brake rod threads before reassembly.

19 Fit the torque arm bolt through its hole and ensure that the shoulder is exposed. The hexagon head of the bolt often fits into a slot or other holding device in the backplate.

Grease the bolt shoulder and fit the torque arm over it, making sure that the arm fits over the shoulder and doesn't rest on the threaded portion. Fit the nut, finger-tight only at this stage.

When the chain has been tensioned, and wheel alignment checked, tighten the torque arm nut to its correct torque setting and fit a new split pin or refit the 'R' clip.

20 Adjust the chain tension and check the wheel alignment (see Section 1).

21 Before tightening the wheel spindle nut, adjust the brake (see below), then apply and hold the brake on whilst tightening the wheel spindle nut. This will centralize the shoes for optimum braking performance.

22 Adjust the rear brake light switch so that the lamp illuminates just before resistance is felt in the pedal.

23 Recheck that ALL nuts/bolts are tight.

Front brake adjustment

Front drum brake adjustment should be carried out every 2000 miles

1 Pull off any rubber cover that is over the handlebar adjuster.

2 Turn the lock ring (A) until it touches the adjuster (B).

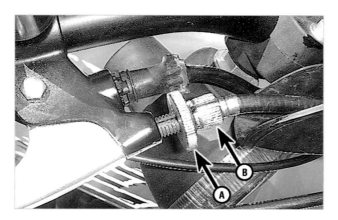

3 Turn the adjuster (B) all the way into the lever assembly until the lock ring touches the assembly.

4 Move to the front wheel and turn the adjuster (C) until there is 3 to 4 mm of freeplay at the handlebar lever. This is the amount of freeplay measured between the lever and bracket before resistance can be felt when operating the lever.

5 Although the manufacturer may recommend 3 to 4 mm of freeplay it is better to allow a little more when adjusting at the wheel. This will mean that final adjustment (to the

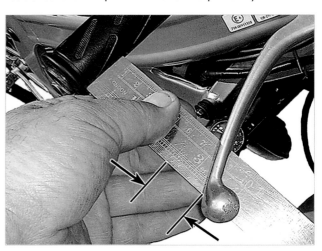

7 Some manufacturers quote a figure for lever freeplay that is measured at the end of the lever, e.g. 10 to 15 mm before resistance is felt. Adjustment is as stated previously.

manufacturer's specification) can be achieved by adjusting the screw (B).

6 When adjustment has been completed, tighten the lock ring (A) against the lever assembly. Refit the rubber cover over the adjuster.

Rear brake adjustment

Rear drum brake adjustment should be carried out every 2000 miles.

Note: *Brake pedal height should be checked, and if necessary adjusted before adjusting the brakes. See Section 5 for details.*

1 Push down on the brake pedal and measure the distance it moves until initial resistance can be felt in the pedal.

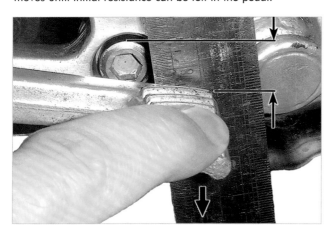

2 Turn the adjuster until there is the correct pedal freeplay when measured at the pedal tip. For this machine, the distance that the pedal should travel before initial resistance is felt is 20 to 30 mm.

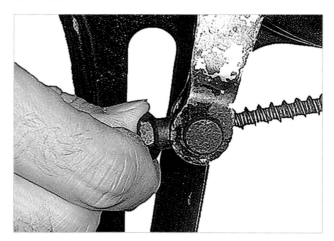

3 Always check the rear brake light switch setting after adjusting the rear brake.

Front brake light switch

The front brake light switch is incorporated in the front brake lever bracket, or on the underside of the master cylinder on disc braked models. The switch is usually non-adjustable.

If the brake light does not work when the lever is operated, the switch may have failed or become stuck due to corrosion. Often removing the switch and giving its plunger a squirt of WD40 will succeed in getting it working again.

Some switches are held in place by plastic 'ears' which extend into a hole in the lever assembly. Use a small screwdriver to press the ear upwards, then gently pull the switch out of its housing.

Grip the body of the switch, do NOT pull on the wires or the switch terminals may break.

With the switch out of its housing, spray the plunger with WD40 and work the plunger in and out. Turn the ignition ON and operate the plunger to see if the brake light comes on. If it does, the remedial action has worked. If it doesn't, yet the rear brake light switch operates the brake light (proves that the bulb has not failed) then there is a wiring fault or the switch has failed.

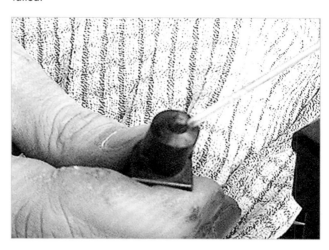

Refit the switch by pushing it back into its housing until the ears clip into place. If the switch has a flat edge, such as on that photographed, this should be positioned against the lever bracket.

Another type of switch fitment is via a single screw and locating lug. To remove the switch, pull off its wire connectors (A) and undo the screw (B). The switch contact can be sprayed with WD40 if it is stuck, but repairs are not possible.

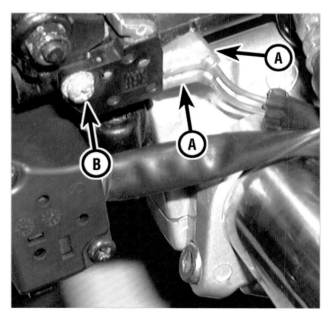

Rear brake light switch

1 Switch the ignition on. Press the rear brake pedal and note its position when the brake light illuminates. The light should come on at the point when resistance can be felt in the pedal.

2 This is a typical rear brake light switch and is a 'pull' type where a spring, connected to the brake pedal operates an internal rod. If the switch needs adjusting, hold the body (B) and turn the nut (A). Turn the nut by a small amount, settle the

switch by pulling it into its seat and operate the brake pedal. Re-adjust as necessary until the light comes on at the correct point.

3 If the switch fails to operate the light, this may be due to corrosion inside the switch. Clean the switch by pulling the switch rod downwards and spraying the rod with WD40 or a similar water-dispersant aerosol. Work the rod up and down.

14 Stands

Centrestand

The centrestand is often ignored until it becomes so stiff in its action that something must be done, or the pin wears to such an extent that the machine rocks from side to side when on the stand, or the pin breaks causing the stand to collapse.

Items required

✔ General-purpose grease and light oil spray
✔ Sockets, spanners and torque wrench
✔ Cleaning cloth and 'wet and dry' paper

Service the stand every 12 months or at major service intervals. Having an assistant to help on the rebuild will be an advantage.

Procedure

1 With the centrestand in the up (retracted) position place the machine on its sidestand. Check whether the exhaust system will prevent access to the centrestand pivot shaft and if necessary remove the exhaust system.

2 Remove the return spring, noting the information in the **Hint**.

HINT

When removing a stand return spring, use a length of string, thin rope or electrical cable around the spring eye (as shown) and pull on the cable/string. This will extend the spring safely and allow the spring eye to come off its peg.

When replacing the spring, use the same technique to get the spring back over its peg. This works equally well for side and centrestand springs. Do NOT be tempted to use a 'blunt instrument' (screwdriver or similar) to attempt to pry the spring off its peg, you will only damage the tool, the spring or yourself.

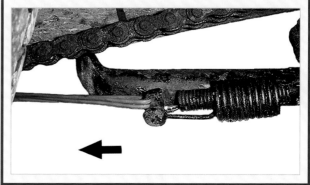

3 Straighten and remove the pivot shaft retaining split pin. Discard the old split-pin and have a new one ready for re-assembly. Do NOT be tempted to re-use the old split-pin; if it should break the first you will know of it will be when the centrestand falls off. Split pins are a 'use once only' item.

4 If the pivot pin is difficult to remove, due to hardened grease or rust, use an aluminium drift (bar) and hammer to gently tap it out. Pull the pin out, lift the stand legs and at the same time push the pivot end of the stand downwards out of its brackets.

5 Clean the pivot pin bore within the centrestand. If it is excessively dirty a length of round wood, wrapped with emery cloth or 'wet and dry' abrasive paper usually does the trick. If it has been regularly serviced a good spray with light oil and a 'pull through' with a clean cloth is all that is usually needed.

> ⚠ **Caution: Resist the temptation to stick your finger (wrapped with cloth) into the shaft to clean it, as it is very likely that you will get your finger stuck in the stand.**

6 Clean the old hardened grease off the pivot pin and clean off any rust with emery cloth or abrasive paper. Insert the pin in the bore of the stand and check that there is only a small amount of play between the shaft and pin. If the pivot pin is a sloppy fit in the stand it may be a case of replacing both the pin and centrestand. If regularly cleaned and greased the components will usually last the life of the machine.

7 Cover the pin with fresh grease prior to reassembly and apply grease to the spring posts.

8 Offer up the stand and ensure that it is central to its brackets. Have your assistant line up the frame bracket and stand while you insert the pin. It may be necessary to wiggle the stand to get it to line up so that the pin can be inserted fully.

9 Fit the spring over the frame spring post and pull the spring over the stand spring post. See **_Hint_**.

10 Turn the pivot pin so that the holes for the split pin are parallel with the ground and insert the new split pin.

Turn the pivot pin so that the split pin is now perpendicular to the ground, with the head of the pin uppermost, and then open the split pin ends. If the ends are too long, such as in the accompanying photograph, cut them below the pivot by about half their length. Excessive bending of the split pin ends may result in weakening, then breakage (due to vibration). Bend the split pin ends around the pivot pin.

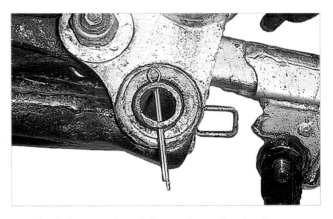

11 Check the operation of the stand ensuring that it returns to its fully up position. Spray the spring with light oil then gently wipe off any excess with a dry cloth or tissue paper. A gentle spray with light oil, once a week, will keep the spring clean and working smoothly.

12 Not all centrestands will be retained by a pivot shaft and split pin arrangement. In the accompanying photo the legs of the stand are retained to the frame brackets by a pivot bolt and nut, with the plain shank of the pivot bolt forming the bearing surface for the stand.

13 To remove the stand, first detach its return spring, then hold the pivot bolt head on the inside of the bracket and unscrew the nut. Repeat this for the other pivot bolt. Withdraw the pivot bolts from both brackets to free the stand. Clean all old grease off the pivot bolts, nuts, frame brackets and stand legs. Apply fresh grease to the pivot bolt shanks, brackets and stand legs. Insert the pivot bolts from the inside, noting that there may be a link plate for the return spring, as shown in the photo, which the pivot bolt passes through. Tighten the pivot bolt nuts to the torque setting specified in the workshop manual. Wipe off any excess grease and reconnect the return spring.

Sidestand

The sidestand should be removed for re-greasing at every major service or every 12 months.

Items required

- ✔ General purpose or Molybdenum grease
- ✔ Emery cloth or 'wet and dry' paper and a wire brush
- ✔ Light oil spray
- ✔ Appropriate sized sockets or spanners
- ✔ Torque wrench

Procedure

1 Support the machine on its centrestand. If no centrestand is fitted, a paddock stand or trolley jack will be needed to support the machine. If your machine has a sidestand switch, refer to the end of this section BEFORE starting work.

2 The pivot bolt will often have a locking nut behind it. Remove this first then unscrew and remove the pivot bolt.

If the spring is weak the sidestand will not return fully to its rest position. This is a potentially dangerous condition. The spring in the accompanying photograph has started to open its coils and needs replacing. If in any doubt – replace the spring.

4 Clean all old grease, dirt and rust from the frame bracket and spring post, then liberally coat BOTH sides of the frame bracket and the spring post with grease.

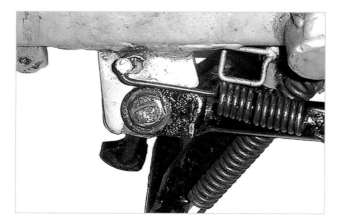

3 Swing the sidestand downwards and out of its bracket. Do not worry about the spring at this stage, just remove it and check that all its coils are touching and that there are no cracks or damage to the spring ends.

Check the condition of the threads on the pivot bolt. They should be clean and undamaged, if in doubt replace the bolt. Check the condition of the shoulder of the bolt. If it has grooves worn into it (from the action of raising and lowering the stand) replace the bolt.

Use a wire brush to clean the threads, shank and head of the bolt and liberally smear the shank with grease.

5 Clean the pivot bolt hole in the sidestand. Fit one end of the return spring to the hook in the sidestand. Note that the spring has different length ends; the longest ear is fitted to the frame bracket so that it clears the pivot bolt head.

6 Slide the stand pivot end over the frame bracket but do not try to line up the holes yet. Whilst the spring is still untensioned, hook its free end over the frame post. Push the stand fully over its frame bracket and line up the bolt hole. It may be necessary to wiggle the end of the stand to facilitate this task.

Insert the pivot bolt and screw it in a couple of turns. Clean off any excess grease.

An alternative would be to fit the spring after the stand; see the centrestand procedure for a hint on fitting the spring.

7 It will be necessary to re-align the stand and bracket to ensure that the shank of the pivot bolt enters the hole in the stand. Tighten the pivot bolt and use a torque wrench to finish

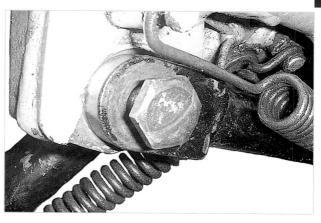

tightening to the value recommended by the manufacturer. Check your workshop manual for this figure.

Fit the retaining nut behind the bracket and holding the bolt head with a spanner, tighten the nut to its torque value.

8 Finally, give the spring a light coating of spray lubricant and check the action of the stand.

Sidestand switch

A sidestand switch is built into the ignition system to prevent you from riding off with the sidestand down (which may cause an accident on your first left-hand turn). The plunger-type switch shown below is the most common fitment, although some machines have a rotary-type switch which locates over the stand pivot bolt head.

If the switch fails, the engine will die when you select a gear, or on certain systems may not even start. When the stand has been serviced, leave it down, start the engine and using the clutch, as normal, engage first gear. If the switch is working, the engine should stall – check that it does.

Push the switch plunger in when refitting the stand. Failure to move the plunger out of the way may cause it to be bent or broken. If you are concerned that it may be damaged, unscrew the switch and move it out of the way. Do NOT forget to replace the switch after you have serviced the sidestand.

With the stand down, spray the plunger (arrowed) with WD40 and work it in and out a few times to keep the plunger free.

15   Bodywork

Fairing panels

Most sports motorcycles have a full fairing as standard. To do even the simplest of tasks requires the removal of some, or all, of the bodywork or fairing.

Considering the high cost of replacement parts, care must be taken removing and replacing the panels so as not to introduce undue stress.

Before attempting removal, take a close look around the fairing panel and note which bolts are used to hold it in place, including any which might be hidden under trim or auxiliary covers. If necessary, draw an outline sketch of the panel and mark the position of each bolt. In this way, when the bolts are removed their size can be recorded on the sketch as an aid to refitting.

Items required

✔ Sockets, Allen keys and screwdrivers as required
✔ Old newspaper – to lay the parts on
✔ A parts tray to store the screws etc.

Procedure

The following removal procedure of a fairing sidepanel is based on a Kawasaki ZXR400, although the principle is similar on most fully-faired machines.

1 Slacken, but do NOT completely undo, each bolt starting with those at the bottom and finishing with the ones at the top.

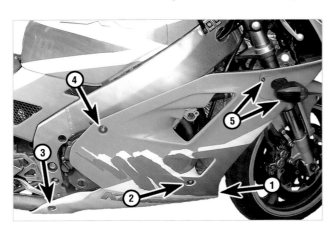

2 The left and right sidepanels are usually joined at the bottom by a bolt, which due to its exposed location is often corroded in place and difficult to remove. Always remove this bolt first.

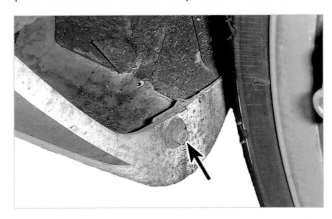

3 After slackening the top bolts which retain the sidepanel to the upper fairing, support the fairing panel with one hand and remove all bolts with the other. Finish by removing these last two bolts and slide out the panel. Place the panel on clean newspaper or cloth to protect the finish, and in a place where it will not be trodden on.

4 Take note of which bolts have rubber or nylon washers fitted. If in doubt, most bolts that do not have a sleeve built in will have a washer fitted.

5 When you refit the panel, slide these two lugs under their clips first. It may be necessary to angle the panel slightly as you fit it.

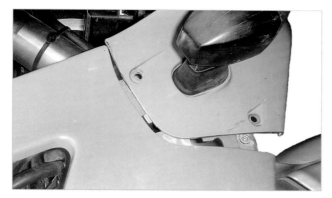

6 Watch out for a clip like this at the rear, lower joint. When you refit the panel, fit this clip into its slot AFTER you fit the top, front lugs (see previous picture) but before you fit any of the bolts.

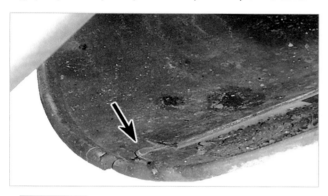

> **HINT**
>
> Lightly coating each bolt thread with copper-based grease will reduce corrosion and make future removal that much easier.

7 Once you have placed the panel in position, start by fitting the top bolts and work your way to the bottom of the panel. Ensure washers are fitted where necessary. Thin rubber or nylon washers protect the fairing paintwork and should always be

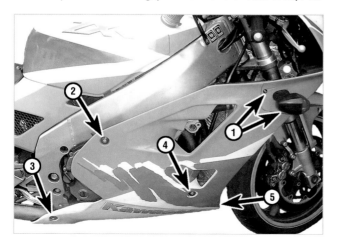

fitted. Secure each bolt by one or two turns ONLY, do NOT tighten any bolt at this stage.

8 With all the bolts fitted, hold the panel closed at the top joint, and tighten the two TOP bolts (1). Now tighten the rest of the bolts, starting again from the top and working your way to the bottom of the panel.

Alternative fittings

The fairing on this Suzuki GSX model comprises four separate pieces. The upper fairing is mounted to the frame, whereas the two fairing lowers are held in place by three screws along the top edge on each side, a rear screw on each side and bridging pieces along the bottom edge. There is also a front, centre section.

The complete lower section (two fairing lowers and centre section) can be removed as one piece but can be a bit tricky to manoeuvre it off the machine.

1 The recommended procedure for removing the fairing piece by piece is to slacken the three upper screws, starting with the centre one first, then move to the lower rear screw and slacken it. Do NOT remove any screws at this stage.

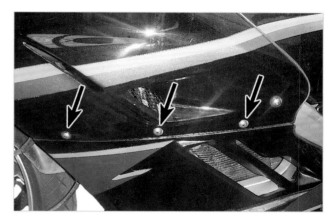

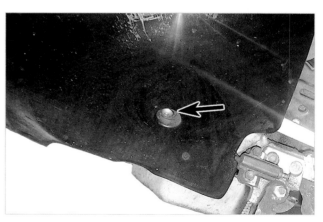

2 Move to the other side of the machine and repeat this process.

3 Remove the six screws which retain the bridging pieces joining the undersides of the fairing lower panels. Remove the three screws which retain the centre section to the fairing lower panels and lift the centre section away.

4 Working on one fairing lower panel at time, support the panel and remove its four mounting screws. Place the panel on old newspapers to protect its finish.

5 Refitting is the opposite of the removal procedure. Fit all screws and secure them by a turn or two, then tighten them completely. Work from the top downwards, noting that the centre screw of the top three should be tightened first.

Sidepanels

Many sidepanels have lugs build into the inside of the panel which locate in rubber grommets in the frame.

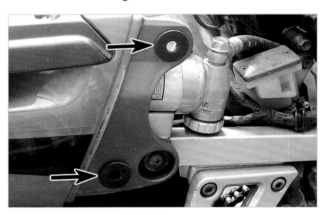

1 Check whether the sidepanel has a screw fastening in addition to the lugs. If it has, remove the screw first.

2 Check the repair manual for the location of the lugs and pull the panel gently as close to this point as possible.

3 If the rubber grommets have hardened with age, now is a good time to replace them.

4 When refitting the sidepanel, lubricate the grommets with WD-40 to aid fitting. Don't use grease because it is possible that the panel lugs might pop out of the grommets whilst you are riding.

Fastener types

Sleeved bolts have spacers built in (like the two photographed), others have the spacer separate from the bolt. Although the thread lengths of the bolts shown are similar, the spacer on bolt A is twice as long as that on bolt B. If you try to fit bolt A into the hole for bolt B the bolt head will stand proud of the panel. Conversely, fitting bolt B into the hole for bolt A will place undue stress on the panel and may fracture it.

Other mounting arrangements use a separate metal bush (tube) within a rubber grommet to prevent the mounting screw squashing the rubber. Make sure that the metal bush is always in place when refitting the panel.

Various 'quick release' type fasteners are often used instead of bolts. Those used on the Ducati photographed secure the top edge of the fairing lower panels to the upper fairing; they are rotated by hand 180° anticlockwise to release them and 180° clockwise to secure them.

Centre-pin type plastic fasteners are used mainly for securing non-load bearing panels or small access panels. Their head design will vary, the type shown here has a screw head which is turned anticlockwise to release, whereas others have a plain centre pin which is either pushed in or pulled out via a slot in its head to release the fastener. Study the type fitted to determine how to remove it.

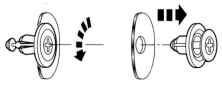

H32767

Body panels and fuel tank

For many service tasks the bodywork, seat and fuel tank must be removed to gain access to the engine, carburettors or air filter. The following is a typical procedure for removing these components, based on a Kawasaki ZXR400. Note that in may cases it is not necessary to remove the rear bodywork in order to remove the fuel tank.

Procedure

1 Use the ignition key to unlock the pillion seat or rear hump. In some instances the seat is held to the machine via a safety line. You can remove this or leave it in place providing it does not interfere with the rest of the work.

2 Undo the Allen screw holding the front of the rider's seat. Lift the front of the seat and slide it forward to pull it from the rear securing lugs.

HINT

You will be removing many bolts/screws with differing heads and lengths. If you are not familiar with this job, draw a few pictures and write on them which bolts go where.

3 Undoing these two bolts will release the rear of the fuel tank.

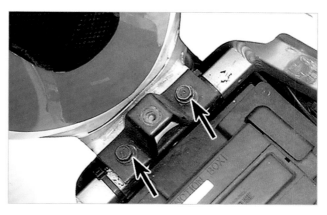

4 Slacken these two sidepanel screws but do not remove them yet. There should be plastic washers under them to protect the paintwork, check they are there are in good condition. Go round to the other side of the machine and repeat this for the opposite panel.

5 Under the pillion seat/tail hump you will find these two screws. Remove the screws and put them into your parts box.

6 Two screws hold the panel halves together at the rear. Remove these two and place them in your parts tray. These screws should have plastic washers under them to protect the paintwork.

7 A third screw holds the panel halves together at the front.

8 Now remove the four main panel screws (two per side) previously slackened in Step 4.

9 Have a look around the panel to check that all its screws have been removed. You will often find tucked away underneath, a screw like this one. There will be another for the opposite panel.

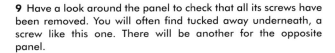

10 Make sure that the screws and bolts have washers on them or the head of the bolt has a washer built in. Carefully pull off the panel and lay it on old newspaper to protect the finish.

11 With the rear bodywork off, you can proceed with removal of the fuel tank. Use an Allen key to remove this bolt.

HINT

Protect the fuel tank paintwork from damage by the tool by placing a cloth in the area or use an Allen socket, long extension bar and ratchet to remove the bolt.

12 Remove these two screws, slacken the clips holding the air hoses and remove the panel.

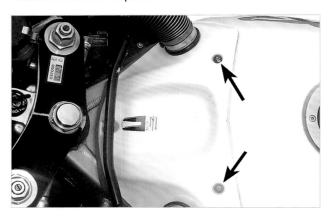

13 With the panel out of the way, the fuel tank bolts can be removed from each side. Note the rubber grommets used at the tank mountings. Check their condition and replace them if they have hardened, are missing or damaged.

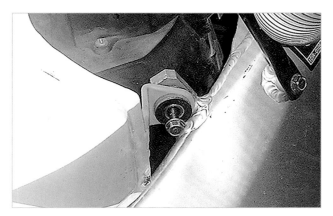

Where the fuel tap has an extended control knob, ensure that the tap is in the OFF position, then unscrew its centre screw and remove the tap control knob.

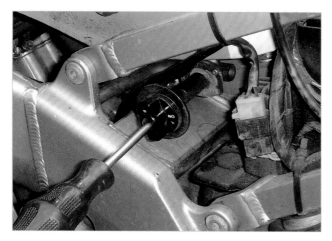

If a vacuum type fuel tap is fitted, which doesn't have an OFF position, ensure that it is turned to the ON position. With the engine stopped there will be no fuel flow when the tap is in the ON or RES positions. Do NOT switch the tap to PRI as this will manually turn on the fuel.

15 Slide back the clip(s), remove the fuel pipe(s) from the tap. If there is more than one pipe, note which one goes where. Note that some fuel tanks have a long breather pipe – note where it is routed.

Lift the fuel tank at the rear and carefully draw it rearwards off the machine. Place the fuel tank upright on old newspapers or cloth to protect its paintwork.

Installation notes

16 The seat for this machine has a spring and catch mechanism holding it in place and is operated by a short cable from the seat lock. Put a smear of silicon grease on the catch and if the cable operation is stiff, lightly oil the cable's exposed ends.

Lubricate the moving parts and operate the mechanism to get the grease well into it.

17 Under the seat, you will find the lug that locates in the catch. Clean any dirt or rust from it and smear silicon grease around it.

18 The front of the seat has a bar, which locates in these catches. Grease the contact surfaces of the catches.

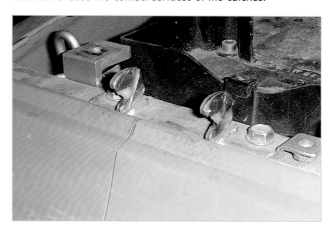

19 Many machines still use the old method of fuel tank mounting which consists of two rubber plugs at the front and a bolt at the rear. To ease the task of pushing the tank's channels fully onto the rubber plugs, apply a smear of silicon grease to the rubber plugs as shown. When fitting the tank, angle its front down at about 30° and slide the tank channels onto the rubber plugs.

Chapter 5

Electrics

Contents

1   Battery safety warnings

Extreme care must be taken when handling the battery. Not only does the lead-acid battery contain dilute sulphuric acid as one of its active constituents, but care must be taken when charging and connecting the battery otherwise you could harm yourself or damage the machine.

Before performing any of the procedures described in the following sections of this chapter, you are advised to read the warnings below.

✔ Always wear medical gloves or barrier cream when topping up a conventional battery or filling a maintenance-free (MF) battery. Dispose of the gloves afterwards and wash your hands. If you get electrolyte on your skin wash it off immediately.

✔ Don't smoke, operate welding or grinding equipment, or allow naked flames near a battery. The gases given off the battery are Oxygen and Hydrogen which when combined with a flame result in an EXPLOSION.

✔ NEVER connect (bridge) the battery terminals with a piece of wire, screwdriver, spanner or other metal object to check if the battery has any life, the resulting flash may cause the battery to explode in your face.

✔ If you need to peer into the top of a black battery, to see the fluid levels, use a battery-operated torch (flashlight) – NEVER a match or cigarette lighter.

✔ The electrolyte in the battery is corrosive. If spilt, mop it up immediately using a rag and plenty of clean water, then neutralize the area with an alkaline solution (baking soda) afterwards.

✔ When charging a conventional battery, remove its caps BEFORE charging to prevent an excessive build up of pressure. Top up with distilled or de-ionised water only, available from motor accessory stockists.

✔ Wear overalls to protect your clothes, and eye protection. It is not 'Wimpish' to wear goggles to protect your eyes, electrolyte stings if it gets into a cut finger, in your eyes it can be very injurious. If you should get electrolyte in your eyes, wash with copious amounts of clean water and seek medical help IMMEDIATELY.

✔ Before and after charging the battery, visually inspect it for any signs of damage or cracks, especially if one or more cells were low on electrolyte.

✔ Don't charge a 6 Volt battery with a 12 Volt battery charger; you will severely damage both items.

✔ The charging area should be uncluttered, well lit and ventilated and the battery should be upright and charged on a level surface.

✔ Connect the battery charger leads BEFORE plugging the charger into the mains and switching it on. Positive lead to positive terminal and negative lead to negative terminal.

✔ When disconnecting a battery from a bike, remove the negative EARTH (–ve) lead FIRST. This prevents an accidental terminal short circuit.

✔ When reconnecting a battery to a bike, connect the positive LIVE (+ve) lead FIRST.

✔ NEVER store an 'in service' battery in a confined space or under a workbench. Vented gases can accumulate with dire results.

2   Conventional battery

The term 'conventional battery' applies to all lead-acid batteries which can be topped up via removable filler caps on their top surface. The case is usually clear or translucent and has upper and lower level markings on one side. The conventional battery also has a breather pipe to vent gases.

The checks in this section should be carried out every 12 months or 4000 miles (6000 km). The author's recommendation is, however, that a 12-volt battery should be checked every 6 months and a 6-volt battery every 3 months.

Items required

✔ Distilled or de-ionised water
✔ Battery hydrometer
✔ Filler bottle
✔ Battery charger
✔ Battery terminal grease or petroleum jelly
✔ Appropriate size socket, 'T' bar or screwdriver

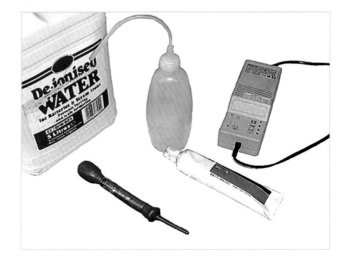

Removing the battery

The battery is usually situated under the seat or hidden behind a sidepanel. Gain access by lifting or removing the seat or sidepanel, then unhitch the battery strap.

If the machine has a starter motor the POSITIVE or 'live' lead (A) will usually be coloured RED, will be thick diameter and short length (to connect with the starter relay, which is usually close by) and be connected to the battery's positive terminal post marked '+'. The NEGATIVE or 'ground/earth' lead (B) is usually BLACK and is connected to the battery's negative terminal post marked '−'.

If the machine doesn't have a starter motor, refer to the table of wiring colours in Section 11.

Battery removal from above the machine

1 You must FIRST undo the screw holding the NEGATIVE lead to its battery terminal post. This is to prevent an accidental short circuit across the battery terminals. Tuck the negative lead out of the way so that it cannot accidentally touch the negative terminal post.

2 Undo the screw holding the positive lead to its battery terminal post.

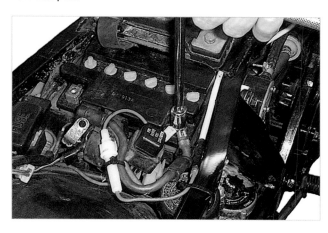

3 Lift the battery up and out of its carrier, disconnecting the breather pipe from its stub once access is available. Thread the lead screws back into the battery terminal nuts to prevent them from becoming lost.

Battery removal from the side of the machine

On some machines the battery is removed from the side of the frame, once the sidepanels have been detached.

1 Take off the left-hand side panel to reveal the '−' terminal. Undo the screw and tuck the negative lead (arrow) out of the way. The silver finned component attached to the battery carrier is the regulator/rectifier. Its purpose is to convert the alternating current (AC) from the generator into direct current (DC) to charge the battery and to control the generator output voltage.

 Warning: Be careful NOT to touch the positive and negative terminals at the same time with something metallic, you'll get a big blue flash and a ruined battery! For this reason use a socket or a 'T' bar to undo the lead screw, NOT a spanner.

2 Move to the other side of the machine and remove the right-hand sidepanel. Undo the screw holding the battery carrier cover in place and unhook it from its mounting.

4 Now slide the battery out of its carrier.

3 Pull off the battery breather pipe, but don't let it fall onto the floor. Undo the battery '+' terminal and tuck its lead (arrow) out of the way.

> **Warning: Be careful how you handle the battery. It vents minute quantities of electrolyte, in an unseen mist. This is not a nice substance to get onto your frame or exhaust, as it will corrode it.**

Checking the battery

1 With the battery removed, inspect the condition of the anti vibration padding inside the battery carrier. Check the rubber padding for damage, hardening of the rubber or bits missing. If this padding is damaged, the battery will rattle around inside the carrier, leading to vibration of its internals, and a shortened battery life.

2 Place the battery on a flat and safe surface and look at the liquid levels. They should all be above the LOWER LEVEL mark. If they are in the same state as the battery shown (the actual

levels have been marked on the photograph) then starter or other electrical troubles are very likely.

3 A 6-volt battery will have 3 cells and a 12-volt battery will have 6 cells, usually with separate filler caps for each cell. Before removing the caps, clean the area around them with a small paintbrush and tissue paper.

4 The screw type cap has a slot in the top and a rubber washer underneath. If there isn't a screw slot, the cap is of the push in type; use a pair of pliers to gently remove this type of cap with a slight twisting and pulling action.

5 With all the caps removed, top up each cell with distilled or de-ionised water to the upper mark shown on the battery. Do not overfill the battery. Note the use of a small bottle with filler spout to add the distilled water.

Charging the battery

Having checked that the cells are topped up with water, you can charge the battery. Leave the caps out.

1 FIRST, connect the charger to the battery terminals. Positive lead (usually red) to the positive terminal post and the negative

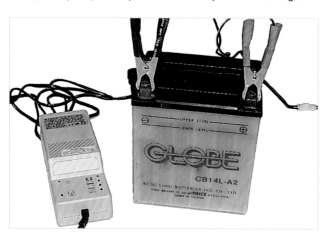

lead (usually black) to the negative terminal post. On dual-voltage chargers set the charger controls to either 6V or 12V to suit the battery type.

2 NOW you can plug the charger into the mains and switch it on. Note that the charger shown has electronic controls and only works on 12V batteries, but does all the charging and testing for you. Battery condition is indicated via a series of lights. See Section 5 for information on the different types of battery chargers.

3 If you have set the charger controls correctly the end of the charging process will be indicated by the release of a lot of gas, i.e. all the cells bubble quite vigorously. It is at this point that you switch off the charger, disconnect the leads and wait a while for the battery to cool down. DO NOT MOVE THE BATTERY FOR AT LEAST 30 MINUTES.

> ⚠ **Caution: Note that it is normal for the battery case to become warm during the charging process because a lot of heat is generated.**

Specific gravity check

Specific gravity (SG) sounds technical but is only a measurement of a liquid's relative density to that of water. Water has a value of 1.0 when measured at 20°C. By measuring the SG of the battery's liquid, the state of charge can be ascertained. Measure SG once the battery has cooled

down, i.e. NOT immediately after charging or running the machine.

1 With the cell caps removed as described previously, squeeze the bulb of the hydrometer and keep it squeezed BEFORE inserting the rubber pipe into the first cell. Now slowly release the pressure on the bulb and liquid will be drawn up into the hydrometer. When the pressure is fully released, the gauge inside the hydrometer will float freely.

2 Leave the hydrometer pipe inside the battery when reading the scale on the gauge. Always lower your head to read the scale on the gauge – DO NOT lift the hydrometer up to your face or you will splash dilute sulphuric acid over yourself.

3 The higher the float, the more dense the liquid. The SG of a fully charged battery will be 1.28 for bikes with starter motors and 1.26 for bikes without (usually 6V types). Many hydrometers have a colour-coded scale: Blue for True, Red for Dead and Yellow for so-so.

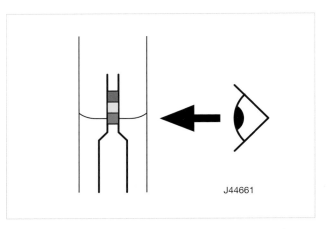

J44661

4 Repeat this process for all the cells. If all cells are good, then top up with distilled water to the upper line, if necessary. Refit the battery caps and refit the battery. If one cell shows a low reading or has lost a lot of liquid, this indicates that it has a cracked case or has a short circuit – the battery should be replaced.

HINT

It is almost impossible to get a full reading from a battery that has been in service for some time. A reading lower than 1.22 after the battery has been charged suggests that the battery is past its prime and should be replaced.

Refitting the battery

1 With the caps refitted and the battery case cleaned, slide the battery back into its carrier and reconnect the LIVE (positive) lead. Hold the positive lead whilst tightening the screw to ensure that it is positioned correctly and not twisted.

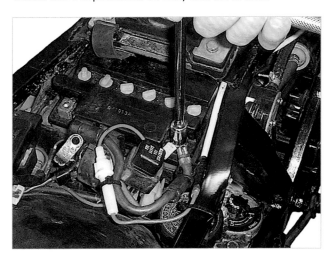

2 Switch to the other side, fit and tighten the EARTH (negative) terminal. Again, hold the lead to ensure that it isn't twisted or kinked.

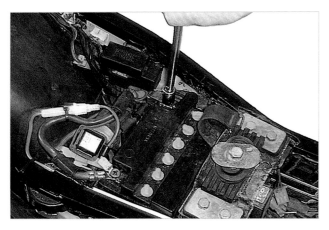

3 At this point carry out a charging voltage test as described in Section 4.

4 Smear both terminals with battery grease or petroleum jelly (Vaseline) to keep the dreaded white powder corrosion at bay. Do NOT use ordinary grease on the battery terminals, as it is a very good insulator and will cause electrical problems. Refit the battery strap. Fit the protective cover over the positive terminal.

> ### HINT
>
> If a build-up of white powder on the terminal posts is a constant problem, remove the battery and pour hot, NOT BOILING, water over the posts. Use an old toothbrush to gently brush the corrosion away. Smear battery grease or petroleum jelly over the posts once the battery is reconnected.

5 With the battery connected, its breather pipe can be installed. First check that the pipe is clean and that it is free from obstructions. DON'T put it in your mouth to blow it out, as it will have had minute quantities of dilute sulphuric acid through it; instead use a bicycle pump with a football inflation adapter to force air through the pipe.

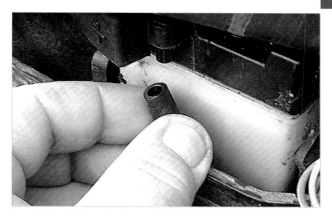

6 Check the battery carrier area, under the seat or behind a side panel for a label like this, which shows the correct routing for the breather pipe. Correct routing is important – the breather pipe vents minute quantities of dilute sulphuric acid and if this gets on the frame it will corrode it. If the pipe is too close to the exhaust system it will be heat welded closed, causing excessive pressure to build up inside the battery; this pressure will only be relieved by the pipe or one of the caps being blown off, or at worst, by a crack occurring in the battery casing. All of which are undesirable events.

Technical

All conventional lead-acid batteries are constructed from lead grids in which lead pastes are forced; red lead is used for the positive plate and grey lead for the negative plate. The electrolyte (liquid) used is dilute sulphuric acid. The normal lead-acid battery uses electrolyte with an SG of 1.28 (1.26 for 6V batteries) whereas the maintenance-free (MF) battery uses electrolyte with an SG of 1.32, both types having special separators to keep the different plates apart.

The chemical action of a normal lead-acid battery, when discharged, causes the lead plates to be converted to lead sulphate (white powder coating) and the electrolyte to become even more dilute. Because of this action it is possible to check the state of charge by measuring the density (SG) of the liquid. If the liquid level is allowed to drop so that the top of the plates become exposed to air then the lead sulphate becomes hardened and this is almost impossible to convert back to lead. This causes a reduction in plate capacity with an equal reduction in battery capacity, which will show itself by a refusal to start the engine (see *Hint*).

During charging the lead sulphate of the plates slowly returns to the lead peroxide of the positive plate and spongy grey lead of the negative plate. This process releases sulphate radicals, increasing the density of the liquid. Once all of the conversion that is going to be done, is done, the charging current attacks the water. This process CANNOT be hastened by increasing the current flow into the battery, all that happens is that the extra current will attack the water causing it to break up into oxygen and hydrogen, which is released in the form of bubbles. If the charging current were correct this would signal the end of the charging process.

> ### HINT
>
> If the starter motor spins reasonably quickly but the engine will not fire, do not assume that there is nothing wrong with the battery.
>
> The starter motors on modern motorcycles (circa 1990 onwards) have permanent magnet bodies. Although this type of starter motor doesn't draw the very high current of the electro-magnet starters fitted to older models, the current draw will cause the voltage of a discharged battery to drop to a level that may be insufficient to operate the ignition system, yet the starter motor still spins quite quickly. Do not be fooled into thinking that the battery is OK.
>
> The starter motors fitted to earlier motorcycles (and all cars) are of the electro-magnet type which draw a high current. If the battery is in a state of discharge, the starter motor will rapidly slow down and the ignition system refuse to fire. This is an extremely good indicator that the battery needs servicing or replacing.

3 Maintenance-free (MF) battery

Maintenance-free (MF) batteries are 'Sealed for Life' and require minimal maintenance. Unlike the conventional lead-acid battery described in Section 2, there is no loss of liquid and therefore no need to top them up. However, you still need to 'grease' the terminals and inspect the casing for signs of cracking and electrolyte leakage.

Preparing a new MF battery

Unless your dealer has prepared the battery beforehand, you will need to fill the battery will electrolyte. This is particularly the case with a battery which has been purchased mail-order. The new battery shown in the accompanying illustration is supplied in the following parts:

✔ The battery with a metallic sealing strip over its filler holes
✔ The electrolyte in a row of six plastic containers sealed inside a bag with the filler hole plug strip
✔ The terminal screws and nuts

> ⚠ **Warning: It is vitally important that you read and understand all the safety information supplied with the battery and printed on its case. You are advised to wear hand and eye protection during the battery filling process.**

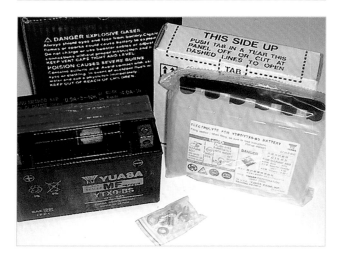

Procedure

1 Place the battery on a FLAT surface and remove the metallic sealing strip from the top of the battery.

2 Remove the electrolyte container from its plastic bag and remove the strip of caps. These will be used later for the battery filler plugs.

Do NOT under any circumstances remove or pierce the metal covers on the electrolyte container. Do NOT cut the tops off the bottles or split them apart from each other.

3 Turn the electrolyte container upside down and line up the six sealed areas with the six filler holes in the battery. When it is perfectly lined up push down with sufficient force to break the seals. Push the container fully home and air bubbles will start to rise in the bottles. Do NOT tilt the container as this may interrupt the flow of the electrolyte.

Make sure that air bubbles are rising in the containers. One or more containers not showing bubbles? Tap the top of the container two or three times with your hand to get things moving.

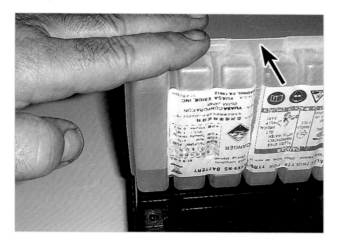

Because of its construction, the electrolyte has been precisely measured at the factory so take care when filling not to spill any electrolyte. If there is some electrolyte left in a bottle, even after tapping the container, gently squeeze the offending bottle to expel the last of the liquid.

Do NOT under any circumstances remove the container from the battery until the ALL the electrolyte has entered the battery. Do NOT be tempted to cut the jointing strip (arrowed above) – this will not speed up the process.

Now leave the battery in this state for at least 20 minutes.

4 Check that ALL the electrolyte has flowed from the bottles into the battery and ONLY then GENTLY pull the container from the battery. Seal the battery by fitting the strip of caps into the filler ports.

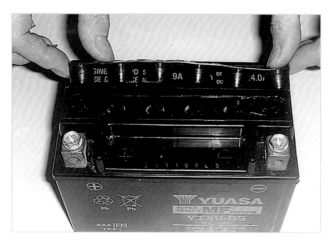

5 Press down gently with your thumbs to insert the caps in the filler ports. Start with the centre pair and push the caps down only half way. Move to the next pair i.e. numbers 2 and 5 and press them down only half way. Finally, move to the outer pair and push them half way down.

If the caps are difficult to fit, use a SMALL smear of silicon grease around the cap lips.

Now return to the centre pair and push them fully home. Repeat this procedure for the remaining caps, working from the centre outwards. Do NOT be tempted to hammer the caps in place. Such action is likely to cause microscopic cracks to appear in the case which will allow the battery to vent acid, resulting in a loss of electrolyte and early death to the battery.

Wipe the top of the battery to remove any moisture.

6 The fill-up procedure is now complete and the battery effectively sealed. There will never be a need to add any more water or electrolyte. NEVER remove the battery caps.

7 It is not normally necessary to charge the new battery before installing it on the machine but if you do wish to do so follow the instructions on the top of the battery. Refer to Section 5 for information on battery chargers and the procedure for charging an MF battery.

8 In terms of maintenance all you have to do is cover the terminals with battery grease or petroleum jelly after you have installed the battery and tightened the screws. An occasional wipe over the top with a clean rag and checking the tightness of the screws is all that is necessary. Basically this is a 'fit and forget' battery.

Technical

The MF battery uses a different construction to the normal lead-acid battery. Its plates are made from a lead calcium alloy, and the separators are made from a special glass fibre which retains the plates within each cell and keeps the active substances on the surfaces. Because of the separator construction the electrolyte is absorbed thus there is no free electrolyte, which allows the battery to be mounted at any angle. Never substitute a normal battery in place of an MF battery, even if it is cheaper. Not only would it be unsuitable, but in cases where it is mounted at an angle, electrolyte will be allowed to escape and corrode the machine.

Because the MF battery is sealed it is impossible to check its state of charge with an hydrometer. Instead connect a DC voltmeter (preferably a digital meter) set to the 0 – 20 DC volt range across the two battery terminals – positive (+) lead to positive terminal and negative (–) lead to negative terminal. At 20°C the terminal voltage for a fully charged battery will be just over 13V. If the battery is 50% discharged it will show approximately 12.5V. Note that a normal battery will show 12V until it is almost exhausted.

Note that the terminal voltage of a new MF battery, at initial fill, will show approximately 12.5V. This represents about 80% of the fully charged state and is due to the SG of the electrolyte around the plates being temporarily lowered. Do not be alarmed – the battery will be perfectly OK after 30 minutes.

The electrolyte in a Gel-cell maintenance-free battery takes the form of a thick gel, which doesn't flow as in a regular MF battery. Gel-cell batteries are supplied complete and do not require filling with electrolyte.

---

4 Charging voltage test

This simple test will confirm that the charging system is working correctly. The only item needed is a voltmeter set to DC Volts. The scale used will depend on the type of meter you have but as a rule of thumb, it should read between 0 – 20 DC Volts.

1 Before testing, make sure that the battery is in good condition and fully charged. Run the engine so that it is at normal operating temperature then stop the engine.

> ⚠️ **Caution: This test should be carried out with the machine in neutral and in a ventilated area.**

2 With your meter set to DC Volts and an appropriate scale, connect its positive probe to the battery positive terminal. Connect the negative probe to the battery negative terminal. Hold the probes in place and start the engine.

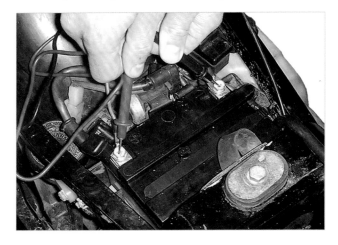

3 Open the throttle twistgrip until you reach the speed recommended by the manufacturer. As a 'rule of thumb' this speed is approximately 3000 revs/min. Don't hold the revs for more than a few seconds whilst you read the voltage – it should be between 13.5 and 15V.

4 Now switch on the lights and select main beam, noting the voltage reading. There may be a slight drop but it should never go below 13.5V. Stop the engine and disconnect the meter.

If the voltage exceeds 15V

✦ The regulator/rectifier is probably faulty and causing overcharging. Have the unit tested by a dealer.

A clue to overcharging is frequent bulb blowing. A second clue may be that your battery always needs topping up. This problem isn't going to go away if you ignore it – get it fixed.

If the voltage does not reach the minimum specification yet rises above 12V

This problem has a multitude of possibilities:

✦ The battery cannot HOLD its charge – even if you have recently charged it (get a new one).
✦ Something in the electrical system requires more current than the charging system can supply. Typically this might be the fitting of an aftermarket twin headlamp set-up or changing the headlamp bulb from a 35W item to a 60W one in the search for better lighting. You then have to decide to either live with the problem, go back to your original set-up, or have the alternator rewound to enable it to cope with the extra demand.
✦ Charging system fault – have the system tested by an electrical expert.

If the voltage does not rise above battery voltage

✦ Charging system fault caused by broken or disconnected wiring between the generator (alternator), regulator/rectifier or battery.
✦ Charging system fault caused by faulty alternator stator, rotor or regulator/rectifier.
✦ Loose battery terminal screws.
✦ The battery has reached the end of its working life.

5   Battery charging

The battery tends to be ignored until it suddenly fails. The failure may be due to a fault in the battery, old age (they don't last forever) or that the battery is exhausted because of a fault in the motorcycle's charging system (see charging voltage test).

Lack of use can also adversely affect the battery. This applies in climates where riding motorcycles in the winter is not practicable or where the owner prefers to take their motorcycle off the road during the winter season. Whatever the reason, the battery could be sitting in the motorcycle for 3 months or more, quietly discharging itself, so that when you want to use the motorcycle the battery will be in no condition to start the engine.

This problem will be exacerbated by the use of an alarm/immobiliser, which can place quite a drain on a battery and can lead to its voltage falling to a level where the alarm believes that the bike is being 'hot-wired' and the alarm sounds (usually around 2am!).

In all cases, particularly if the motorcycle is taken off the road, the battery should be given regular care and attention otherwise it will pay you back with interest come the nice weather.

Battery charging

There are a few myths about battery chargers:

✔ Any 12 volt charger will do – WRONG.
✔ The greater the charging current the quicker it will charge – WRONG.
✔ There is no difference between a car and a motorcycle battery, as far as charging rate goes – WRONG.

Each battery has an Amp/hour rating (either at the 10hr or 20 hr rate), which simply means that for a given load a battery will supply X amps for 10 or 20 hours. This is an important figure for charging as it gives the correct, MAXIMUM safe charging rate for each battery. The battery capacity will be marked on its case and the charging rate printed on its top surface – see the photos in Section 3.

For example:
A 14 amp/hour (AH) rated battery (typical large motorcycle) has a maximum charging rate of 1/10th of its amp/hour rating at the 10-hour rate, i.e. 1.4 amps. This value should not be exceeded when charging the battery, otherwise damage to the battery plates, due to excessive heat, will occur. In addition, the excess current attacks the water breaking it down into gas and fooling you into thinking that it is fully charged.

Note that you may see a 'quick charge' rate printed on the battery, e.g. 4.0A x 1 hr, instead of the regular 0.9A x 5 – 10 hr rate. This 'quick charge' can only be applied to MF batteries, not to conventional batteries.

Battery chargers

If you have a battery charger where you are able to control or adjust the charging rate, all well and good. If not, then it would be advisable to get one of the many electronically controlled chargers that are on the market. There are basically two types of battery charger, the CONSTANT CURRENT CHARGER and the CONSTANT VOLTAGE CHARGER.

Constant voltage charger

This is a very good charger for what it was designed for, but it has a maximum output of 4 amps. This is virtually 3 times the charging current for the biggest motorcycle battery. There are some motorcycle batteries that this type of charger can be used on, but they are few.

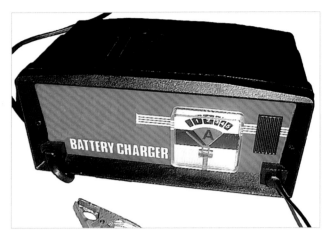

With this type of charger you must constantly check to see when charging has been completed, as there is no control built in to prevent overcharging. The minimum sized battery this can safely be used on has a rating of 40 amp/hours, i.e. a small car battery. The more sophisticated constant voltage charger will have a high/low switch and sometimes a 6V/12V switch as well.

Constant current charger

With the advent of the maintenance-free battery there are now many new chargers appearing on the market, some are 12V only, others are combined 6V and 12V.

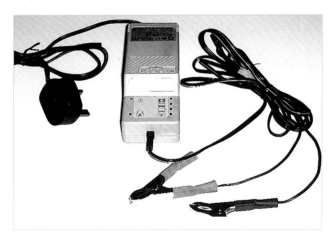

All control the charge rate electronically using programs that assess the state of charge and increase the voltage until charging starts. The voltage then drops to a lower level and the electronics monitor the battery's state of charge to prevent overcharging. These chargers can be left connected to the battery, even when it is connected to the motorcycle, as the unit will switch itself on and off assessing the battery and acting accordingly – this is particularly useful to ensure the battery receives a 'trickle' charge when in storage.

Despite the many advantages of the MF battery, it has one major drawback in that it can drop into a state of 'deep discharge'. Constant voltage battery chargers will generally NOT pull the battery out of this state, and many a good battery has been condemned because of this problem.

Use of a constant current charger can overcome 'deep discharge' and in the author's opinion is well worth the extra cost. For those who store their motorcycle over the winter these chargers can be left on permanently and save the hassle of removing the battery and remembering to trickle charge it once a month. This is even more important on machines that have an alarm fitted because although the drain on the battery may be small, over a long period (winter) it can cause the battery to become fully discharged. This also applies to a lesser extent, to motorcycles fitted with a clock.

The 'Drop' test

A battery charger cannot restore a battery if it has an internal short circuit or will not hold its charge. Most dealerships will have a piece of equipment that charges the battery and then puts a heavy load, say 25 Amps or more, across the battery for 15 seconds; the electronics show the battery condition via a series of lights. This process takes the best part of a day as the battery must first be charged – be prepared to wait a day or so.

If you suspect the battery is not holding its charge, evidenced because the starter will not turn the engine, or if it does the ignition system will not fire, this simple test will give some guidance.

✔ Charge the battery and refit it to the machine.
✔ Connect a DC voltmeter across the battery terminals. Select the appropriate scale (0 – 20V DC) and connect the positive lead to the positive terminal and the negative lead to the negative terminal.
✔ Switch on the ignition AND lights and operate the starter for a few seconds whilst looking at the voltmeter scale. The battery voltage will drop but should not drop below 9.5V for a 12V battery. If the voltage drops below this value the battery is faulty. Either fit a new battery, or if in doubt take the battery to a dealer to confirm your findings.

6   Bulb changing

Stop/tail lamp

The most common cause of either the stop or tail lamp not working is a broken filament in the bulb. On most machines the bulb is accessed by removing the tail lamp lens which will be retained by two screws. On some machines, however, you have to access the bulbs from inside the tail unit, under the seat. Select the appropriate procedure below.

Procedure – access by removing the tail lamp lens

1 Undo the two screws holding the lens cover to its housing.

2 Carefully remove the tail lens noting any washers that may be on the screws. Place the tail lens in a safe place, NOT on the floor where you are likely to tread on it.

3 Hold the bulb by its glass and push it inwards against the spring, whilst turning it in an anti-clockwise (left-hand) direction. This will release the bulb from the bulbholder.

4 Check that you have the correct new bulb. The usual stop/tail bulb is a dual filament 21/5 watt type, the 21W filament being for the stop lamp, and the 5W filament for the tail lamp.

Careful inspection of the stop/tail bulb (right) and turn signal bulb (left) will show that the dual filament stop/tail bulb has its pins offset and a different base connector.

5 With the old bulb removed, check the condition of the bulbholder within the housing. Clean off any corrosion with fine emery paper, then finish off with a clean lint-free rag.

6 To fit the new bulb, line up the pins with the slots in the bulbholder and push it in against its spring. Now turn the bulb in a clockwise direction until it locks into place. If it pops out or won't turn you have the pins out of alignment, turn the bulb 180° and try again.

7 Before refitting the lens, turn on the lights and operate the brakes to ensure that the bulb works. It is not unknown for a new bulb to be defective.

8 Check the condition of the rubber sealing ring. Any damage here and water will get into the unit and corrode the bulbholder. This causes all sorts of problems not least of which is that the corrosion acts as a resistance to the electricity flow and reduces the brightness of the lamp.

9 Fit the lens ensuring that it is a good fit against the rubber sealing ring. Check that any sealing washers are fitted on the lens screws then tighten them gently. Do NOT over tighten the screws or you will break the lens.

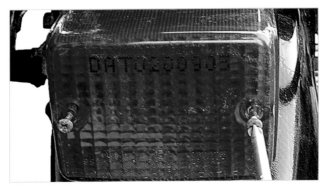

Procedure – access from inside the tail unit

10 Lift the seat and peer into the dark recesses of the tail unit at the back of the bike to locate the bulbholder. You may need to remove the toolkit to access the bulbholder.

11 Grip the bulbholder and twist it anti-clockwise (left-hand) direction. About a quarter of a turn will suffice. Do NOT grab hold of the wires and try to pull the holder out with them. You

will only break the wires where they join the holder necessitating a replacement part or a solder repair.

12 The bulb can be removed from the holder by pushing it in and twisting it anticlockwise. When fitting the new bulb ensure that you line up the pins correctly with the slots in the bulbholder. Push the bulb in gently and turn it clockwise to lock it in place.

13 Refit the holder and twist it clockwise to lock it in place. Note the different size tabs on the holder shown. Make sure that when replacing the holder the tabs line up with their corresponding slots in the tail unit.

Turn signal lamps

A common failure of the turn signal system is that one side works fine, whereas the other side won't flash and one of the bulbs doesn't light. This can usually be traced to one of the following:

✔ A broken feed wire or faulty earth return
✔ Bulb failure

Turn signals with the lens retained by two screws

1 To change the bulb, undo the two screws holding the lens in place. Note the sealing washers on this type. Place the lens and screws in a safe place – NOT on the floor where you are likely to tread on it.

2 Gently hold the bulb glass and push it inwards against its spring and at the same time turn it in an anti-clockwise (left-hand) direction. This will release the bulb pins from their locking mechanism and allow removal of the bulb.

3 To fit the new bulb, line up the metal pegs on the bulb body with the slots within the holder. Push the bulb home and at the same time, twist it clockwise until it locks into the holder. Now operate the turn signals to check that they work properly.

4 Check the condition of the sealing-rubber ring; any damage here and water will get in corroding the bulbholder, reducing its efficiency.

5 Line up the screw holes in the lens with the lugs in the housing and push the lens into place. Ensure that the lens is the correct way up. Keep hold of the lens and fit the top screw, a few turns, then fit the lower screw. Take care not to over-tighten them or the lens will crack.

Turn signals with the lens retained by a single screw

1 On some models, the lens is retained by a single screw on the back or underside of the turn signal. Hold the assembly with one hand whilst undoing the screw with the other, although be careful not to stab yourself with the screwdriver.

2 Have a good look around the edges of the lens and you will probably see a slot between the lens and the body, usually at the bottom. Use a flat-blade screwdriver to pop off the lens; be gentle and use a twisting motion to the screwdriver.

3 There will probably be a couple of projections within the housing, opposite the screw, that hold the lens in place. GENTLY ease the lens out of the housing.

4 Push and twist the bulb in an anti-clockwise (left-hand) direction to free it from the holder. With the bulb out, check the holder for corrosion and if present, clean up with fine emery paper. Finish with a clean, lint-free rag or kitchen paper.

5 To fit the new bulb, line up the pegs on its metal body with the slots in the bulbholder. Push the bulb home, against its spring, and turn the bulb in a clockwise direction to lock it into its holder. Now operate the turn signals to ensure that all is ok.

6 Before fitting the lens, check that the rubber sealing ring is in good condition. If in doubt replace it. If water gets into the unit it will corrode the bulbholder.

7 Line up the lens with the two lugs, ensuring that the screw hole and threaded portion of the lens also line up. GENTLY push the lens into its housing until it 'snaps' fully home.

8 Fit the screw to secure the lens; take care not to over-tighten it.

Turn signals set into the fairing or body panels

Where the front turn signals are set into the fairing, the bulb is often accessed from inside the fairing, leaving the lens in place.

1 Reach up inside the fairing and twist the bulbholder anticlockwise to free its tabs from the back of the turn signal.

2 Remove the bulb by pushing it in and twisting it anticlockwise.

'Mini' turn signals

For machines which have been fitted with 'mini' turn signals there are some important differences to note.

1 Undo the screws (three in this case) from the back of the turn signal and remove the lens.

2 The bulb inside is a Small Bayonet Cap (SBC) type and has a pointed end to the glass. Removal and replacement is the same as previously described.

3 When refitting the lens do NOT over-tighten the screws or it is possible that you will break the screw mounts

Turn signal bulb types

Three different types of single filament bulb are shown.

Turn signals bulbs are usually of the conventional type (B) and rated at 21W. Those used in 'mini' turn signals are usually of the Small Bayonet Cap type (SBC) type (A); these miniature bulbs can be obtained for 6 Volt and 12 Volt systems and are rated at 23 Watts.

The 'pilot' bulb (C) would be used for the rider warning lamp. It is a very low rate bulb usually 1.7W, 3.4W or 4W. Bulbs may be of the bayonet fitting type (as illustrated) or of the capless, plug-in, type shown on page 143.

Turn signal circuit and relay

The system consists of four lamps, a relay, the battery, ignition switch and turn signal switch. A separate circuit fuse can often be found and many machines have a self-cancelling function and hazard function.

If one side refuses to flash or only one bulb lights, switch the other side on. If this works fine then there is nothing wrong with the relay. In the case of only one bulb working check for poor or broken earth return wires as well as a faulty bulb. If both light up but don't flash, check the wattage of both bulbs.

It is essential that you only use the bulbs that are rated for your system. Lower wattage bulbs will slow down the rate of

flash and if too low, will cause the system to cease to flash altogether.

Look up the details in your owner's manual or refer to the information on the turn signal relay. The relay is usually a round, silver coloured unit or a small black box (see accompanying photo) and will have the voltage, wattage and the flash speed details on its surface. A typical example would be:

12.8V – 2 x 21W + 3.4W – 85 C/M.

This is for a 12V system using 21W bulbs front and rear and a rider warning bulb of 3.4W. The rate of flash would be a nominal 85 flashes per minute.

Headlamp

If you have a fully faired sports bike the headlamp bulb is usually accessed from the inside of the fairing – refer to your owners or workshop manual for details. Many machines still use the shell and headlamp system and this is described below.

1 If the headlamp has been on, allow it time to cool before removing the bulb, otherwise you will burn yourself.

2 This machine has two screws – one on each side (arrowed) – which hold the headlamp assembly to the shell. Undo the screws but hold the glass to prevent it falling when the screws are removed. Do NOT disturb the headlamp beam alignment screws – these are usually set in the rim of the headlight itself, and not in the side of the shell.

There will be a method of locating the headlamp and shell. This is often a spigot on the headlamp, which locates in a slot in the shell; check the fitting as you remove the headlamp.

3 If a rubber cover is fitted over the back of the headlamp, peel it back to gain access to the bulbholder.

Support the headlamp glass to prevent it falling on the floor and breaking. Release the bulb assembly, then twist and pull the bulb out of its holder. Note that this bulbholder has a small spigot (arrow) that locates in a slot in the reflector, which is held in place by a spring. Check the condition of the spring.

4 This headlamp uses a plastic bulbholder that also incorporates the pilot light. The bulbholder is held in place by a spring clip (A); check that it locks on assembly.

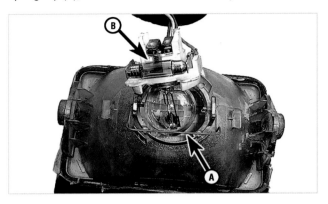

Note the pilot bulb (B); it is a 'festoon' type bulb held between two blades. It is also badly discoloured, which is a sure sign that it isn't going to last much longer. Replace it before it fails.

Headlamp bulb types

Two of the more common bulbs used in a headlamp are shown in the accompanying photo. Both are of the dual filament type (main beam and low beam) and use a three-pin connector.

The conventional bulb on the right has a glass envelope. The bulb on the left is a quartz-halogen bulb and has a special construction. Its envelope is made from clear quartz, not glass, and it is able to give more light for the same power as a conventional bulb. Quartz-halogen bulbs are commonly available as H1, H3, H4 and H7 types for motorcycle use; the dual-filament H4 type is illustrated above.

The important point when handling the quartz-halogen bulb is NOT to touch the envelope with your fingers. Even if your fingers are clean, the natural oils in your skin will affect the envelope, weakening it. This leads to premature failure of the bulb. If you do inadvertently touch the envelope, clean it with methylated spirit and a clean cloth. If you have no option but to hold the envelope of a quartz-halogen bulb, the use of a clean paper tissue or clean card to cover the bulb's envelope is a necessity.

Instrument panel bulbs and warning bulbs

The two common types of panel or warning bulbs are shown, bayonet fitting on the left and capless fitting on the right. Both are available for 6V and 12V systems and in a range of different wattages. To remove a bayonet fitting bulb, push it in and twist it anti-clockwise. To remove a caples bulb, simply pull it out of the bulbholder.

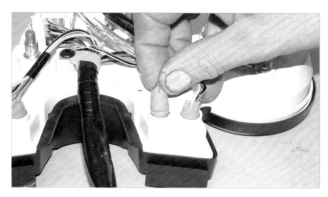

Access to these bulbs can be difficult, particularly where a fairing is fitted. Check with your owner's manual or workshop manual to establish the best way to get to the bulb. Also check whether it is actually a bulb, or an LED (light emitting diode) – LEDs cannot usually be replaced, although are unlikely to fail.

Once the bulbholder has been located it is just a case of pulling the holder (not by the wires) from the back of the instrument panel.

Gently remove the bulb from the holder. A capless type bulb is shown below.

Technical

Bulbs either last five minutes or seem to go on forever, but it can be guaranteed that they will invariably fail at the most in-opportune time. The two major causes of failure are:

✔ Switching them from on to off and vice versa.
✔ Being subjected to excessive vibration.

Switching from high beam to low beam or applying the brakes causes the filament (that little curly bit inside the glass) to heat up and then cool down, and it is this change that causes the life of the bulb to be shortened.

Vibration is the biggest cause of failure of a motorcycle bulb because the engine vibrates at a high frequency (older riders will remember the tingle we felt, through the bars at certain revs/min). To combat this the manufacturers rubber mount everything, but it doesn't last forever. Rubber hardens with age so check that the rubber grommets which hold the lamp assembly are in good condition.

The motorcycle manufacturer has determined the voltage of the system and the wattage of each individual bulb. Changing the wattage of any bulb can have an adverse effect.

Changing a 35W headlamp bulb to a 60W bulb or fitting a twin headlamp fairing in the search for better lighting can lead to a rapidly discharged battery. The purpose of the battery is to start the engine (via an electric starter where fitted) and supply all electrical needs at low engine speeds. The alternator supplies all the electrical requirements at higher engine speeds, and at the same time replenishes any electricity taken from the battery.

The alternator was designed for the electrical load of the original components, so if you have subsequently increased the current demand by approximately 2 Amperes or more when the lights are on, the alternator will try to supply this extra demand but something will have to give. The give in this case will be a reduction in charging voltage such that this voltage may not be enough to drive electricity into the battery. If the conditions are severe, the alternator may not be able to supply the system with a high enough voltage and the battery will do it instead, causing the battery power to drain rapidly. In this situation, the engine may start, but die as soon as the lights are turned on. Many a mechanic has scratched their head trying to work this out!

It is important when replacing a failed panel bulb that the wattage of the new bulb matches the manufacturer's specifications. For example, if a 1.7W bulb is specified for the clock illumination and you change it for a 3.4W or 4W bulb it will be too bright and can be a distraction for the rider. Electrically this will not be too much of a problem for large machines but can be a nightmare for smaller ones whose alternators often cannot cope with this slight increase.

Small machines, many of which are 6 volt and have generator-fed lighting systems (lights that only work when the engine is running) can have a detrimental effect on the battery's state of charge due to this slight increase in Wattage. In this instance, the charging output voltage, with the lights being supplied by a separate generator coil is very closely matched to the needs of the battery. Increasing the wattage

and therefore current demand, will cause the voltage to decrease with a corresponding reduction in lamp brilliance. There will also be a reduction in the battery charging voltage such that the battery may receive no charge at all. This often shows itself by the turn signals failing to flash. Changing the battery for a new one or one of greater capacity only puts off the day when you are going to have to do something about it.

If you suspect there is a problem with electrical load, first charge the battery, then check that all bulbs are of the correct wattage, replacing any that differ from the manufacturer's specification. If the problem is still evident, carry out a charging voltage test to check for a fault elsewhere in the system (see Section 4).

7 | Horn

Adjustment

If the horn has started to squeak rather than blare out, it is likely that adjustment is required to restore its sound.

Items required
✔ Screwdriver – usually a crosshead type.
✔ Small pot of paint and tiny paintbrush or dead matchstick pared to a point.
✔ Small spanner to fit the adjuster screw locknut.

Procedure

1 The horn is usually situated at the front of the bike, often on the steering lower yoke, frame downtubes or radiator mounts. Locate the adjusting screw on the back of the horn. This may be locked in place by a small nut or held in place by an internal plastic locking mechanism.

2 Loosen any locknut, switch the ignition on, press the horn button for a second, and note the tone.

3 Turn the screw, one way or the other, by no more than an 1/8th of a turn, and press the horn button again. If the sound gets better, continue turning the screw in small increments until

the optimum sound it achieved. If the tone quietens, you are turning the screw the wrong way.

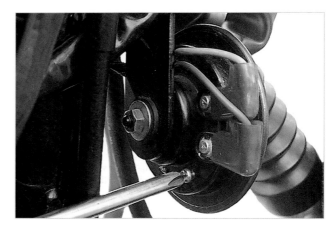

4 Tighten the locknut, if fitted. Apply a small blob of paint to the thread of the screw. This will hold the adjustment in place against the rapid vibrations of the horn body.

Fault finding

If the horn has stopped working and adjustment shows no improvement, it is likely that its electrical circuit has failed. This simple test will determine whether it is the horn or the circuit wiring/button which is at fault.

Items required
✔ A working bulb. For a 12 volt system a 12V, 35W bulb is ideal. For a 6 volt system use a 6V, 25W or 6V, 35W bulb.
✔ Two lengths of insulated cable with suitable connectors fitted.

Procedure

1 With the ignition switched OFF disconnect the wires at the horn, and connect your two wires and lamp to the loom as shown. This takes the horn out of circuit and puts the lamp into circuit in its place. You can connect any bulb wire to any horn wire – polarity is not important.

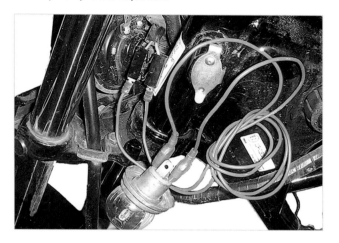

2 Switch the ignition ON and press the horn button.

If the lamp lights the circuit is proved good and horn is confirmed faulty.

If the lamp does not light, the fault is in the circuit wiring, fuse or horn button, or your test lamp is faulty. Check your lamp is working by connecting its two wires to the battery terminals. The horn button can be inspected by separating the handlebar switch (see Section 8) and the fuse can be checked (see Section 9), but if the problem is due to a wiring fault you may need to consult your dealer or an electrical expert.

3 If the horn only has one wire connector, its earth return will be via the frame. To test, disconnect the horn wire and connect either of your two lamp cables to the loom wire and your other cable to a good 'earth' point on the frame or direct to the battery ground terminal (negative). Switch on the ignition and press the horn button. Interpret the results as in Step 2 above.

4 Replacement of the horn is a simple case of switching off the ignition, disconnecting the horn wires, undoing the mounting screw and fitting the new horn. Re-connect the wires to the new horn and if necessary, adjust its tone.

8 Handlebar switchgear

Although electrical failures can be a real problem to sort out, the weakest link is often where an electrical circuit is operated by a mechanical switch. Water ingress of the switch causes its internal contacts to corrode, reducing the efficiency of the system and possibly causing the switch to break up. The handlebar switchgear does not usually appear as part of the service schedule, but a few minutes spent each year doing the following tasks will help to reduce the possibility of switch failure.

1 First peer underneath the switch and locate the two (sometimes three) screws that hold the two halves together. Note that the switches split vertically on some machines, with the screws at the top and bottom of the front section. Often the throttle twistgrip pulley shares the right-hand switch housing and the choke lever shares the left-hand switch housing, so make sure you take careful note of how they locate as the switch housings are separated.

2 Slacken the screw that is to the rear of the machine then

slacken the screw that is forward of the machine BEFORE removing either. If the switch has been correctly assembled, the front screw will be extremely tight and trying to undo it first will only chew up the head. Make sure that you use the correct size screwdriver on these screws.

3 With the screws removed, separate the two halves of the switch. If there is moisture inside the switch or its contacts are visibly corroded, spray with a water-dispersant fluid such as WD40. Apply silicone grease along the leading edge of the switch joint (arrowed), i.e. the joint which faces forwards. This will help to keep rain water out of the switch.

4 Before fitting the screws, open the throttle by about 1/4 of its movement and refit the two switch halves. Hold the two halves together with one hand and operate the throttle with the other to ensure that it works freely. If it doesn't, separate the two halves and start again.

Note that some switches have a locating peg which engages a hole in the handlebar, thus ensuring that the switches themselves are in the correct position.

5 Fit BOTH screws but only tighten them by a TURN or TWO to start with. First, fully tighten the forward screw to bring the two switch halves firmly together on the front edge. Now tighten the rear screw. This will cause the gap between the two halves of the switch to be facing towards the rear of the machine. In addition to the grease applied previously, this will prevent rain water from being driven into the front facing joint of the switch. Note that the tightening sequence will cause the front screw to be very tight as the second screw pulls the two switch halves together.

HINT

The screw locations are quite often deeply recessed in the underside of the switches. To keep the screws in place try putting a dab of grease on the end of the screwdriver, then placing the screw onto the driver and feeding the screw up into the switch.

9   Fuses

The fuse is a safety device, designed to fail if the current flow exceeds a safe limit, thereby protecting electrical components from damage.

Fuse holders

Fuse holders are usually located in a place which is protected from the elements, such as under the seat, behind a side panel or in the tail section. The accompanying photo shows a selection of typical fuse holders.

A typical under-seat fuse box is shown below. The decal on the inside of the lid contains a key to the circuits protected and fuse rating. Most fuse boxes also have provision for spare fuses to be carried.

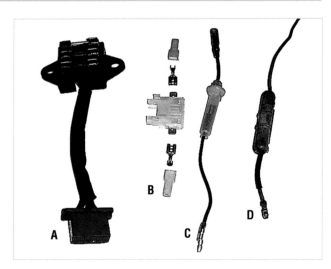

A is a fuse box which, in this case holds three glass fuses.

B is a single fuse holder which takes the modern, plastic coated 'blade' fuse. It can be connected to other fuse holders to form a bank of fuse holders.

C and D are in-line fuse holders for housing glass fuses.

Fuses

The accompanying photo shows the typical fuse types. All fuses have their Ampere rating (current rating) marked on them in some way.

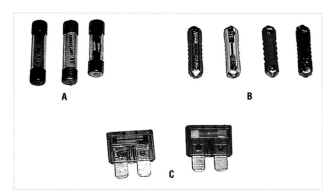

A Glass fuses. They are in various lengths with the most common being 20 mm and 32 mm. The fuse rating is on a piece of paper within the glass or printed on one end cap.

B European ceramic fuses. These are 20 mm long and have the fuse wire on the outside. The fuse rating is stamped on the metal strip or incorporated in the colour-coded body moulding.

C Blade type fuses. A pair of 6 mm (1/4 in) blades connected by the fuse wire and encapsulated in plastic. As well as being colour-coded (see table), the fuse rating is printed on the end of the fuse. Modern versions can now be purchased that become illuminated if the fuse should fail; this can be a boon on a dark wet night when you are hunting an electrical failure.

The blade type fuses tend to fit so well in their holders that they can be difficult to remove without breaking your fingernails. Use of the tool shown makes removal of the fuse extremely easy.

Blade fuse colour coding

Continuous	Fusing	Colour
3 Amps	6 Amps	Violet
4 Amps	8 Amps	Pink
5 Amps	10 Amps	Tan
7.5 Amps	15 Amps	Brown
10 Amps	20 Amps	Red
15 Amps	30 Amps	Light blue
20 Amps	40 Amps	Yellow
25 Amps	50 Amps	White
30 Amps	60 Amps	Light green

Ceramic fuse colour coding

Continuous	Fusing	Colour
5 Amps	10 Amps	Yellow
8 Amps	16 Amps	White
16 Amps	32 Amps	Red
25 Amps	50 Amps	Blue

10   Crimping cable connectors

There are two distinct types of cable connectors and each is used with its corresponding cable crimping tool. Referring to the accompanying photograph, the set on the right are the 'Japanese type' of connectors with their crimping tool; the 'female' connector has a full, plastic or rubber cover whereas the 'male' connector is only partially covered. When the two connectors are joined, the complete joint is covered in plastic. The set on the left are the 'Pre-insulated' connectors with their crimping tool; these are commonly found in auto-spares stores etc.

Japanese type connectors can accommodate cables with a cross-sectional area of up to 2 mm. Pre-insulated connectors can accommodate cable sizes up to 6 mm.

'Japanese' connector and crimping tool

Procedure

1 Use the cutting blade to remove about 1/4 inch from the end of the cable. This will give you a neat, squared end to start with.

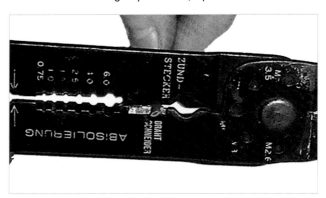

2 You can see from the photo that when closed the tool has a number of 'holes' down its length. These are the 'stripping' holes. Select a hole that is approximately the same size as the wire inside the plastic sleeve of the cable. Put approximately 1/4 inch of wire through the hole and squeeze the handles shut.

3 With the handles held completely shut, pull the tool away from you and the outer, plastic coating will be stripped away. This is what you should be left with after stripping the cable.

If any of the strands are damaged or broken then you probably used a hole that was too small. Repeat steps 1 and 2, but this time use the next size larger hole.

HINT

The tool seems to strip easier if you use it backwards and hold the cable right by the tool as shown in the centre left-hand photo.

4 The crimping end of the tool. Note the three, different sized sets of teeth; each set is used to close differing size sets of connector 'ears'. To find which set of teeth are best for which set of ears.

✦ Place a crimp into the largest set of teeth, with the ears uppermost (into the 'M' shape).
✦ Gently close the jaws until they just hold the crimp.
✦ Now wiggle the crimp about inside the jaws. If the jaws hold the crimp firmly you have the correct size. If not, try the next size down.

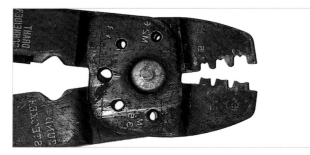

HINT

The larger set of connector ears (cable crimp) is often closed with the largest set of teeth, whereas the wire crimp is usually closed with the middle set of teeth.

5 Slide the cover over the cable FIRST then place the cable into the connector as shown. The plastic coating is to be crimped by the rear pair of ears and the wire by the front pair.

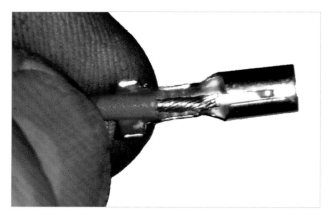

Check the length of wire, it should just pass the end of the ears but not protrude too far into the body of the connector. If it does it will get in the way of the male bullet; trim it to fit if necessary.

6 Place the tool around the rear pair of ears, ensuring that the tool is central to the ears.

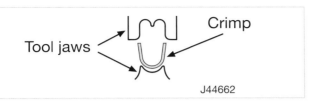

Close the jaws and squeeze hard on the handles. This action will fold the ears over and clamp them to the plastic sleeve.

Note that the plastic sleeve is tight up against the inner pair of ears.

7 Repeat this process for the inner pair of ears. The inner ears are smaller than the outer pair so this time use the centre section of the tool. Squeeze hard to get a good, tight joint.

8 The finished joint should look like this. There is no need to reinforce this with solder, as it is quite strong enough. Slide the cover up over the connector.

HINT

When you are linking the male and female connectors together make sure that the male cover slides inside the female cover for a waterproof connection.

Pre-insulated connector and crimping tool

Pre-insulated connectors are available in many different terminal designs, but all conform to three cable sizes. The smallest cable size has red covers, the next size up has blue covers and the largest size has yellow covers. The cable sizes which these connectors can accommodate are as follows:

- ✦ Red   0.65 to 1.5 mm²
- ✦ Blue   1.5 to 2.5 mm²
- ✦ Yellow   3.0 to 6.0 mm²

Note the three corresponding different size 'teeth' to the jaws and the colored paint marks. The inner set clamp the largest connectors (yellow), the centre set clamp the smallest size (red) and the outer set clamp the medium size (blue).

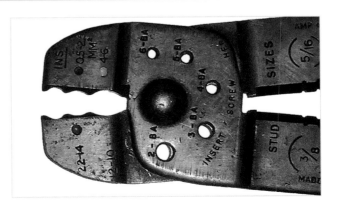

Procedure

1 Follow steps 1 to 3 of the 'Japanese connector' section to trim the cable and strip the plastic coating.

2 Note the two bulges in the plastic; these are the two ends of the metal crimp. Line up the trimmed cable with the plastic and cut the wire to match the plastic.

3 Hold the cable in place and fit the tool jaws around the lower part of the plastic. Squeeze the handles of the tool together to make the first clamp.

4 With the first clamp made, release the pressure on the handles, slide the tool up the crimp and squeeze again.

5 The finished connection should look like this. Note the two indentations in the plastic created by the tool jaws, and the length of wire showing through.

The one disadvantage is that this type of connection, when mated with its counterpart, should really have a plastic cover over it to exclude water (see 'Heat shrink sleeve' in Chapter 1 for details of this process).

11   Cable sizes

Cables are made up of a number of strands of copper wire (generally 0.30 mm diameter per strand) and insulated with a plastic sheath. The specification is described below:

Number of strands	**14**/0.30, 1 mm², 8.75 Amps
Diameter of each strand in mm.	14/**0.30,** 1 mm², 8.75 Amps
Cross sectional area in sq. mm.	14/0.30, **1 mm²,** 8.75 Amps
Continuous current carrying capacity in Amps.	14/0.30, 1 mm², **8.75 Amps**

The table below lists the cross-sectional area and continuous current carrying capacity of the common cable sizes.

Size	Cross-sectional area	Continuous current carrying capacity (single run cable)
9/0.30 mm	0.65 mm²	5.75 Amps
14/0.30 mm	1.0 mm²	8.75 Amps
28/0.30 mm	2.0 mm²	17.5 Amps
44/0.30 mm	3.0 mm²	27.5 Amps
65/0.30 mm	4.5 mm²	35.0 Amps

To calculate the cable size for a given application you will need to know the voltage applied (from your battery) and the wattage of the component. Use the formula: WATTS ÷ VOLTS = AMPS

For example, if you are fitting a quartz-halogen headlamp of 12 volts, 60 watts. Applying the formula to work out the cable size required:

60W ÷ 12V = 5 Amps. Therefore a 9/0.30 mm size cable would be able to carry the current.

There is a proviso to this. If the cable is to be run in a loom with other cables then they will be heating each other. To ensure that the cable does not overheat increase the current by 50%, i.e. select a cable capable of carrying 7.5 Amps (5 Amps + 50%), thus a 14/0.30 mm cable.

Motorcycle manufacturers apply their own standard colours for battery positive feed and earth return negative feed. The main types are listed in the table.

Manufacturer	Battery positive lead	Battery negative lead
Aprilia	Blue	Black
Honda	Red/White tracer	Green
Kawasaki	White	Black/Yellow tracer
Suzuki	Red	Black/White tracer
Yamaha	Red	Black

12   Soldering

Items required

- ✔ Soldering iron – A 25 or 40Watt iron is adequate.
- ✔ Multi-core solder. This has the flux (soldering agent) within the solder, and does not affect the copper wire. Other fluxes can weaken the wire under the sheath causing the joint to fail.
- ✔ Soldering iron stand. There is nothing more painful than resting part of your flesh on a hot iron.
- ✔ Piece of wood to rest the iron and work on (see text).
- ✔ Wire cutters and strippers.
- ✔ Insulating sleeve and PVC tape or heat shrink sleeve.

Making a soldered joint

1 Strip the two wires to be joined, leaving about one inch of wire showing. See the previous section on Crimping for details of how to strip back the wire insulation.

Place the two wires together as shown, and trim the wires so that they are of equal length.

2 Spread the wires and feed them into each other so that the end of one wire butts up to the sheath of the other.

Note the yellow insulating sleeve on one wire. Fit this BEFORE you make the joint. The sleeve needs to be approximately 1 1/2 times the length of the joint.

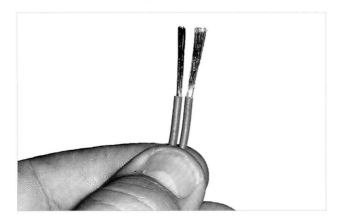

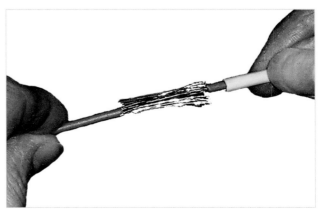

3 Hold one end of the joint and twist the strands together. When you have completed this hold the other end and complete the twist.

Some people prefer to lay the wires side by side and solder them rather than twisting them together. This method, however, allows the electrical current to flow through the solder joining the wires. If the current is sufficiently high, the joint may weaken and even part. By twisting the stands together it ensures that the current flows through the wire and the solder only holds the joint together.

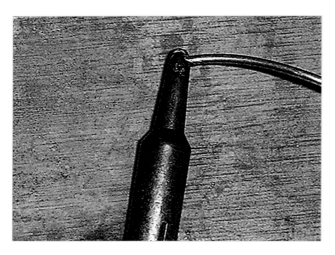

4 Switch the soldering iron on and place it in the stand provided with the iron (see Chapter 1). When the iron is hot (only takes a couple of minutes) lay it on the block of wood and apply solder to its tip. The solder will melt and form a 'blob' on the tip.

Remove the solder wire and, taking great care to avoid burning your hands, clean the blob of solder from the iron tip with a DAMP rag. The iron is now 'tinned'.

5 Place the hot iron tip UNDER the centre of the joint and wait a few seconds. Count to ten before carrying on to the next stage.

Now apply the solder to the soldering iron tip at the exact junction of wire and tip. This is where the magic happens – the solder will run through the joint all by itself.

6 Keep the iron in the middle of the joint and run the solder along the top. There is no need to move the iron, just the solder wire.

When the joint is completely covered with solder, remove the solder wire and SLIDE the iron away from the joint. Do NOT lift the joint off the iron or you will leave a large unsightly blob of solder on the joint.

Have a damp rag handy to immediately wipe the excess solder from the joint because you are bound to use far too much solder when you first practice this.

7 Whilst the solder is still warm, slide the sleeve over the joint until it is completely covered.

If using heat shrink sleeve, use a hairdryer to reduce the sleeve in size (see Chapter 1). If using PVC tape, wait a few moments for the joint to cool, then wrap a small amount of tape around each end.

Soldering a connector

1 Cut and trim the cable as described in the previous section on Crimping. Twist the wire stands together and feed it into the eyelet until the plastic sheath is tight up against the metal end. If necessary, trim the wire so that it extends about half way up the tag as shown.

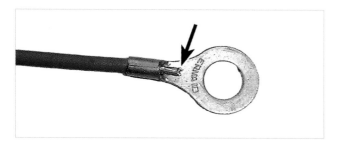

2 Prepare ('tin') the soldering iron as described in Step 4 of the previous section on making a soldered joint.

3 Remove the wire from the eyelet make sure that it is still twisted and 'tin' the exposed wire stands of the cable.

This entails laying the wire on the iron tip so that the centre of the wire is about halfway down the tip. Leave it on the iron for a few seconds.

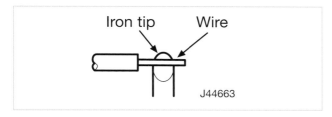

Iron tip   Wire

J44663

Now apply solder to the WIRE. Capillary action will cause the solder to run into the wire.

Remove the iron and solder. Taking care to avoid burning your hands, wipe any excess solder from the wire using a damp cloth.

4 Slide the tinned wire into the eyelet until the plastic sheath is tight up against the eyelet, then lay the assembly on the wood.

Place the soldering iron on the wire, leaving a gap between the end of the iron and the eyelet that is the same width as the solder. Wait a few seconds then apply the solder to this gap. Again, capillary action will work its magic. Remove the iron and solder and hold the cable until the joint hardens (a few seconds).

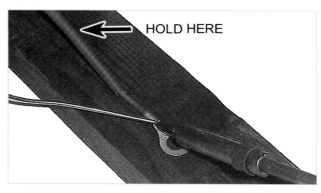

HOLD HERE

5 Switch the soldering iron off when the job is complete and place it in its holder to cool. If you lay it on the wood, you are bound to rest your hand on its hot end – very painful.

6 Allow the solder to cool and harden (takes only a few seconds) BEFORE lifting the wire from the wood. Slide the sleeve over the warm end to insulate it and the job is done.

If you have been a bit heavy with the solder wipe the excess from the joint with a damp cloth before it hardens.

Chapter 6
Accessories

Contents

1 Twin horn conversion

Converting from a single to a twin horn system is not as difficult as it first appears and will enhance the horn sound considerably.

Items required

- ✔ A second horn – similar to the original or purchase a pair from an auto accessory store.
- ✔ A relay – 30Amp is sufficient.
- ✔ A variety of connectors and lengths of different coloured wire (see the section on cable sizes in Chapter 5).
- ✔ In-line fuseholder and fuse. The rating of the fuse will depend upon the type of horns used. Those used in this example draw approximately 2.5 Amps each, so a 7 Amp fuse is used.
- ✔ Crimping tool and soldering iron (see Chapter 5).

Procedure

1 Before commencing work, disconnect the earth cable (negative) from the battery and tuck it out of the way. This will prevent any accidental short circuits that may cause fuses to fail or even cause an electrical fire.

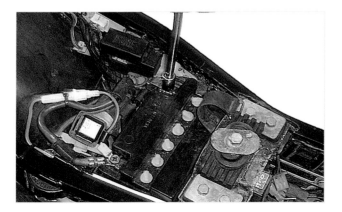

2 Remove the fuel tank, side panels, seat and headlamp to gain access to the main loom etc.

3 Decide where to mount the horns. Select a position that gives sufficient clearance between the horns and any frame or body panels, then install the horns securely via their mounting brackets so that they are not obstructed by body panelling, and do not interfere with free steering movement or suspension travel.

4 Find a suitable location for the relay where it will not become waterlogged or covered in road dirt, will not affect the steering or get in the way of cables or wiring. In the example shown, the relay is mounted inside the headlamp shell.

5 Disconnect the two original horn wires and connect them to the relay terminals 85 and 86. Which lead connects to which terminal doesn't matter. It may be necessary to make up extension leads so that they reach the relay.

The relay

A relay is a remote switch which allows a small current to control a much larger current. The reason for using a relay is to ensure that large currents do not flow through the control switches. A typical example of this is the starter motor circuit, where the relay allows the use of a small current to switch the starter circuit on, thereby making it unnecessary to route the heavy starter cable via the handlebar switch.

Illustrations 1 to 6 show the internal circuitry of the different types of relay and their applications. Current flow through the coil, via pins 85 and 86, creates an electromagnetic force that operates the internal contacts. This allows current to flow through the contacts via the input pin 30 and the output pin 87.

Most relays will have some form of information on the body. The relay shown on the right, has four pins, 12 Volt 30 Amp capacity, is normally open, and closes when activated. Look closely at the pin area, there will often be very small numbers next to the pins that relate to the circuit shown on the body. Most relays are of the 'normally open' type (illustrations 1 to 4). The 'normally closed' type of relay (illustration 5) is sometimes used – one application is for a carburettor warmer circuit which is on until switched off by a thermoswitch.

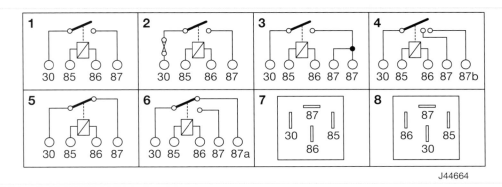

1 4-Blade, single on – off relay. Used for spot-lamps, horns etc.
2 Same as shown in illustration 1 but with a replaceable fuse built into the accessory circuit.
3 5-Blade, twin make-and-break. Same as shown in illustration 1 but with two output pins at 87.
4 5-Blade, Double make-and-break. Powers two circuits that are independent when off.
5 4-Blade, normally closed relay. Breaks the circuit when activated.
6 5-Blade, changeover. Circuit 87a is on until the relay is activated, then it switches off and circuit 87 switches on.
7 Pin layout number 1. Look at the base of the relay and each pin will have its own number.
8 Pin layout number 2. A variation of number 1. It is necessary to fit the correct type if you are replacing an existing relay.

Two basic original equipment horn circuits are shown in diagrams A and B. The conversion for a twin horn circuit is shown in diagram C.

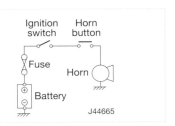

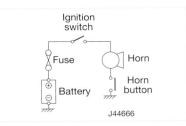

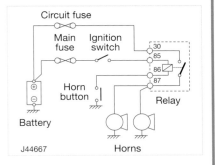

A Original equipment circuit (push button switch before horn)

B Original equipment circuit (push button switch after horn)

C Twin horn circuit and relay wiring

6 Make up a double lead and connect one end to relay terminal 87 and the other two ends to one terminal of each horn.

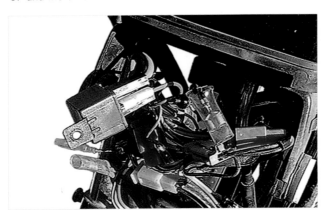

7 Make up a second double lead but connect this to the other horn terminals and run the single end down towards the battery. Do NOT connect it to the battery's negative terminal yet. Lay the New Wires Alongside the Main Loom

8 Make up a single lead with an in-line fuseholder close to the battery or relay end and connect one end to relay terminal 30 run the other end down towards the battery's positive terminal. Again, do not connect it to the battery yet.

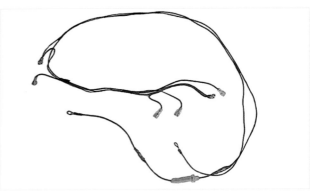

9 With the relay mounted and all wires connected to it, use tape to produce a mini loom and tape the battery leads (shown above) to the main loom.

10 Disconnect the battery positive lead and connect the relay lead with the fuseholder and the main positive lead to the battery's positive terminal.

11 Connect the negative lead and the lead from the horns to the battery's negative terminal.

12 Finally, check that the steering is not affected by any wires, switch on the ignition and test the horn system. Replace all components that have been removed, i.e. headlamp etc.

2   Fitting fork gaiters

Chapter 4, Section 7 included an example of a front fork stanchion pitted by stone chips. If the stanchion's working surface becomes chipped, rust will set in and the rough edges of the mark will tear the fork seal lips. Fork oil will be lost leading to uneven damping and poor handling. Replacing the seal only puts off the inevitable stanchion replacement, or regrind and re-chrome, both of which are very expensive.

This sort of damage can be prevented by fitting fork gaiters. Although not aesthetically pleasing on sports machines, fork gaiters are a practical solution for machines which are in everyday all year round use. Fork gaiters can be fitted to conventional forks, but not upside-down forks.

Items required

✔ Spanners, sockets etc. for removing the front forks and mudguard.
✔ A pair of gaiters – the diameter and length will depend upon your own motorcycle. Measure the diameter of the fork stanchion directly below the bottom yoke and the length from the bottom yoke to the top of the slider – then select a pair that is bigger than these measurements.
✔ Four plastic cable ties or metal screw-type 'Jubilee' clips.

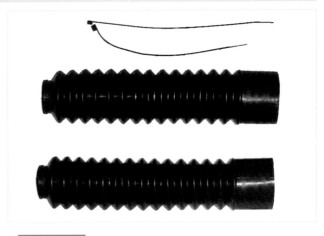

HINT

As fitting fork gaiters requires the forks to be removed from the machine, you could combine this job with a fork oil change.

Procedure

1 Refer to Chapter 4, Section 7 and remove one fork leg from the machine.

2 If the fork has a dust cover which fits over the fork slider, prise this off the slider and slip it off the stanchion (keep the dust seal safe for when you sell the machine). If the fork has a dust seal which fits inside the slider it can be left in place.

3 Clean all dirt and grime from the stanchion and top few inches of the slider. Check that there is no sign of oil leakage past the seal – if so this must be rectified before fitting the gaiters.

4 Slide the gaiter down over the fork stanchion (wide end first), then push it over the slider as far as the end piece will allow. If the gaiter is difficult to push over the slider use a small amount of water to act as a lubricant. The gaiter will usually have an air vent hole – position the gaiter so that it will be facing the back of the fork when it is installed.

5 If you are going to use metal clips to secure the gaiter, install the bottom clip (large one) first followed by the smaller, top clip. Tighten the bottom clip so that it clamps the gaiter to the top of the fork slider. Do NOT tighten it until it 'surrenders', just tight enough so that the gaiter will not rotate or move.

6 Refit and tighten the fork leg in the yokes. When both forks and the wheel have been installed, slide the top end of the gaiter up the fork leg until it is tight against the underside of the bottom yoke. Hold it in this position and fit and tighten the second cable tie or screw-type clip. If using plastic cable ties cut off the excess once they are secure.

---

3   Fitting a top box

There are two important points to bear in mind when considering fitting a top box:

✦ Unless a rear carrier is already fitted, purchase a carrier which is specifically designed for your machine.
✦ It is also essential that you purchase a box that relates to the size of your machine. A large box may be the correct thing for a touring motorcycle but will be far too much for a 50cc scooter.

Before fitting the top box, observe the following guidelines:
✦ Lay the parts on the floor (in the correct order) and check that everything is there. This also allows you to see how they fit together.
✦ Read the instructions supplied before fitting any part.
✦ Leave all bolts/nuts loose as you go and tighten them at the end.

The quickly-detachable top box

The top box illustrated here is supplied complete with a mounting plate, suitable for fitting to many different types of rear carrier. The mounting plate allows the top box to be easily removed from the machine.

1 Lay the plate on the carrier and fit the red plugs and screws into the appropriate square holes (arrows).

2 Working from underneath, offer up each clamp in turn and check that they grip the carrier bars. Note that it may be necessary to move the red plugs and screws to different holes to ensure that the clamps fit correctly.

Many clamps are double ended, with a different shape to each end, thus making the clamps almost universal. Choose which end is the better shape for the bar diameter of your carrier. Fit the nuts (Nyloc nuts in this case) but do NOT tighten them fully at this time.

3 Fit the top box to the mounting plate and ensure that it does not foul the seat or any part of the machine. Also, check that it is not overhanging the back of the machine by too much. If all is well, tighten the nuts and recheck the box position.

The permanently fixed top box

If you are fitting one of the older style of top boxes, where it is necessary to drill holes in the box, follow these guidelines.

1 Put the box on the carrier and place the clamps in their respective positions.

2 While holding each clamp in turn, mark the holes for drilling.

3 Make sure that the position of the box is central to the carrier and allows the lid to fully open without fouling any part of the machine. The strap on the right hand side prevents the lid opening too far.

4 When fitting the screws, use large washers under the heads of the screws to spread the load. This will help to prevent the box splitting at the drilled holes.

5 Use self-locking (Nyloc) nuts or lock washers.

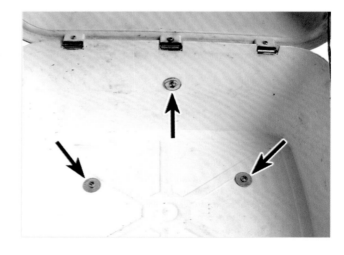

HINT

Do not be tempted to fill the top box with a lot of heavy items or a single heavy item which is allowed to slide from side to side. Excessive weight may place too great a strain on the carrier causing it to break. Too much weight extended behind the machine will cause the steering to be light, resulting in less grip from the front tyre.

4   Fitting an automatic drive chain oiler

The drive chain oiler operates off engine vacuum to dispense a measured amount of oil onto the drive chain whilst the engine is running. There are a number of automatic drive chain oiler kits available, all of which are relatively easy to fit. The following procedure illustrates the fitting of a Scottoiler kit.

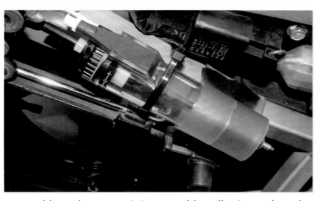

. . . and here the reservoir is secured by adhesive pads and a cable-tie.

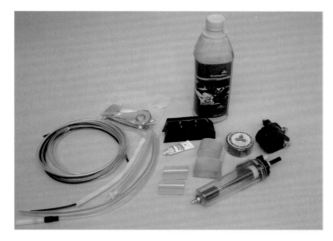

There are a few important points to note before you start:

✦ Remove all parts from the box and check that everything has been supplied.
✦ Read the fitting instructions thoroughly. Familiarise yourself with the various parts, how they connect to each other and in what order you want to fit them. There is no 'hard and fast' rule as to which is the correct order, as this will depend on the system you have purchased and your make and model of machine.
✦ Have a few extra cable-ties to hand.

1 The oil reservoir can be mounted in any position, but aim to position it as vertical as possible.

Mount the unit away from sources of heat such as the engine, exhaust, radiator etc; typical locations are behind a body panel, under the seat, to the main frame or rear sub-frame tubing, or even behind the licence plate bracket. Make certain that the filler hole is uppermost (allows the unit to breathe) and that the adjuster knob is accessible. Most kits contain several mounting attachments for the oil reservoir.

There is often space under the rear bodywork for the reservoir. Here a right-angled bracket is used to mount the reservoir . . .

On this small capacity machine, the kit's mounting cradle is positioned in place of the tool roll and the rubber strap used to hold the reservoir securely.

2 There are various ways to connect the dispenser assembly. Ensure that the installation is as neat, durable and safe as you can make it with the parts supplied.

The dispenser tube can be secured to the swingarm or chainguard with cable-ties or the fixing strips/adhesive provided. Here the tube is fixed to the underside of the swingarm and cable-ties used for extra security – trim the ends of the ties to prevent them contacting the chain.

Use a hairdryer or paint gun to heat the dispenser tube sufficiently to bend it so that its cut end is a few millimetres from the chain sideplate and with its open facing outwards. The tip of the dispenser should be in the 6 or 7 o'clock position relative to the sprocket and there should be no contact with the sprocket mounting nuts.

Here the bracket (arrowed) supplied in the kit is mounted to the wheel spindle and enables the end of the dispenser to be held in the correct position.

When routing the delivery tube to the reservoir, be sure to avoid contact with the chain and the exhaust and check that the tube doesn't

interfere with suspension components that could fatigue to wear through it. Try to follow the route of existing wiring or cables and use cable-ties to keep the delivery tube in place, taking care that it doesn't become pinched or trapped at any point. A little slack in the tube at the swinging arm pivot will allow for suspension movement.

3 Connect the delivery tube to the stub on the base of the oil reservoir and the small-bore vacuum pipe to the top of the reservoir.

4 The kit is supplied with a variety of vacuum connectors. Select a vacuum source appropriate to the fittings on your machine.

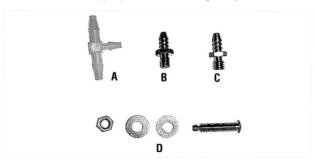

✦ The 'T' piece (A) is used when a vacuum operated fuel tap is fitted. Locate the vacuum pipe which runs from the fuel tap to the inlet tract and cut it. Fit the 'T' piece between the two cut ends. Note that on many fuel injected models, the vacuum pipes link each inlet tract or throttle body.

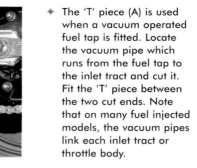

✦ Vacuum take-off point adaptors B (5 mm) or C (6 mm) fit where there are vacuum take-off points provided in the inlet tracts (arrow). If you use this type, ensure that you fit a sealing washer under the adaptor.

✦ Adaptor D can be used where there is no facility to use the types described above. Remove a rubber inlet tract and drill a 3 mm hole in it. Apply a sealant to the threads (Silicon RTV or similar), fit the adaptor through the hole, with a washer on each side, and tighten the nut.

✦ This vacuum take-off stub has a rubber cap fitted over it in normal use. It provides an ideal take-off point for the vacuum pipe, although check that the stub diameter is the correct size for the vacuum pipe.

Whichever vacuum source has been selected, connect the vacuum pipe elbow to the adaptor. Route the vacuum pipe to the top fitment of the reservoir and cable-tie it in place. When cutting the pipe to length, make sure that the cut end is open and not squashed. The pipe should be routed as neatly and safely as possible, away from the throttle linkage and components which might crush, damage or melt the pipe.

Caution: It is essential that vacuum pipe connections are air-tight. This is particularly important if using the T-piece joint in the fuel tap vacuum pipe.

5 Fit the oil bottle to the reservoir filler hole using the connector and hose provided, and squeeze the bottle to fill the reservoir to a level just below the filler hole.

6 It is now necessary to prime the system. Connect the oil bottle to the filler plug and fit the filler plug to the reservoir.

Set the adjuster to the prime position (maximum opening). Hold the oil bottle upright, then squeeze it (pump it) to pressurize the system until the delivery tube is completely full. You should be able to see the diaphagm in the reservoir lift and the oil travel down the delivery tube.

When the delivery tube is full, oil will appear from the dispenser and drop onto the chain. Place a rag under the dispenser to catch the oil and continue priming the system until no more air bubbles are visible in the tube.

At this point, disconnect the oil bottle and connect the breather hose to the filler plug; position the open end of the hose in a position which allows air to enter but not water or dirt.

7 Start the engine and allow it to idle. Hold the dispenser nib away from the sprocket face and carefully time the drops of oil per minute. Rotate the adjuster ring slowly anti-clockwise (away from the prime position) until the rate is as specified in the kit instructions (approximately 1 drop every 40 seconds in this case). Reposition the nib so that the oil drops onto the chain and turn off the engine.

HINT

We found that the dispenser could be held more securely in the delivery tube by applying a piece of heat-shrink over the joint between the two.

8 Before you take the machine for a test ride:
✦ Refit any parts that were removed.
✦ Tighten any nuts/bolts such as the rear wheel spindle that have been loosened/removed.
✦ Start the engine and once again check the operation of the chain oiler.

> ⚠ **Warning: High oil flow rates will increase the risk of oil getting on the tyre. It is essential that the tyre is monitored for oil contamination; turn the adjuster further anti-clockwise to reduce the oil flow rate if necessary.**

Length (distance)

Inches (in)	x 25.4	= Millimetres (mm)	x 0.0394	= Inches (in)
Feet (ft)	x 0.305	= Metres (m)	x 3.281	= Feet (ft)
Miles	x 1.609	= Kilometres (km)	x 0.621	= Miles

Volume (capacity)

Cubic inches (cu in; in^3)	x 16.387	= Cubic centimetres (cc; cm^3)	x 0.061	= Cubic inches (cu in; in^3)
Imperial pints (Imp pt)	x 0.568	= Litres (l)	x 1.76	= Imperial pints (Imp pt)
Imperial quarts (Imp qt)	x 1.137	= Litres (l)	x 0.88	= Imperial quarts (Imp qt)
Imperial quarts (Imp qt)	x 1.201	= US quarts (US qt)	x 0.833	= Imperial quarts (Imp qt)
US quarts (US qt)	x 0.946	= Litres (l)	x 1.057	= US quarts (US qt)
Imperial gallons (Imp gal)	x 4.546	= Litres (l)	x 0.22	= Imperial gallons (Imp gal)
Imperial gallons (Imp gal)	x 1.201	= US gallons (US gal)	x 0.833	= Imperial gallons (Imp gal)
US gallons (US gal)	x 3.785	= Litres (l)	x 0.264	= US gallons (US gal)

Mass (weight)

Ounces (oz)	x 28.35	= Grams (g)	x 0.035	= Ounces (oz)
Pounds (lb)	x 0.454	= Kilograms (kg)	x 2.205	= Pounds (lb)

Force

Ounces-force (ozf; oz)	x 0.278	= Newtons (N)	x 3.6	= Ounces-force (ozf; oz)
Pounds-force (lbf; lb)	x 4.448	= Newtons (N)	x 0.225	= Pounds-force (lbf; lb)
Newtons (N)	x 0.1	= Kilograms-force (kgf; kg)	x 9.81	= Newtons (N)

Pressure

Pounds-force per square inch (psi; lbf/in^2; lb/in^2)	x 0.070	= Kilograms-force per square centimetre (kgf/cm^2; kg/cm^2)	x 14.223	= Pounds-force per square inch (psi; lbf/in^2; lb/in^2)
Pounds-force per square inch (psi; lbf/in^2; lb/in^2)	x 0.068	= Atmospheres (atm)	x 14.696	= Pounds-force per square inch (psi; lbf/in^2; lb/in^2)
Pounds-force per square inch (psi; lbf/in^2; lb/in^2)	x 0.069	= Bars	x 14.5	= Pounds-force per square inch (psi; lbf/in^2; lb/in^2)
Pounds-force per square inch (psi; lbf/in^2; lb/in^2)	x 6.895	= Kilopascals (kPa)	x 0.145	= Pounds-force per square inch (psi; lbf/in^2; lb/in^2)
Kilopascals (kPa)	x 0.01	= Kilograms-force per square centimetre (kgf/cm^2; kg/cm^2)	x 98.1	= Kilopascals (kPa)
Millibar (mbar)	x 100	= Pascals (Pa)	x 0.01	= Millibar (mbar)
Millibar (mbar)	x 0.0145	= Pounds-force per square inch (psi; lbf/in^2; lb/in^2)	x 68.947	= Millibar (mbar)
Millibar (mbar)	x 0.75	= Millimetres of mercury (mmHg)	x 1.333	= Millibar (mbar)
Millibar (mbar)	x 0.401	= Inches of water (inH_2O)	x 2.491	= Millibar (mbar)
Millimetres of mercury (mmHg)	x 0.535	= Inches of water (inH_2O)	x 1.868	= Millimetres of mercury (mmHg)
Inches of water (inH_2O)	x 0.036	= Pounds-force per square inch (psi; lbf/in^2; lb/in^2)	x 27.68	= Inches of water (inH_2O)

Torque (moment of force)

Pounds-force inches (lbf in; lb in)	x 1.152	= Kilograms-force centimetre (kgf cm; kg cm)	x 0.868	= Pounds-force inches (lbf in; lb in)
Pounds-force inches (lbf in; lb in)	x 0.113	= Newton metres (Nm)	x 8.85	= Pounds-force inches (lbf in; lb in)
Pounds-force inches (lbf in; lb in)	x 0.083	= Pounds-force feet (lbf ft; lb ft)	x 12	= Pounds-force inches (lbf in; lb in)
Pounds-force feet (lbf ft; lb ft)	x 0.138	= Kilograms-force metres (kgf m; kg m)	x 7.233	= Pounds-force feet (lbf ft; lb ft)
Pounds-force feet (lbf ft; lb ft)	x 1.356	= Newton metres (Nm)	x 0.738	= Pounds-force feet (lbf ft; lb ft)
Newton metres (Nm)	x 0.102	= Kilograms-force metres (kgf m; kg m)	x 9.804	= Newton metres (Nm)

Power

Horsepower (hp)	x 745.7	= Watts (W)	x 0.0013	= Horsepower (hp)

Velocity (speed)

Miles per hour (miles/hr; mph)	x 1.609	= Kilometres per hour (km/hr; kph)	x 0.621	= Miles per hour (miles/hr; mph)

Fuel consumption*

Miles per gallon (mpg)	x 0.354	= Kilometres per litre (km/l)	x 2.825	= Miles per gallon (mpg)

Temperature

Degrees Fahrenheit = (°C x 1.8) + 32

Degrees Celsius (Degrees Centigrade; °C) = (°F - 32) x 0.56

** It is common practice to convert from miles per gallon (mpg) to litres/100 kilometres (l/100km), where mpg x l/100 km = 282*

A

ABS (Anti-lock braking system) A system, usually electronically controlled, that senses incipient wheel lockup during braking and relieves hydraulic pressure at wheel which is about to skid.

Aftermarket Components suitable for the motorcycle, but not produced by the motorcycle manufacturer.

Allen key A hexagonal wrench which fits into a recessed hexagonal hole.

Alternating current (ac) Current produced by an alternator. Requires converting to direct current by a rectifier for charging purposes.

Alternator Converts mechanical energy from the engine into electrical energy to charge the battery and power the electrical system.

Ampere (amp) A unit of measurement for the flow of electrical current. Current = Volts ÷ Ohms.

Ampere-hour (Ah) Measure of battery capacity.

Angle-tightening A torque expressed in degrees. Often follows a conventional tightening torque for cylinder head or main bearing fasteners **(see illustration)**.

Angle-tightening cylinder head bolts

Antifreeze A substance (usually ethylene glycol) mixed with water, and added to the cooling system, to prevent freezing of the coolant in winter. Antifreeze also contains chemicals to inhibit corrosion and the formation of rust and other deposits that would tend to clog the radiator and coolant passages and reduce cooling efficiency.

Anti-dive System attached to the fork lower leg (slider) to prevent fork dive when braking hard.

Anti-seize compound A coating that reduces the risk of seizing on fasteners that are subjected to high temperatures, such as exhaust clamp bolts and nuts.

API American Petroleum Institute. A quality standard for 4-stroke motor oils.

Asbestos A natural fibrous mineral with great heat resistance, commonly used in the composition of brake friction materials. Asbestos is a health hazard and the dust created by brake systems should never be inhaled or ingested.

ATF Automatic Transmission Fluid. Often used in front forks.

ATU Automatic Timing Unit. Mechanical device for advancing the ignition timing on early engines.

ATV All Terrain Vehicle. Often called a Quad.

Axial play Side-to-side movement.

Axle A shaft on which a wheel revolves. Also known as a spindle.

B

Backlash The amount of movement between meshed components when one component is held still. Usually applies to gear teeth.

Ball bearing A bearing consisting of a hardened inner and outer race with hardened steel balls between the two races.

Bearings Used between two working surfaces to prevent wear of the components and a build-up of heat. Four types of bearing are commonly used on motorcycles: plain shell bearings, ball bearings, tapered roller bearings and needle roller bearings.

Bevel gears Used to turn the drive through 90°. Typical applications are shaft final drive and camshaft drive **(see illustration)**.

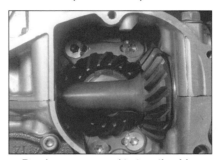

Bevel gears are used to turn the drive through 90°

BHP Brake Horsepower. The British measurement for engine power output. Power output is now usually expressed in kilowatts (kW).

Bias-belted tyre Similar construction to radial tyre, but with outer belt running at an angle to the wheel rim.

Big-end bearing The bearing in the end of the connecting rod that's attached to the crankshaft.

Bleeding The process of removing air from an hydraulic system via a bleed nipple or bleed screw.

Bottom-end A description of an engine's crankcase components and all components contained there-in.

BTDC Before Top Dead Centre in terms of piston position. Ignition timing is often expressed in terms of degrees or millimetres BTDC.

Bush A cylindrical metal or rubber component used between two moving parts.

Burr Rough edge left on a component after machining or as a result of excessive wear.

C

Cam chain The chain which takes drive from the crankshaft to the camshaft(s).

Canister The main component in an evaporative emission control system (California market only); contains activated charcoal granules to trap vapours from the fuel system rather than allowing them to vent to the atmosphere.

Castellated Resembling the parapets along the top of a castle wall. For example, a castellated wheel axle or spindle nut.

Catalytic converter A device in the exhaust system of some machines which converts certain pollutants in the exhaust gases into less harmful substances.

Charging system Description of the components which charge the battery, ie the alternator, rectifer and regulator.

Circlip A ring-shaped clip used to prevent endwise movement of cylindrical parts and shafts. An internal circlip is installed in a groove in a housing; an external circlip fits into a groove on the outside of a cylindrical piece such as a shaft. Also known as a snap-ring.

Clearance The amount of space between two parts. For example, between a piston and a cylinder, between a bearing and a journal, etc.

Coil spring A spiral of elastic steel found in various sizes throughout a vehicle, for example as a springing medium in the suspension and in the valve train.

Compression Reduction in volume, and increase in pressure and temperature, of a gas, caused by squeezing it into a smaller space.

Compression damping Controls the speed the suspension compresses when hitting a bump.

Compression ratio The relationship between cylinder volume when the piston is at top dead centre and cylinder volume when the piston is at bottom dead centre.

Continuity The uninterrupted path in the flow of electricity. Little or no measurable resistance.

Continuity tester Self-powered bleeper or test light which indicates continuity.

Cp Candlepower. Bulb rating commonly found on US motorcycles.

Crossply tyre Tyre plies arranged in a criss-cross pattern. Usually four or six plies used, hence 4PR or 6PR in tyre size codes.

Cush drive Rubber damper segments fitted between the rear wheel and final drive sprocket to absorb transmission shocks **(see illustration)**.

Cush drive rubbers dampen out transmission shocks

D

Degree disc Calibrated disc for measuring piston position. Expressed in degrees.

Dial gauge Clock-type gauge with adapters for measuring runout and piston position. Expressed in mm or inches.

Diaphragm The rubber membrane in a master cylinder or carburettor which seals the upper chamber.

Diaphragm spring A single sprung plate often used in clutches.

Direct current (dc) Current produced by a dc generator.

Decarbonisation The process of removing carbon deposits - typically from the combustion chamber, valves and exhaust port/system.

Detonation Destructive and damaging explosion of fuel/air mixture in combustion chamber instead of controlled burning.

Diode An electrical valve which only allows current to flow in one direction. Commonly used in rectifiers and starter interlock systems.

Disc valve (or rotary valve) A induction system used on some two-stroke engines.

Double-overhead camshaft (DOHC) An engine that uses two overhead camshafts, one for the intake valves and one for the exhaust valves.

Drivebelt A toothed belt used to transmit drive to the rear wheel on some motorcycles. A drivebelt has also been used to drive the camshafts. Drivebelts are usually made of Kevlar.

Driveshaft Any shaft used to transmit motion. Commonly used when referring to the final driveshaft on shaft drive motorcycles.

E

Earth return The return path of an electrical circuit, utilising the motorcycle's frame.

ECU (Electronic Control Unit) A computer which controls (for instance) an ignition system, or an anti-lock braking system.

EGO Exhaust Gas Oxygen sensor. Sometimes called a Lambda sensor.

Electrolyte The fluid in a lead-acid battery.

EMS (Engine Management System) A computer controlled system which manages the fuel injection and the ignition systems in an integrated fashion.

Endfloat The amount of lengthways movement between two parts. As applied to a crankshaft, the distance that the crankshaft can move side-to-side in the crankcase.

Endless chain A chain having no joining link. Common use for cam chains and final drive chains.

EP (Extreme Pressure) Oil type used in locations where high loads are applied, such as between gear teeth.

Evaporative emission control system Describes a charcoal filled canister which stores fuel vapours from the tank rather than allowing them to vent to the atmosphere. Usually only fitted to California models and referred to as an EVAP system.

Expansion chamber Section of two-stroke engine exhaust system so designed to improve engine efficiency and boost power.

F

Feeler blade or gauge A thin strip or blade of hardened steel, ground to an exact thickness, used to check or measure clearances between parts.

Final drive Description of the drive from the transmission to the rear wheel. Usually by chain or shaft, but sometimes by belt.

Firing order The order in which the engine cylinders fire, or deliver their power strokes, beginning with the number one cylinder.

Flooding Term used to describe a high fuel level in the carburettor float chambers, leading to fuel overflow. Also refers to excess fuel in the combustion chamber due to incorrect starting technique.

Free length The no-load state of a component when measured. Clutch, valve and fork spring lengths are measured at rest, without any preload.

Freeplay The amount of travel before any action takes place. The looseness in a linkage, or an assembly of parts, between the initial application of force and actual movement. For example, the distance the rear brake pedal moves before the rear brake is actuated.

Fuel injection The fuel/air mixture is metered electronically and directed into the engine intake ports (indirect injection) or into the cylinders (direct injection). Sensors supply information on engine speed and conditions.

Fuel/air mixture The charge of fuel and air going into the engine. See **Stoichiometric ratio**.

Fuse An electrical device which protects a circuit against accidental overload. The typical fuse contains a soft piece of metal which is calibrated to melt at a predetermined current flow (expressed as amps) and break the circuit.

G

Gap The distance the spark must travel in jumping from the centre electrode to the side electrode in a spark plug. Also refers to the distance between the ignition rotor and the pickup coil in an electronic ignition system.

Gasket Any thin, soft material - usually cork, cardboard, asbestos or soft metal - installed between two metal surfaces to ensure a good seal. For instance, the cylinder head gasket seals the joint between the block and the cylinder head.

Gauge An instrument panel display used to monitor engine conditions. A gauge with a movable pointer on a dial or a fixed scale is an analogue gauge. A gauge with a numerical readout is called a digital gauge.

Gear ratios The drive ratio of a pair of gears in a gearbox, calculated on their number of teeth.

Glaze-busting see **Honing**

Grinding Process for renovating the valve face and valve seat contact area in the cylinder head.

Gudgeon pin The shaft which connects the connecting rod small-end with the piston. Often called a piston pin or wrist pin.

H

Helical gears Gear teeth are slightly curved and produce less gear noise that straight-cut gears. Often used for primary drives.

Installing a Helicoil thread insert in a cylinder head

Helicoil A thread insert repair system. Commonly used as a repair for stripped spark plug threads **(see illustration)**.

Honing A process used to break down the glaze on a cylinder bore (also called glaze-busting). Can also be carried out to roughen a rebored cylinder to aid ring bedding-in.

HT (High Tension) Description of the electrical circuit from the secondary winding of the ignition coil to the spark plug.

Hydraulic A liquid filled system used to transmit pressure from one component to another. Common uses on motorcycles are brakes and clutches.

Hydrometer An instrument for measuring the specific gravity of a lead-acid battery.

Hygroscopic Water absorbing. In motorcycle applications, braking efficiency will be reduced if DOT 3 or 4 hydraulic fluid absorbs water from the air - care must be taken to keep new brake fluid in tightly sealed containers.

I

lbf ft Pounds-force feet. An imperial unit of torque. Sometimes written as ft-lbs.

lbf in Pound-force inch. An imperial unit of torque, applied to components where a very low torque is required. Sometimes written as in-lbs.

IC Abbreviation for Integrated Circuit.

Ignition advance Means of increasing the timing of the spark at higher engine speeds. Done by mechanical means (ATU) on early engines or electronically by the ignition control unit on later engines.

Ignition timing The moment at which the spark plug fires, expressed in the number of crankshaft degrees before the piston reaches the top of its stroke, or in the number of millimetres before the piston reaches the top of its stroke.

Infinity (∞) Description of an open-circuit electrical state, where no continuity exists.

Inverted forks (upside down forks) The sliders or lower legs are held in the yokes and the fork tubes or stanchions are connected to the wheel axle (spindle). Less unsprung weight and stiffer construction than conventional forks.

J

JASO Quality standard for 2-stroke oils.

Joule The unit of electrical energy.

Journal The bearing surface of a shaft.

K

Kickstart Mechanical means of turning the engine over for starting purposes. Only usually fitted to mopeds, small capacity motorcycles and off-road motorcycles.

Kill switch Handebar-mounted switch for emergency ignition cut-out. Cuts the ignition circuit on all models, and additionally prevent starter motor operation on others.

km Symbol for kilometre.

kmh Abbreviation for kilometres per hour.

L

Lambda (λ) sensor A sensor fitted in the exhaust system to measure the exhaust gas oxygen content (excess air factor).

Lapping see **Grinding**.
LCD Abbreviation for Liquid Crystal Display.
LED Abbreviation for Light Emitting Diode.
Liner A steel cylinder liner inserted in a aluminium alloy cylinder block.
Locknut A nut used to lock an adjustment nut, or other threaded component, in place.
Lockstops The lugs on the lower triple clamp (yoke) which abut those on the frame, preventing handlebar-to-fuel tank contact.
Lockwasher A form of washer designed to prevent an attaching nut from working loose.
LT Low Tension Description of the electrical circuit from the power supply to the primary winding of the ignition coil.

M

Main bearings The bearings between the crankshaft and crankcase.
Maintenance-free (MF) battery A sealed battery which cannot be topped up.
Manometer Mercury-filled calibrated tubes used to measure intake tract vacuum. Used to synchronise carburettors on multi-cylinder engines.
Micrometer A precision measuring instrument that measures component outside diameters **(see illustration)**.

Tappet shims are measured with a micrometer

MON (Motor Octane Number) A measure of a fuel's resistance to knock.
Monograde oil An oil with a single viscosity, eg SAE80W.
Monoshock A single suspension unit linking the swingarm or suspension linkage to the frame.
mph Abbreviation for miles per hour.
Multigrade oil Having a wide viscosity range (eg 10W40). The W stands for Winter, thus the viscosity ranges from SAE10 when cold to SAE40 when hot.
Multimeter An electrical test instrument with the capability to measure voltage, current and resistance. Some meters also incorporate a continuity tester and buzzer.

N

Needle roller bearing Inner race of caged needle rollers and hardened outer race. Examples of uncaged needle rollers can be found on some engines. Commonly used in rear suspension applications and in two-stroke engines.
Nm Newton metres.
NOx Oxides of Nitrogen. A common toxic pollutant emitted by petrol engines at higher temperatures.

O

Octane The measure of a fuel's resistance to knock.
OE (Original Equipment) Relates to components fitted to a motorcycle as standard or replacement parts supplied by the motorcycle manufacturer.
Ohm The unit of electrical resistance. Ohms = Volts ÷ Current.
Ohmmeter An instrument for measuring electrical resistance.
Oil cooler System for diverting engine oil outside of the engine to a radiator for cooling purposes.
Oil injection A system of two-stroke engine lubrication where oil is pump-fed to the engine in accordance with throttle position.
Open-circuit An electrical condition where there is a break in the flow of electricity - no continuity (high resistance).
O-ring A type of sealing ring made of a special rubber-like material; in use, the O-ring is compressed into a groove to provide the sealing action.
Oversize (OS) Term used for piston and ring size options fitted to a rebored cylinder.
Overhead cam (sohc) engine An engine with single camshaft located on top of the cylinder head.
Overhead valve (ohv) engine An engine with the valves located in the cylinder head, but with the camshaft located in the engine block or crankcase.
Oxygen sensor A device installed in the exhaust system which senses the oxygen content in the exhaust and converts this information into an electric current. Also called a Lambda sensor.

P

Plastigauge A thin strip of plastic thread, available in different sizes, used for measuring clearances. For example, a strip of Plastigauge is laid across a bearing journal. The parts are assembled and dismantled; the width of the crushed strip indicates the clearance between journal and bearing.
Polarity Either negative or positive earth (ground), determined by which battery lead is connected to the frame (earth return). Modern motorcycles are usually negative earth.
Pre-ignition A situation where the fuel/air mixture ignites before the spark plug fires. Often due to a hot spot in the combustion chamber caused by carbon build-up. Engine has a tendency to 'run-on'.
Pre-load (suspension) The amount a spring is compressed when in the unloaded state. Preload can be applied by gas, spacer or mechanical adjuster.
Premix The method of engine lubrication on older two-stroke engines. Engine oil is mixed with the petrol in the fuel tank in a specific ratio. The fuel/oil mix is sometimes referred to as "petroil".
Primary drive Description of the drive from the crankshaft to the clutch. Usually by gear or chain.
PS Pfedestärke - a German interpretation of BHP.
PSI Pounds-force per square inch. Imperial measurement of tyre pressure and cylinder pressure measurement.
PTFE Polytetrafluoroethylene. A low friction substance.

Pulse secondary air injection system A process of promoting the burning of excess fuel present in the exhaust gases by routing fresh air into the exhaust ports.

Q

Quartz halogen bulb Tungsten filament surrounded by a halogen gas. Typically used for the headlight **(see illustration)**.

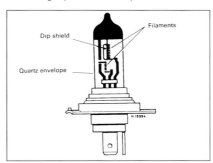

Quartz halogen headlight bulb construction

R

Rack-and-pinion A pinion gear on the end of a shaft that mates with a rack (think of a geared wheel opened up and laid flat). Sometimes used in clutch operating systems.
Radial play Up and down movement about a shaft.
Radial ply tyres Tyre plies run across the tyre (from bead to bead) and around the circumference of the tyre. Less resistant to tread distortion than other tyre types.
Radiator A liquid-to-air heat transfer device designed to reduce the temperature of the coolant in a liquid cooled engine.
Rake A feature of steering geometry - the angle of the steering head in relation to the vertical **(see illustration)**.

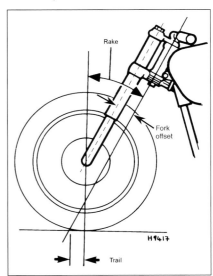

Steering geometry

Rebore Providing a new working surface to the cylinder bore by boring out the old surface. Necessitates the use of oversize piston and rings.

Rebound damping A means of controlling the oscillation of a suspension unit spring after it has been compressed. Resists the spring's natural tendency to bounce back after being compressed.

Rectifier Device for converting the ac output of an alternator into dc for battery charging.

Reed valve An induction system commonly used on two-stroke engines.

Regulator Device for maintaining the charging voltage from the generator or alternator within a specified range.

Relay A electrical device used to switch heavy current on and off by using a low current auxiliary circuit.

Resistance Measured in ohms. An electrical component's ability to pass electrical current.

RON (Research Octane Number) A measure of a fuel's resistance to knock.

rpm revolutions per minute.

Runout The amount of wobble (in-and-out movement) of a wheel or shaft as it's rotated. The amount a shaft rotates 'out-of-true'. The out-of-round condition of a rotating part.

S

SAE (Society of Automotive Engineers) A standard for the viscosity of a fluid.

Sealant A liquid or paste used to prevent leakage at a joint. Sometimes used in conjunction with a gasket.

Service limit Term for the point where a component is no longer useable and must be renewed.

Shaft drive A method of transmitting drive from the transmission to the rear wheel.

Shell bearings Plain bearings consisting of two shell halves. Most often used as big-end and main bearings in a four-stroke engine. Often called bearing inserts.

Shim Thin spacer, commonly used to adjust the clearance or relative positions between two parts. For example, shims inserted into or under tappets or followers to control valve clearances. Clearance is adjusted by changing the thickness of the shim.

Short-circuit An electrical condition where current shorts to earth (ground) bypassing the circuit components.

Skimming Process to correct warpage or repair a damaged surface, eg on brake discs or drums.

Slide-hammer A special puller that screws into or hooks onto a component such as a shaft or bearing; a heavy sliding handle on the shaft bottoms against the end of the shaft to knock the component free.

Small-end bearing The bearing in the upper end of the connecting rod at its joint with the gudgeon pin.

Spalling Damage to camshaft lobes or bearing journals shown as pitting of the working surface.

Specific gravity (SG) The state of charge of the electrolyte in a lead-acid battery. A measure of the electrolyte's density compared with water.

Straight-cut gears Common type gear used on gearbox shafts and for oil pump and water pump drives.

Stanchion The inner sliding part of the front forks, held by the yokes. Often called a fork tube.

Stoichiometric ratio The optimum chemical air/fuel ratio for a petrol engine, said to be 14.7 parts of air to 1 part of fuel.

Sulphuric acid The liquid (electrolyte) used in a lead-acid battery. Poisonous and extremely corrosive.

Surface grinding (lapping) Process to correct a warped gasket face, commonly used on cylinder heads.

T

Tapered-roller bearing Tapered inner race of caged needle rollers and separate tapered outer race. Examples of taper roller bearings can be found on steering heads.

Tappet A cylindrical component which transmits motion from the cam to the valve stem, either directly or via a pushrod and rocker arm. Also called a cam follower.

TCS Traction Control System. An electronically-controlled system which senses wheel spin and reduces engine speed accordingly.

TDC Top Dead Centre denotes that the piston is at its highest point in the cylinder.

Thread-locking compound Solution applied to fastener threads to prevent slackening. Select type to suit application.

Thrust washer A washer positioned between two moving components on a shaft. For example, between gear pinions on gearshaft.

Timing chain See **Cam Chain.**

Timing light Stroboscopic lamp for carrying out ignition timing checks with the engine running.

Top-end A description of an engine's cylinder block, head and valve gear components.

Torque Turning or twisting force about a shaft.

Torque setting A prescribed tightness specified by the motorcycle manufacturer to ensure that the bolt or nut is secured correctly. Undertightening can result in the bolt or nut coming loose or a surface not being sealed. Overtightening can result in stripped threads, distortion or damage to the component being retained.

Torx key A six-point wrench.

Tracer A stripe of a second colour applied to a wire insulator to distinguish that wire from another one with the same colour insulator. For example, Br/W is often used to denote a brown insulator with a white tracer.

Trail A feature of steering geometry. Distance from the steering head axis to the tyre's central contact point.

Triple clamps The cast components which extend from the steering head and support the fork stanchions or tubes. Often called fork yokes.

Turbocharger A centrifugal device, driven by exhaust gases, that pressurises the intake air. Normally used to increase the power output from a given engine displacement.

TWI Abbreviation for Tyre Wear Indicator. Indicates the location of the tread depth indicator bars on tyres.

U

Universal joint or U-joint (UJ) A double-pivoted connection for transmitting power from a driving to a driven shaft through an angle. Typically found in shaft drive assemblies.

Unsprung weight Anything not supported by the bike's suspension (ie the wheel, tyres, brakes, final drive and bottom (moving) part of the suspension).

V

Vacuum gauges Clock-type gauges for measuring intake tract vacuum. Used for carburettor synchronisation on multi-cylinder engines.

Valve A device through which the flow of liquid, gas or vacuum may be stopped, started or regulated by a moveable part that opens, shuts or partially obstructs one or more ports or passageways. The intake and exhaust valves in the cylinder head are of the poppet type.

Valve clearance The clearance between the valve tip (the end of the valve stem) and the rocker arm or tappet/follower. The valve clearance is measured when the valve is closed. The correct clearance is important - if too small the valve won't close fully and will burn out, whereas if too large noisy operation will result.

Valve lift The amount a valve is lifted off its seat by the camshaft lobe.

Valve timing The exact setting for the opening and closing of the valves in relation to piston position.

Vernier caliper A precision measuring instrument that measures inside and outside dimensions. Not quite as accurate as a micrometer, but more convenient.

VIN Vehicle Identification Number. Term for the bike's engine and frame numbers.

Viscosity The thickness of a liquid or its resistance to flow.

Volt A unit for expressing electrical "pressure" in a circuit. Volts = current x ohms.

W

Water pump A mechanically-driven device for moving coolant around the engine.

Watt A unit for expressing electrical power. Watts = volts x current.

Wear limit see **Service limit**

Wet liner A liquid-cooled engine design where the pistons run in liners which are directly surrounded by coolant **(see illustration)**.

Wet liner arrangement

Wheelbase Distance from the centre of the front wheel to the centre of the rear wheel.

Wiring harness or loom Describes the electrical wires running the length of the motorcycle and enclosed in tape or plastic sheathing. Wiring coming off the main harness is usually referred to as a sub harness.

Woodruff key A key of semi-circular or square section used to locate a gear to a shaft. Often used to locate the alternator rotor on the crankshaft.

Wrist pin Another name for gudgeon or piston pin.

Index